ETHNIC ISSUES, SECULARISM AND CONFLICT RESOLUTION IN NORTH EAST INDIA

Books Published for NEICSSR, Shillong

- Reorganisation of North East India Since 1947,
  B. Datta Ray and *S.P. Agrawal.*
- Sociological Constraints to Industrial Development in N-East India
  B.K. Datta Ray et. al.
- Population, Poverty and Environment in North East India,
  B. Datta Ray, et. al.
- Agenda for North East India,
  B. Datta Ray (Ed.)
- Development Priorities in North East India,
  Bimal J. Deb (Ed.)
- Linguistic Situation in North East India
  Mrinal Miri (Ed.)
- Perspective of Security and Development in North East India,
  B. Datta Ray and *S.K. Agnihotri*

About the Editor

Bimal J. Deb is Professor and Head, Department of Political Science, North-Eastern Hill University, Shillong. He has several prestigious publications to his credit, including *Development Priorities in North East India* published by Concept Publishing Company.

Ethnic Issues, Secularism and Conflict Resolution in North East India

Edited by
BIMAL J. DEB

Published for
NORTH-EAST INDIA COUNCIL FOR SOCIAL SCIENCE RESEARCH, SHILLONG

By
CONCEPT PUBLISHING COMPANY PVT. LTD
NEW DELHI-110059

Cataloging in Publication Data—DK
Courtesy: D.K. Agencies (P) Ltd. <docinfo@dkagencies.com>

Seminar on Ethnic Issues, Secularism and Conflict Resolution in North-east India (2001 : Shillong, India)
Ethnic issues, secularism and conflict resolution in North East India / edited by Bimal J. Deb.
p. cm.
Papers presented at the Seminar on Ethnic Issues, Secularism and Conflict Resolution in North-east India, held at Shillong during 25-26 April 2001.
Includes bibliographical references.
Includes index.
ISBN 9788180691348

1. Ethnicity—India, Northeastern—Congresses. 2. Secularism—India, Northeastern—Congresses. 3. Conflict management—India, Northeastern—Congresses. I. Deb, Bimal J. II. North East India Council for Social Science Research. II. Title.

DDC 305.800 954 1 22

ISBN 978-81-8069-134-8

First Published 2006

Published and Printed by
Concept Publishing Company (P) Ltd.
A/15-16, Commercial Block, Mohan Garden
New Delhi-110059 (INDIA)
Phones : 41101460
Email : publishing@conceptpub.com, Email: www.conceptpub.com

FOREWORD

The chapters included in this volume were presented to the seminar on Ethnic Issues, Secularism and Conflict Resolution in North-East India held on 25-26 April, 2001 organised by North-East India Council for Social Science Research, Shillong. There are more than one hundred ethnic groups in North-East India. The migration of ethnic groups occurred spread over time by different routes and topography has shaped the ethnological distribution in North-East India. In the imperial days major ethnic groups remained essentially in excluded and partially excluded areas. As a result they were not integrated with social and economic systems of the rest of India. Some ethnic groups remain encircled by a notional Inner Line Policy. Independent India inherited and continued the same Inner Life Policy. As a result they remained more underdeveloped than other parts of underdeveloped States of North-East India.

The motivation of different ethnic groups for preserving their identities has been a dynamic force in the reorganization of North-East India. In course of time the agrarian and economic issues found place in the ethnic movements. The process of alienation of rural land by the tribals themselves to the rich tribals has been going on all over North-East India. The notional egalitarian communities have given way to slow process of class formations.

The ideology of ethnic separatism is a worldwide phenomenon. In many parts of the world, the ethnic identities bypassed the overarching unifying force of the national unity. It resulted in interethnic conflicts and disintegration of some nation-states. The feeling of ethnic separation cannot be suppressed by military operations. The alternative is political dialogue. The dialogue is an essential process for formulations and execution of development plans for achieving equal society for increased volume of production and its fair distribution. This only can generate the feeling of emotional integration among different ethnic groups based on a solid material infrastructure. The conflict resolution is a slow process.

Ethnic and religious minorities are becoming concerned with their freedom of faith. We must realise that without reassertion of secular and human values, conflicts cannot be resolved. There is a constitutional separation of the religious institutions from the State machineries. Cultural pluralism is what India represents as the rich mosaic of her traditional values. The other road will lead to disintegration of our plural cultural fabric; intolerance is spreading to deny freedom of speech and expression. The tradition of tolerance is an underlying strength of India. Any other kind can only have limited acceptance. North-East India has a long tradition of secularism and conflict resolution.

We are thankful to Mr. Ashok Kumar Mittal and to Concept Publishing Company of New Delhi for undertaking the expeditious publication of this volume.

16 June, 2003

B. DATTA RAY
Secretary
North-East India Council for
Social Science Research,
Shillong - 793 003

PREFACE

In the recent decades ethnicity occupies a space of importance in civil society discourse in the North-East Region of India. There was a time when ethnic issues and aspirations were brushed aside as law and order questions and were never understood in correct perspective. The change of scenario is characterised by positive postures by those in the corridors of power in responding to the demands of ethnic-territorial mobilizations. No doubt, protection of cultural identities is clearly entrenched in any effort at conflict resolution, although fulfilment of economic and political goals is more often than not, hedged by considerations of State dominance and its centripetal nature. At the same time, ethnic diversities of north-eastern region and elite manipulation of cultural sentiments and symbols also find expressions in extra-constitutional demands. Such mobilization arising out of economic deprivation, uneven development, internal colonialism etc. have often had the effect of strengthening group identity and cultural exclusivism. However, revivalistic tendencies and cultural intolerance arising out of ethno-cultural paranoia produced alarming outbursts of Naga-Kuki clashes of 1994 in Manipur and Dimasa-Hmar killings of 2003 in Assam. Ethnic issues also form the core of secessionist demands in certain parts of North-East India. It is against this background that the contributors have looked at ways and means of resolving ethnic issues within the framework of secular polity.

BIMAL J. DEB

CONTENTS

ABOUT THE CONTRIBUTORS

Athparia, R. P., Anthropological Survey of India
Banerjee, Amalesh, Professor of Economics, Jadavpur University
Bhattacharjya, N. N. Professor of Geography, Gauhati University, Guwahati
Bhattacharjee, R. P., Asstt. Registrar, NERIST
Bhuyan, Vashyati, Department of Geography, Tezpur College, Assam
Biswas, P. C., Scholar From Calcutta

Chakraborty, Gorky, Department of Economics, Doom Dooma College, Doom Dooma, Assam.
Chakraborty, Minakshi, Deptt. of Political Science, Haflong College
Chandra, Ramesh, Deputy Director, A.S.I., Shillong
Chakravarti, Mahadev, Mahatma Gandhi Professor, Tripura University
Choudhury, Abhijit, St. Edmund's College

Das, Samir Kumar, Reader in Political Science, Calcutta University
Das, M. M., Professor of Geography, Gauhati University
Datta, P. C., S. S. College, Hailakandi
Datta, Lakhahira, Reader in Geography, Gauhati University, Guwahati.
Deb, Bimal J., Professor and Head, Department of Political Science, North-Eastern Hill University, Shillong.
Devi, Premalata, State Resource Centre, NEHU
Ganguly, J. B., Former Vice Chancellor, Tripura University
Ghosh, Lipi, Reader, Department of South & South East Asian Studies, Calcutta University
Goswami, Momita, Research Scholar, Gauhati University, Guwahati
Mazumdar, Sukhendu, Scholar from Assam Rifles
Mukherjee, S. K., Anthropological Survey of India
Nandi, S. D., Principal, Oriental College, Kohima
Nath, Lopita, Cotton College, Assam
Pyal, Gita, Goodwill College, Shillong
Prasad, R. N., Professor of Public Administration, Mizoram University
Priyadarshini, Susmita, D.C.B. Girls' College
Pradhan, B. C., S. S. College, Hailakandi
Phukan, Girin, Professor of Political Science, Dibrugarth University
Rizvi, B. R., Deputy Director, Anthropological Survey of India, Udaipur
Sharma, Dhruba Pratim, Gauhati University

1

ETHNO-NATIONALISM AND SELF-DETERMINATION

BIMAL J. DEB

The engima of nationalism admittedly defies any cut and dried approach for unravelling its mystery and charm. Nevertheless no one can dispute the fact that the force of nationalism is most compelling and pervasive. Undoubtedly, membership in a nation provides "a powerful means of defining and locating individual selves in the world through the prism of collective personality and its distinctive culture". At the same time popular mobilization is ignited and set in motion by the driving force of nationalism. Over the years it has been rather evident that the crystallization of national identity on ethnic lines eventually fosters collective identity often decisively and in a manner inconceivable by either religion or class. The fact, therefore, remains ethnic national identity is relatively more meaningful and promising than other identities more because it fulfils the test of stability.

Various scholars attribute the force of ethnic nationalism to the perception of the nation as a community of shared fate. One may not agree with Gellner who has opined that nationalism "invents nations where they do not exist" on the ground that there would be an element of fabrication in the process primarily because the elite in all cases construct social reality in terms of "cultural artifacts" and expressed through imagination which undoubtedly includes ethnic distinctiveness. There is no disputing the fact that the notion of the nation needs to be imagined. It is worth quoting Anderson who made theoretical formulation succinctly clear by stating that "members of even the smallest nation will never know most of their fellow members – yet in the mind of each lives the images of their community". Ethnic communities are, therefore, not necessarily historically precise and consistent reality. The fact however remains that ethnic nationalism is a 'powerful drive that induces millions across the globe to nurture the vision of better political existence'. In the construction of an ethnic community's image and also in the evolution of the entity several attributes matter such as culture, language and above all national consciousness. Indeed, the common denominator of all ethnic communities is national consciousness, which fosters, by all means, a feeling of belongingness and fraternity.

Of the various typologies of national movements, ethnic nationalism stands out to be the most significant because of its volatile nature, although examples of ethnic secession are very few indeed. The end of cold war, dissolution of the USSR and loosening of authoritarian shackles have no doubt seen the emergence of a number of ethnically defined states in the past one decade, the demonstration effect of which looms large in a number of other cases.

The gravitational pull of ethnic nationalism can be traced to certain basic urges. It goes without saying that membership in a nation promotes a sense of identification, which in turn instils a sense of pride in the tradition and institutions. Tradition remains the sheet anchor of ethnic identity and mobilization. Persistence of tradition has been found to be both socially and practically acceptable as a means of strengthening ethnic bond and overcoming anonymity. The result is anything but spectacular so much so that individuals consciously or unconsciously submerge themselves in the vortex of ethnic pride and prejudice to kindle the hope of governance in tune with some sense of equality. The inroads of modernization loom large in their lifestyle but tradition holds the sway, for it is at once uniting and rewarding. Evidently, ethnic aspirations get directed towards identity formation and consolidation. Over the years several ethnic categories have transformed themselves into ethnic communities.

Significantly, the crystallization process of ethnic community does not however take place at a rapid pace and at the same time no uniform pattern is discernible either. The properties of ethnic nationalism explain the explosive power rooted in the myth of a common ancestry and homeland. It is well acknowledged that prevalence of a common culture too facilitates the emergence of a collective personality. Above all, language and religion add to a sense of solidarity and are considered to be the important resources of ethnic community.

Over the past two decades ethnic nationalism has taken deep root in several parts of North-East India projecting the need for collective destiny. Side by side the idea of self-determination ignites and motivates individual members to take recourse to agitational path and often political extremism. The movement is not self-propelled because intelligentsia and political elite play the vital role of educating and mobilizing the masses along the path of ethnic separateness. Over and above, the rationale of the move as interpreted by the elite holds sway in the society. Generally speaking political autonomy and statehood are projected as the ultimate prize of ethnic nationalism. Elsewhere in the world stateless ethnic communities clamour the same sentiments even though the right of self-determination is no more than a political fiction.

The dissolution of the USSR led to the emergence of a number of new states and this development in its wake virtually reopened debate about the ethnic components of national identity along with the right of self-determination. However the guiding principles as enunciated by the former UN Secretary-General Boutros Ghali in Agenda for Peace have been by and large found to be acceptable to the members of the world community. It was held that if every ethnic, religious or linguistic group claimed statehood, there would be no limit to fragmentation and peace, security and economic wellbeing for all will become ever more difficult to achieve. In his prescription, all rival claims of sovereignty and self-determination could be resolved through respect for human rights particularly the rights of minorities on the one hand and democratization on the other.

Despite ethnic movements and upsurge, the conventional interpretation of self-determination as de-colonization remains largely intact at the beginning of a new century. However, the advocates of ethno-nationalism harp on the secessionist element of the right of self-determination, which in their view is a fundamental human right. Even the African Union held that only the ex-colonies could claim statehood. The emergence of Bangladesh was no doubt a triumph of ethnic nationalism but it was largely facilitated by external intervention. Again the emergence of post-Soviet States on ethnic line is considered to be a reiteration of the conventional interpretation of self-determination as new entities emerged after the collapse of an empire. Further, the Eritrean independence from Ethiopia and the recent success of nationalist movement in East Timor too remain within the ambit of this understanding. It is not out of place to mention that the Canadian Supreme Court in 1996 ruled out Quebec's secession stating 'outside the colonial context, there is no recognition to a right to secession whether or not such population has any distinctive cultural identity.

Against this background the emphasis remains on democratic government, human rights and political autonomy within the existing borders. The legitimacy of state remains undiluted. Nevertheless, politicization of ethnicity and ethnic militancy continue to pose challenge to the power and stability of the state and competing theories may be cited to explain the clamour for political bargaining. Michael Hechter has argued that relatively most backward region of country will exhibit the strongest desire for ethnic autonomy. On the other hand, Innamuel Wallerstein argues that the richest ethnic group living on the geographic periphery will express the strongest desire for sovereignty. In another explanation Rothschild holds that ethnicity can be seen as a highly conscious political and new mode of interest articulation. The fact however remains undisputed that politicization of ethnicity on the plank of socio-economic demands is a legitimate instrument in the pursuit of political power.

REFERENCES

Freeman, Michael, Democracy and Dynamite : The People's Right to Self-determination, *Political Studies,* Vol. XLIV, 1996.

Moore, Margaret, National Self-determination, *Political Studies*, Vol. XVI, 1997.

Never, Renee de, Democratization and Ethnic Conflict, *Survival*, Vol. 35, No. 2, Summer 1993.

Tamir, Yeal, The Enigma of Nationalism, *World Politics,* Vol. 47, April 1995.

2

ETHNIC ISSUES, SECULARISM AND CONFLICT RESOLUTION IN NORTH-EAST INDIA

J. B. GANGULY

In colonial India the freedom movement was launched, organized and sustained on the praxis of the ideology of nationalism. This served as the unifying force for the submergence of various ethnic, social, cultural, linguistic and religious identities and emergence of the pan-Indian national identity. The colonial rulers kept the tribal areas of North East India (NEI) as 'Excluded' and 'Partially excluded areas' and promulgated the Inner-Line Regulation for restricting the free entry of people from other parts of India into these areas. By such measures the colonial rulers succeeded in keeping the different ethnic communities of NEI away from the nationalist freedom movement. Of course the tribal people themselves fought against British penetration into their respective areas. In these fights both the sides inflicted heavy casualties on each other. But ultimately the British subdued tribal resistance and established special systems of administrative, legal, judicial, land settlement, fiscal arrangements, etc.

The tribal communities never reconciled themselves to their subjugation by the British. Their micro-level freedom struggles continued and they consistently asserted their respective ethnic identities and insisted on enjoying exclusive control over their resources like land, water, forests, minerals etc.

Many members of the north-eastern tribal communities were aware of India's freedom movement and they admired the Indian nationalist leaders like Gandhi, Nehru, Bordolai, *et al.* In some cases the tribal leaders organized their freedom agitations taking inspiration from the ideas upheld by these leaders. Until India's independence, however, no express tie-up between the tribal and the nationalist freedom fighters was built up.

The post-colonial Indian state is structurally a federal one but it contains strong unitary elements in many spheres. The state policy *vis-a-vis* the tribal peoples of NEI was initially to provide some opportunities for self-rule at the district level. Later in response to continued agitations and movements of tribal peoples more autonomy was given at the state level for which purpose Assam was vivisected and separate states of Nagaland, Meghalaya, Mizoram and Arunachal Pradesh were created as units of the Indian Union. Manipur and Tripura, the former princely states, were also elevated to the status of full-fledged statehood.

Several positive discriminatory constitutional provisions were made in favour of the tribal peoples to give them preferential opportunities for their education, job, seats in legislatures and preservation of their exclusive rights over their lands, water, forests, etc. In matters of central resource transfer also the north-eastern states get preferential allocations both for plan and non-plan expenditures. Despite such preferential treatments some of the ethnic groups have been carrying on insurgent agitations by asserting their separate ethnic identities which they claim should be the basis of separate sovereign state formations outside the Indian Union.

Such an ideology of ethnic separatism is not a unique one in this part of India. During the later part of the twentieth century in many parts of the world ethnic identities bypassed the overarching unifying bond of the ideology of nationalism resulting in inter-ethnic clashes and disintegration of some nation-states. This global phenomenon, phenomenal development of information and communication technology, easy availability of sophisticated arms in many parts of the world, support provided by external agencies and, finally, the upholding of ethnic separatism in certain cases by even the UN agencies and some foreign powers etc. have been helpful in carrying on ethnic insurgency in NEI on a sustained basis despite military intervention by the Government of India. There are other contributing factors also. The people of NEI resent dominance of the larger ethnocentric groups in state affairs enabling them to promote their exclusive interests and deprivation of minority groups and growing inequalities, etc.

"Ethnic separatism", rightly states J. Bandyopadhya, "is not fundamentally a problem of law and order but one of collective existential alienation". Therefore, this cannot be suppressed by military operations and/or granting of limited local autonomy and "pseudophilanthropic economic 'packages'.

The cult of ethnic separatism is getting further boosted by the trend of dilution of secular values and growing signs of religious intolerance which must be effectively contained. The ethnic minorities of NEI are becoming concerned about their freedom of faith as a religious minority group. Therefore, without reassertion and pursuance of true secular values ethnic disturbances cannot be resolved.

Some myths about the commonness of cultural identity of the north-eastern ethnic communities and that of the so-called mainstream communities which is presumed in certain quarters from some mythological accounts and archaeological findings of some religious symbols and sculptures and building ruins need to be objectively verified and corrected in certain respects. Amartya Sen has pointed out in his discourse on interpreting India's past that it is natively simplistic to claim that there is an 'overarching unity of Indian culture and history'. In reality cultural plurality is what India represents as the rich mosaic of her cultural tradition and values. As the trend to ignore this fact gets going and the so-called traditional cultural oneness of all peoples is propagated, the lurking suspicion in the minds of the minority ethnic cultural groups gets heightened and the assertion of distinct and separate cultural identities of the peoples of the North-East gets boosted. India is a land of unity in diversity and by trying to enforce uniformity at the cost of real and rich diversity will only jeopardise the value of unity among all ethnic, cultural, religious groups.

Finally, it needs to be admitted that instead of trying to resolve ethnic insurgencies by military means more emphasis should be laid on political dialogues on a sustained basis by the government with the insurgent groups. In such negotiations the civil societies of both from North-East India and other regions of India should be involved for evolving constitutional and administrative measures for decentralization of state power and empowerment people the grassroots level. Participation of civil societies is also required for formulating and executing developmental plans for achieving egalitarian and just methods of generating increased volume of production and its distribution among different sections of population. It should be also ensured that people enjoy access to powers of control over their natural resources at the grassroots level. These should be the building blocks of promoting ethnic unity and amity and solving the problem of ethnic separatism. But this cannot be achieved quickly, without generating the feeling of emotional integration among the minority and majority ethnic groups. The process will be a slow one and any attempt at hastening it will only be counter-productive.

3

GROWING CHALLENGE TO THE CONCEPT OF SECULARISM AND ITS SPECIAL IMPACT ON NORTH-EAST REGION

P. C. BISWAS

Introduction

Though it may sound somewhat curious, we would first like to understand what is actually meant by secularism. There is utter confusion about the true meaning of the term, even amongst the topmost political leaders and high intellectuals. Those who want to strike at the very root of the concept of secularism, try to pose themselves as the votaries of true secularism, and depict their opponents as supporters of pseudo-secularism in the way of pampering and appearing the minority communities. In fact, there cannot be secularism and pseudo-secularism.

Our constitution makers, in their wisdom, considered the incorporation of the term 'Democratic Republic' in the Preamble as enough to protect and promote, the inherent secular character of our state. In the following articles (Articles 14, 15, 16, 21 and 25 to 30), fundamental rights of citizen are enumerated, whereby equality before law, prohibition of discrimination, on grounds of religion etc., equality of opportunity, protection of life and personal liberty, freedom of conscience, freedom to manage religious affairs, freedom to pay taxes for promotion of any particular religion, freedom of interests of minorities, right of minorities to establish administer educational institution are guaranteed. All these are ingrained in the very concept of modern Democratic Republic.

But within 25 years of the working of our Constitution, the political leaders were confronted with a challenge to the democratic structure of our state. To protect its erosion, it was thought necessary to add the term 'secular', (in addition to 'socialist') in the preamble of the

Constitution by the 42nd Amendment in 1976. But even then, the concept of democracy and secularism are being faced with growing challenge. And this is being done in the name of democracy itself. Fundamentalism and autocracy can now, easily go in the name of majority (i.e. Hindu majority *vis-a-vis* different minority communities). That is why, it is of utmost importance to define the term 'secularism'.

Secularism Defined

According to the Oxford Dictionary 'secularism' is concerned with the affairs of the world, not anything spiritual, sacred, ecclesiastical or monastic. The modern democratic republic deals with mundane day-to-day matters of the people for the preservation and promotion of the political and social life. Therefore, the state have or should have nothing to do with anything metaphysical, mythical or religious, which are essentially matters of individual faith and cannot be put under the scrutiny of reason or any scientific research. An individual or group of people adopt their religious faith in the historical and economic circumstances they live in. The different circumstances and geo-political conditions determine their mental make-up and give birth to different faith and customs. To sum up, state is concerned with people's relationship with people, not people's relationship with God or anything supernatural and in that, it is secular. If a state is based on religion, or if it meddles with any religion, it cannot be called a secular state. There were many examples of the Heads of our state and the Government, visiting different religious shrines and paying obeisance to particular symbols, in the name of showing their equal treatment to all religions. This is nothing but distorting the basic principles of secularism. From the birth of our Democratic Republic, our political leaders were confronted with the problem of defining the basic democratic structure of the state. While Pakistan choose to be an Islamic state, people of India resolved to be Democratic Republic and not a theocratic state, based on the religion of the Hindu majority and that is why more Muslims continued to live in India, than in Pakistan itself. Now-a-days, this basic secular character of our state is sought to be eroded.

Heritage of Our National Movement

Our national movement aimed at freeing the country from the foreign rule to promote the unhindered development of all sections of the people by achieving a free democratic republic. It is through this national movement, that the Indian nation building process got strengthened and unity of all sections of people was sought to be achieved. But in reality, the message of national movement could not reach to all areas and sections of people of our vast country, even though it assumed mass character in many areas, often of militant type. The movement was however dominated by the Hindu leaders of the upper class, with consequent limitations. But the concept that India is only for the Hindus was never entertained during the freedom struggle. However, the negligence of the class interests of the workers and peasants, who were deep in abject poverty, illiteracy and superstition, influence of religion on our national movement to some extent, restricted the parameter of our national movement. In order to rouse the majority Hindu population to unite in the struggle for Independence, some of the national leaders injected religious sentiments in the freedom struggle and portrayed the country as 'Bharat Mata' and invoked God's blessings for giving strength to fight the foreign enemy (often referring them as demon) instead of depending on people's strength. Bankim Chandra's 'Vande Mataram' became the rallying cry of our national movement. 'Ganpati Puja' and 'Shivaji' *utsav* in Maharashtra, became a part of our national movement. Swami Shradhananda's purification movement (*Suddhi Karan*) and Swami Dayananda's Arya Samaj also tended to give a religious orientation to the freedom movement. Naturally it had a counter-reaction amongst Muslim masses in the way of organising *Tabling* and '*Tanjim*' movement. It may be mentioned that Tilak's co-worker B.S. Munje was one of the five founder members of the Rastriya Swayam Sangha (RSS) which was founder on the Vijya Dasami Day in 1925. The ideological basis for Hindu revivalism and propagation of Hindutva was laid by Vir Savarkar, one of the foremost revolutionary patriots in the book *Who is a Hindu* published in 1923. Many other revolutionaries also sought inspiration from *Gita* and took oath with their blood before goddess Kali. So there was a running streak of religious colour in our national movement itself.

How and why Religious Sentiment Arose

Religious sentiments is the product of the existing social system, where people suffering under the grindstone of feudal exploitation, from generation to generation, could not find any wayout of their misery, sought solace and peace of mind from religion. After independence, to remove their misery, what was necessary was to adopt a programme and policy to eradicate their misery by changing the exploitative social and economic system and isolating the feudal conservative forces, which was not done because of the class interest of the rulers and they were left more and more addicted to superstition and religious beliefs. The communal leaders could easily take advantage of their ignorance and helplessness, with a view to serve their own political purpose, – Gandhiji in his attempt to draw the Muslim masses in the non-cooperation movement in 1920, incorporated 'Khilafat' in his programme, but when the *Khilafat* movement collapsed in Turkey itself the non-cooperation movement also lost its spirit. Following this, the Hindu communal movement got a fillip. According to R.S.S. leader Hedgewar, "Gandhiji's non-cooperation movement, raised the ugly head of evil forces in our national life and *yavan* snake, with its poisonous fangs, provoked communal riots after getting stronger by drinking the milk of non-cooperation." In the aftermath of communal riots the Hindu Mahasabha was established at Nagpur. Congress leaders like Madan Mohan Malaviya and Lala Lajpat Rai became active members of the same. As a matter of fact, there were many who simultaneously, worked in both the organisations, so nationalism and communalism existed side by side or even together. That is how, communalism could grow without any concerted resistance from any quarter and one form of communalism fostered the other form from the opposite side and British rulers skilfully utilized both forms of communalism in their divide and rule policy. Both types of communalism kept aloof from the struggle against the British. It may sound somewhat enigmatic how even after the British rule ended, communal divide, along with caste and ethnic problems still existed and deepened further. That is, because, our basic social and economic system remained unchanged with feudal legacies still persisting.

Face of Hindutva and Hindurashtra

The danger has grown all the more when religion began to be utilized for political purpose. And that is being done openly with a sense of pride. The medieval superstitions, belief in myths and the glorification of the past and distortion of history, is being carried on with the avowed purpose of establishing Hindu Rashtra. *Hindutva* will be the basis of this *Rashtra*.

As is being said this *Hindutva* is synonymous with *Bharatiyata,* i.e. Indian nationalism. In a book, *Our Nationhood Defined,* Golwalkar bemoaned that the Hindus had forgotten their nationhood and called upon them to rise to defend their nation. He stated only those movements are truly national as aim at rebuilding, revitalising and emancipating them Hindu nation from the present stupor. Further, 'Those only are nationalistic patriots, who, with the aspirations to glorify the Hindu race and nation to their heart, are prompted to strive and achieve that goal. All others are either traitors and enemies to the national cause, or to take a charitable view, idiots'. According to him, all those who are not Hindus, have no place in national life, unless they abandon their differences, adopt the religion, culture and language of the nation and completely merge themselves in the national race. So long, however, as they maintain their racial, religious and cultural differences, they cannot but be only foreigners. Hindusthan exists and must exist as the ancient Hindu nation. In fact, originally, the word '*Hindusthan*' was not related to any caste, or religion, but used to denote a geographical area and not to denote as the place (*sthan*) of the Hindus. A nation is generally defined as a historically developed stable community whose residence, language, economic life, psychological make-up and cultural traits are one. As these factors do not apply in our country as a whole and because of the existence of different languages, religions, cultures and customs, ethnicity, it is a multinational state and cannot be made a single state, based on one religion, i.e. Hinduism. The proponents of the slogan 'Hindi, Hindu, Hindusthan' overlook the fact that Hindi is not the language of all the Hindus, that the Hindus, themselves are not a compact community, their culture and psychological make-up etc. are also different in different regions. Their social system and economic conditions also vary. So even though Hindus formed the majority (82.41%, 1991 Census) of the population (out of whom scheduled castes formed 16%) followed by Muslims (11.69%) and tribals (6.9%). Hindu religion cannot be the yardstick to determine a nation. Pakistan which was formed on the basis of religion, broke down. India sustained itself as it must, as a multinational country and if religion is sought to be accepted as the basis of our state, it will disintegrate into pieces.

Looking Back to History

Apart from the different sects of aboriginals, Indian population, grew out of the many streams of invaders from outside. The Indo-European invaders, known as 'Aryan, were closely related to Iranians, and they were supposed to have brought civilization to India. But after excavation in Mohenjodaro and Harappa, we come to know that Indus valley civilization had originated around 2500 B.C. and Aryans came as pastoral race, much later. There are evidences of the presence of Proto-Austroloid, Mediterranean, Alpine and Mongoloid racial elements who contributed to the growth of Indian civilization. As the different races spread eastward and intermixed with the indigenous people, conflicts amongst them subsided and they started living a settled life (when the growth of agriculture) for mutual subsistence. In the later period, other immigrants, Greeks, Saythians, Parthanians, Shakas, Kushans and Huns settled down in India. In this context we may recall Tagore's famous poem *Bharata-tirtha*. There were waves of Mongoloid groups from the north-east and northern passes, who entered Assam. Anthropologists got evidences of Nigrito and Austric groups living in north-east region in distant past. In the Assam plains, people of diverse origin, after absorption into Hinduism intermixed with a large number of original inhabitants, speaking Bodo language of the Tibeto-Burman family, and they formed the bulk of Assamese population.

Many of the Hills and plain tribes retained their own languages (dialect), religion and customs etc., but a large number adopted Christianity. It would be however wrong to suppose that the non-Christians have adopted Hindu religion of culture. Assamese population embraced other ethnic clusters who had linguistic affinity with the Burmese and Kachins. People of Tai and Shan origin, known as Ahoms, who were believed to have entered Assam from Yunan in China and upper Burma, formed an important sector of Assamese people. Besides, many other groups of people from other parts of India migrated to Assam and got absorbed in Assamese population, while some sections retained their language. The Hindu Assamese population itself had different religious sects within it, like Shakti cults, Vaishnavism, Buddhism etc. Assam illustrates a composite character and a prototype of India where 'unity in diversity' existed. So any attempt to draw North-East region into a so called homogeneous 'Hindu Rashtra' would be disastrous, as it would foster separatist forces further.

The texture of Hindu society in South also are quite different from that of the northern and central India and it had strong separate regional traditions, with strong anti-Hindu bias of the type *Rama Puja*. So it is entirely wrong to depict India as a uniform and compact body on the basis of Hindu religion. Hindus are divided in different *varnas*, and castes and women also did not occupy the same position as men. Besides, class divisions among the Hindus cannot be ignored. So unity of India cannot be achieved through formation of Hindu Rashtra on the basis of Hindu religion.

False Cry of Hindus in Danger

Fanatic Hindus raise this slogan with a view to hide the interests of the upper class exploiters and try to divert the attention of the simple, religious minded Hindu masses against an imagined enemy, mainly the Muslims. There cannot be any danger to the Hindus with a 82.41 per cent majority from a Muslim minority community (11.69%) or Christians who formed only 2.6 per cent. Because they draw their religious inspirations from foreign sources, so they cannot be loyal to the nation and they have to be subdued unless they embrace Hindu religion and culture — This argument as advanced by the Hindu fundamentalists is tenuous.

India is the homeland of multi-lingual, multi-religious and multi-national communities and no community, living here is foreigner. Nobody can claim to be purely of Aryan race. Indian population comprises of people speaking different languages and having different religions. However, in the midst of these diversities, unifying forces also are at work and have to be promoted. Towards the end of the last century, 500 anthropologists of the Anthropological Survey of India in their research work for 10 years collected some glaring statistics in this respect, which showed :

1. People of India are not uniform and of the same religion. As many as 4,635 communities have divergences.
2. Most of the communities are of mixed character, i.e., proto-Austroloid, Mediterranean, Caucasians, Afriki, Mongoloid, elements of Aryan, Greek, Hun, Arab, Turkey and Europeans are intermingled in such a way that it is difficult to scan their original identities.

3. There are 325 languages, derived from many sources and there are 25 scripts; besides there are thousands of dialects.
4. There are 775 inseparable special features beyond the boundaries of religion.
5. Hindus and Muslims have 96.17 per cent common features. Buddhists and Muslims 91.18 per cent, Sikhs and Muslims 89.95 per cent.

All these figures show that there cannot be any demarcation line to identify who is an idigenous and who is a foreigner. All are equal citizens with some well defined specialities as recognized by our Constitution and all citizens are entitled to equal rights.

Amartya Sen, the Nobel laureate, in his speech in Cambridge University (1993) on 'Idealism of India' pointed out that there are three different, but connected trends which can be noticed in the deepening crisis faced by secularism and spirit of tolerance of different beliefs. These are (i) communal fascism, (ii) sectarian nationalism, and (iii) militant conservatism.

But people are not sufficiently conscious about the implication and consequence of these trends if not checked soon. Specially, in the context of the North-East region which is already in the vortex of ethnic, linguistic and sectarian national or sub-national troubles, these trends will be disastrous. Any policy of steam-rolling over these diversities, with a view to imposing an autocratic theocratic state in the name of unity will strike at very root of our democratic, socialist and secular republic. The intellectuals and social scientists should face the impending peril and come forward to organise public opinion about the danger of communal fundamentalism and make people conscious about the necessity to combat these forces. There is an apt saying : 'the best ground for the evil to succeed is, for the good people, to remain silent.

REFERENCES

Basu, Tapan et al., *Khaki Pant Geroa Jhanda.*

Chakravarty, Debashish, *Sangha Parivar – Why enemy of people.*

Dube, S. S., *Indian Society.*

Sen, Amartya, *Indian Secularism.*

Yachury, Sitaram, *Pseudo Hinduism exposed.*

4

ETHNICITY AND ETHNIC MOVEMENTS IN NORTH-EAST INDIA

B. R. RIZVI

Ethnicity refers to a common tradition, a system of shared values and culture by a group of people who identify themselves as a district entity different from other cultures. Besides this element of self-conceived identification, the group demanding a place under the sun may have a number of other characteristics that define its distinctiveness and maintain a social distance from other groups. These attributes may roughly include a distinct language (or dialect), social customs, traditions, dress patterns, food habits, and other modes of life. Close to the heels of ethnicity comes the concept of ethnic minorities who consider themselves distinguished from the larger societies by showing certain traits already mentioned above. Subjected to discrimination and outright repression by the dominant group in their society, they may respond by seeking to blur distinctions between themselves demanding recognition and better tolerance for their group.

Ethnic movements in North-East India involve the assertion of identity around certain social problems, historic-cultural legacies and political exigencies by way of organising themselves into an ethnic body to concretise their identity. Subsequently they raise a demand for a separate administrative unit comprising the areas where a distinct ethno-cultural group forms a majority.

The methods adopted achieve their goals range from peaceful persuasion to militant tactics, extortions, kidnapping, indiscriminate homicide and ethnic-cleansing for creation of a homogeneous land of their dreams.

Here an effort has been made to identify and describe a few common denominators of ethnic movements in North-East India.

Before discussing ethnic movements it will be worthwhile to

understand the meaning of ethnic groups. Ethnic group has been defined as a population which is biologically self-perpetuating; shares fundamental cultural values realised in overt unity in cultural forms; make up a field for communication and interaction; has a membership which identifies itself and is identified by others as continuous a category distinct from other categories of the same order. Boundary of an ethnic group is not a static phenomenon.

Depending upon the circumstances and specific goals at a certain point or a period of time fission or fusion of ethnic groups or segments thereof may occur. It is important to see the genesis, organisation and function of ethnic groups in interactional situation especially the maintenance of ethnic boundary in multi-ethnic situation where a tribe or a group of people live in its traditionally defined territory. The ethnic boundary is maintained through cultural likeness and village, inter-village and regional solidarity. The village solidarity is primarily maintained by clan and lineage affiliation and economic, political and religious organisation. Inter-village solidarity is maintained by marriage alliances, exchange of visits during village festivals, participation in the local market and wider political organisation. Regional solidarity is realised mainly by shared cultural traits like language, myths of origin, oral tradition, social system, beliefs, practices and social organisation. Regional or inter-ethnic solidarity is bolstered further in freedom struggle for preservation of self-interest and to counter the oppression and exploitation by the intruders and outsiders.

In a multi-ethnic situation the process of maintaining the ethnic boundary is somewhat different from that of uni-ethnic situation. In a multi-ethnic situation connubium, commensality and language are three major attributes by which ethnic groups maintain their ethnic boundary. No single ethnic group enjoys a decisive numeral dominance and spatial and socio-cultural hold for nurturing and sustaining its ethnic boundary. Each group has to communicate and interact face to face with a number of other groups involved in the same economic activities. Even in the spheres of connubium, commensality and language they have to evolve a compromising formula and an attitude of tolerance. In order to elaborate as to how does this mechanism operate let us discuss marriage alliance as an important factor of ethnicity.

A large number of North-East Indian tribes prescribe marriage of a boy with his mother's brother's daughter (MBD) but prohibit his marriage with father's sister's daughter (FSD). Here there appears to be a unidirectional flow of brides. Most of the tribal groups in North-East India prohibit marriages within the same clan. The lineages among the Khamti of Arunachal Pradesh play main role in regulating marriage alliances. While negotiating matrimonial prospects of a marriageable boy his family members will first see if there is a marriageable girl in boy's mother's brother's family. Though there is a relaxation about selection of a bride from outside one's mother's brother's lineage, there is a strict prohibition regarding taking any girls from father's sister's lineage. Such prohibitions operate at the level of 'minimal lineage' more strictly upto three descending generations. This leaves an alternative for lineage 'A' which provides a girl as bride to lineage 'B' for going in search of a bride for another lineage which once provided a bride. Between two such minimal lineages which prohibit exchange of bride thus a relationship is established in which there are 'wife giver' and 'wife taker' lineages. In such a system a statistically regularised marriage pattern emerges as a result of marriage rules which do not indicate whom one must marry but instead whom one must not marry.

The Wancho of Arunachal Pradesh show an interesting marriage system wherein a particular social division acts as 'wife taker' from another named social division but avoids giving any girl to that social division. The Wancho practice village endogamy. The 'wife giver' division among the Wancho enjoys a lower position contrary to other tribes where 'wife givers' enjoy privileged position. The Konyak and Nocte who are also divided into 'aristocratic' and 'commoner' show a similar marriage system. The Adi, Hill Mizo, Nishi and Ao permit both FSD and MBD allowing the exchange of brides at the level of two families/lineages to avoid the payment of bride price.

Clan exogamy is the rule among the matrilineal Garo and Khasi of Meghalaya. Cousin marriages among the latter are prohibited. Now-a-days deviations from the strict marriage code do occur especially among the Christians but clan endogamy is still rare.

The process of maintaining ethnic boundary in a multi-ethnic situation has been well depicted by the tribal groups from various parts of the country immigrated to the tea gardens of Assam in search of making a livelihood in the growing tea industry. In the past, the garden labourers used to be recruited through agents who would visit tribal villages and advance money to them. There used to be a large scale seasonal migrations during plucking season. As the tea plantations took the shape of an organised industry, the labourers also began to settle down with their families in the tea gardens. At present the seasonal migration has almost ceased.

The labourers now live in a number of multi-ethnic labour settlements within the garden (*basti*) under the command of a *sardar* (headman). Social solidarity and community feeling was primarily reflected on social occasions like marriage, funeral, community worship and festivals etc.

Besides the tea garden labourers, a good number of tribal people coming in search of jobs in the tea gardens or the retired tea garden labourers also established a number of settlements nearby after cleaning forests or purchasing agricultural land in the neighbouring villages. Such settlements for all practical purposes, bear a similarity with a tribal village having a headman each who happens to be a retired labourer. The prevailing demographic situation, hence, does not create any problems in procuring a spouse. An ethnic group maintains its ethnic identity through marriage not only within a micro-region but also within a macro-region. Commensality differentiates ethnic group in the present context. The groups who have migrated from the same region sharing the similar cultural attributes behave like one distinct group so far as commensality is concerned. The Munda, Oraon and Kharia, for example, behave like a homogeneous group and accept food and drinks from each other. The principle does not operate in case of taking liquor and rice beer together but it does operate on social occasions like marriage and funeral feasts, etc.

The interaction of ethnic groups living on the international borders presents a different picture wherein ethnic groups act as a link between different ethnic groups while in some cases they serve as a shield to lessen the shock of concussion between aggressive groups. The tribal communities inhabiting areas around international borders were frequently entering into the circulation of goods and services through non-monetised system from one country to another. Now under the changed circumstances, market forces are substantially at work even in the remote corners of the country and the communities working as a shield between the warring tribal groups have changed their character since peace returned in the border areas after formation ethnic-based states in the North-East India. It is a different matter however that the communities working as shield in the past are now directly involved in conflict with hitherto friendly communities.

Language, as said, is an important marker in fastening the ethnic identity. It is a rallying point and a important symbol of group consciousness and solidarity. A language conflict invariably leads to an ugly political issue. One language may unconsciously tend to destroy another language. The speakers of weaker languages at first tend to be bilingual and ultimately come to depend entirely on the vital language. Assamese is the state language of Assam but the right of other ethnic groups to seek education at least at the primary level in their respective languages has not been denied. Till recently these smaller languages spoken by linguistic minorities remained more or less out of picture and had a precarious existence. Tribals have now become politically conscious and even assertive and nurse a sense of deprivation. In fact languages like Mishing and Kachari are not enjoying the status achieved by the Assamese. The ethnic languages except for Kachari, are rather in a sorry state as they hardly have text books even for lower classes. The Government of Assam have declared Bodo as an associate official language in Kokrajhar and Nalbari districts and Udalgiri sub-division but the state government have not issued orders for publication of important rules, regulations and notices etc. in the languages concerned. In Arunachal Pradesh people have evolved an independent Nephamese language along the lines of Nagamese. This is yet another pidgin language used in intra-ethnic communication. The Government of Arunachal Pradesh too has also failed to issue orders for providing instructions through mother tongue at the stage of education and the state denies even the existence of recognised linguistic minority there. In the state of Manipur English is the official language and Manipuri has been declared as second official language of the state. No arrangement exists for receipt and reply of representations submitted to the government written in minority languages. The Government of Manipur is yet to frame any guidelines for recognition of institutions run by a linguistic minority. Rongmei (written in Roman script) is emerging as a substitute Naga language in Manipur. Similarly Thadou written in Roman script is fast emerging as another potential common language in Manipur but it is disowned by the Kukis, who consider

Thadou as a lineage of the greater Kuki tribe which does not fulfil the aspiration of the entire Kuki tribe.

The linguistic scenario of Nagaland is somewhat bizarre. Each of 16 or so Naga sub-groups speak in their respective dialect. The pidgin Nagamese attributed to be a common Naga language is dismissed by most of the Naga sub-groups as their own.

The Tripuris demand for preservation and safeguards for Kok-Brok in Tripura whereas the Lalung demand for protection and preservation of Tiwa language in Assam. Mizos claim to possess separate languages possessed by each of their sub-groups. The 15 sub-groups of Tangsra speak fourteen different dialects such as Havoy, Jugli, Chamchang, Lungchang, Lungsi, Mungrey, Mosang, Muklem, Roorah, Sangwal, Sechudial, Tihkok and Tanglin, Six groups of Monpa speak in nine dialects, viz., Monpa, Cung, Kalaktang, Lispha Kishpignag, Matchopa, Nangnuo, Munkit and Sangla. The Zeliang language consists of two dialects Zemi and Liangmei. Tloshai Siaha is reported to be one of the five dialects of Marh language.

I find myself in full agreement with Samual Johnson, when he stated: "I am always sorry when any language is lost, because languages are a pedigree of a nation".

The strength of Indian society is its diversity of ethos encompassing a mutual co-existence of various ethnic groups and their shared cultural heritage. Languages/dialects need to be preserved in order to preserve the cultural diversity of India.

North-East India is in a state of flux. Many tribes living on international border shared ethnic and cultural affinities with the people living across the frontiers. Any development across the borders influences the situation in North-East India and may lead to tribal movement of one type or the other.

The dominant form of tribal movement in North-East India is political with varied goals ranging from waging struggle within the constitutional framework to demanding full autonomy through armed insurgency. Even cultural movements have clear political overtones. After independence political processes in North-East India picked up consolidating the democratic and secular systems; older tribes assumed new identities, smaller tribal groups merged with the larger ones to form new ethno-territorial identity which helped to create states to accommodate tribal aspiration for autonomy. In the process the Sixth Schedule model of political autonomy in N.E. was acceded. Nagaland today enjoys more autonomy than other states. The political process emerging from the merger of tribes to formation of new territorial identity and the formation of states is a unique feature of North-Eastern situation.

While the perception of the tribal groups of this region was clear and there emerged a sort of consensus on the formation of states, they, however, differ on the question of their relationship with nation-state. A section of the Nagas chose the path of insurgency followed by the Mizos, Meiteis and Tripuris. The tribal demands again ranged from the formation of states to autonomy of varying degrees under the Fifth and Sixth Schedules of the Indian Constitution.

The phenomenal rise of Christianity all over North-East except AP added a dimension to political processes as a symbol of tribal identity and status. North-Eastern states remained almost immune from the process of "sanskritisation". The Brahma movement among the Bodo Kachari remained parochial. There have been attempts aimed at "desanskritisation" in Manipur, an impulse to return to pre-vaishnava pristine form of Meitei culture is quite clear. The Seng Khasi, a socio-cultural organisation was established to preserve the Khasi way of life with its ancient system of clan relationship which was disturbed by a large scale conversion of the Khasis to Christianity. The Zeliangrong movement under Jadonang started with socio-cultural overtones assuming subsequently a political nature and became the only movement to have established linkages with the national freedom struggle. Under Rani Gaidinliu it remained strongly nationalistic, promoted tribal solidarity and demanded creation of a separate administrative unit to be formed out of territories inhabited by the constituent tribes in the contiguous regions of Manipur and Nagaland.

The post-1976 situation in the North-East India is marked by the continuing process of political integration, the changing dimension of the geopolitical factors, the problem of foreigners and the spread and control of insurgency.

There had been attempts at the government and political levels to seek the merger of regional political parties with Indian National Congress. The Nagaland Nationalist Organisation decided to merge in spite of opposition from United Democratic Front on the premise that the merger would result into Naga loss of identity. The Mizo Union of Mizoram also merged with the Congress Party rather reluctantly. Five organisations of Manipur—the Zou, Paite, Gangte,

Vaiphei and Simte National Councils also joined the Congress. Even All Party Hill Leaders' Conference (APHLC) decided to merge with the Congress for the larger interest of the people of Meghalaya. These moves aroused a suspicion that the diversity of North-East region was sought to be forced into merger with a single political organisation. This creeping suspicion was fully exploited by the opposition parties. Consequently many of the merged (regional) parties suffered in next elections. The parties who identified themselves with the regional ethos emerged stronger. It looked as if the national parties had no room in mainstream parties in the regional politics. However, even those regional parties which came to power sought to build bridges with mainstream opposition national parties. Some of Congress leaders in Arunachal Pradesh and Sikkim lost no time to change their labels in order to identify themselves with the ruling party or the ruling coalition of the parties at the Centre.

Since the signing of Assam Accord, Nagaland has remained more or less peaceful but for sporadic clashes sparked by hostility between National Socialist Council of Nagaland and armed forces. N.S.C.N. under the leadership of T. Muivah and Isak Swu are committed to the objective of military resistance by their followers operating from across the borders in Myanmar. They seek to establish the People's Republic of Nagaland and while they profess Christianity they denounce the Naga church for its rapprochement with the Central Government.

The Manipuris have been nurturing feelings of neglect and deprivation in matters of education and employment, the tribals being given special treatment under the official policy. The most important development since 1976 has been the spread of insurgency led by People's Revolutionary Party of Kangleipak (PREPAK) and People's Liberation Army (P.L.A.). Making a common demand for secession of Manipur from India, PREPAK is closely allied with Meitei revivalism. The P.L.A. is relatively a better trained and more resourceful body with its base in rural areas, committed to a radical ideology which envisages a union of insurgents in all states of North-East. The P.L.A., PREPAK and Red Army have been banned.

While the Meiteis have preferred to play down their traditional differences with the tribal groups, in fact these lay at the root of their resentment against the Centre. The tribals have been kept out of all forms of struggles spearheaded by the above Meitei outfits. They have demanded the creation of a separate state for themselves to be carved out of the tribe-dominated areas of the state. The Nagas of late have demanded the expulsion of the Kukis. Mizoram has shown a growing desire for peace as the bouts of insurgency have not paid off. The Mizos in general and the Mizo National Front (MNF) in particular realised in mid-eighties that a solution to the Mizo problem would be found within the framework of the Indian Constitution. The grant of statehood to Mizoram has met the long standing aspirations of the Mizos. In fact peace in Mizoram holds the key to stability in the North-East.

Meghalaya witnessed in late eighties serious disturbances involving the tribal and non-tribal segments of population. The tribal youth demanded measures to put an end to the influx of foreign nationals and introduction of Inner Line permit for entry as in the case of Nagaland. The state government has always been determined to preserve the identity of the tribal people of Meghalaya and the State Legislative Assembly had passed Transfer of Land (Regulation) Act, 1971 subsequently amended in 1975. The above protective measures have somehow helped to create a land cartel covering the creamy layer of the local tribals who now carry political clout in the state government.

Inhabited by 29 major and 100 sub-tribes at various stages of cultural exposure, Arunachal Pradesh has suffered in the past a sort of political upheavals. Even though the Inner Line Permit system is in vogue and the non-tribals constitute only a fraction of the total population, the All Arunachal Pradesh Students' Union (AAPSU) demanded the withdrawal of trade licences and land allotment permits from non-locals, deportation of refugees and imposition of an effective check on the influx of foreign nationals.

The Assam movement was viewed with misgivings by the Assam tribals themselves. Though they were sympathetic to the demands of expulsion of outsiders yet they expressed concern over the efforts to turn Assam from multi-lingual and multi-ethnic state to uni-lingual and uni-ethnic state. They also considered certain features of this movement as anti-tribal such as abolition of tribal belt and blocks, and demand for recognition of Assamese as the only medium of instruction in colleges. The plain tribals, therefore, kept out of the movement. The Progressive Plain Tribal Council of Assam (PPTCA) demanded the formation of Mishing *Bodo* Land to be carved out of the northern tracts of Goalpara, Kamrup, Darang, Lakhimpur and Sibsagar districts. They also demanded the recognition of English as the medium of instruction and eviction of all immigrants and foreigners including non-*bonafide* encroachers who have settled down in tribal belts/blocks. The Assam government accepted the demand for opening Bodo-medium schools and teachers were being recruited. The Karbis, however, demanded the recognition of English as the medium of instruction, reservation of jobs for the sons of soil and expulsion of foreign nationals. The Mishing Language Movement in Assam appears to be a symbol of assertion of Mishing ethnic identity and a higher level of awareness of their heritage consciousness and self-development. Mishings claim their distinct identity from the linguistic point of view. The Hmars of N.C. Hills of Assam earlier grouped themselves with old Kuki/Kuki-Lushai group now asserted a separate tribal identity. The higher level of literacy added a sense of political awareness amongst them and in spite of having close affinity with Kuki/Lushai group they hankered after an independent identity. The Koch of Assam and Meghalaya also, find themselves amidst an identity crisis. Earlier all of them followed the matrilineal system of descent and inheritance, though some of them adopted patriliny under the influence of Hinduism but the relics of matriliny still continue. Their changed identity from Koch to Koch Rabha or constitutional benefits of being classified as a Scheduled Tribe has aggravated the confusion about their ethnic identity. They seek affinity with matrilineal Rabha than with the patrilineal Bodo Kachari or groups alike. As a result of changing ethnic assertion a process of fission and fusion is still on among the Koch simultaneously.

Most of the communities of N.E. India were not conscious about their ethnic identities in the pre-colonial period and their ethnic world view was confined to their families, clans and villages. The subsequent colonial administration made them aware of their ethno-cultural identity. Different cultural-linguistic communities wanted to retain their tradition and relative prestige while desiring to improve their social, economic and political status with the concomitant issues of competition, conflict and power struggle. Besides attempting to improve their social, economic and political status while retaining tradition and relative prestige they attempted to bolster ethnic identities. The forces of modernisation operating in North-East inculcated a culture of 'conspicuous consumption' or consumerism among the tribal group. The dumping of cheap but durable and better quality products from the neighbouring countries has provided a flip to this culture of consumerism which can hardly be sustained by the traditional economies of the tribes of North-East. Insurgency and political pro-activism comes handy to fill the yawning gap between a myriad of spiralling needs and the scarce resources possessed by them to fulfil their aspirations.

5

ETHNIC CULTURAL DIVERSITY OF NORTH-EAST INDIA

N. N. BHATTACHARJYA

The people of India display a very high degree of diversity and this has been acquired through a long process of settlement by heterogeneous ethnic groups drawn from the neighbouring countries of Asia and Europe. Due to poor accessibility and difficult terrain condition, this region of India is regarded as a *cul-de-sac*[1] where culture and civilization had retarded growth. The rays of modern civilization have only recently penetrated into a vast part of this hilly region. In spite of the geographical isolation, human groups of different ethnic stocks having diverse socio-cultural backgrounds entered North-East India from different directions at different points of time through the river valleys and the mountain passes and settled in this region. The peopling of the region in the prehistoric, ancient and medieval periods has left a deep imprint on the ethnic cultural characteristics of its seven states. The Australoids are believed to be the earliest settlers of North-East India and they were known as Nishada. This group today is represented by the Khasis and Jaintias of Meghalaya. This group was followed by the Mongoloids who belonged to the Kirata group. It is believed that they came to North-East India from different directions and at different intervals of time. The Mongoloid racial stock is mainly concentrated in the hilly region of North-East India and this racial stock is sub-divided into two types, namely Palaeo Mongoloids and the Tibeto-Mongoloids. Adi, Nishi, Mishing, Mismi, Khamti, a variety of Naga tribes, Bodos, Garos etc. are the members of the Mongoloids. After the Mongoloids came the Caucasoids. The non-tribal Hindus and Muslims of Assam are of Caucasoid origin. The Ahoms, who are of Mongoloid origin came to Assam in the thirteenth century through the north-eastern routes. During the British regime, the construction of railway and motorable roads and the opening of tea gardens in Assam opened new avenues of employment which led a large number of people to migrate to this region from other parts of India, Bangladesh and Nepal. Besides, at the time of partition, North-East India had to receive a large number of refugees from East Bengal. The wave of immigration has been continued unabated till today affecting the demography and socio-cultural scenario of North-East India.

The inter-mixture of different racial traits complicated the logic of selecting race as a criterion of ethnic diversity. The frontier location of North-East India with feeble mainstream characteristics have made the make up of socio-cultural groups of the region very complicated.

It is a bit safer to divide the indigenous population of North-East India into four ethnolinguistic groups : Austro-Asiatic, Tibeto-Burman, Siamese-Chinese and Indo-Aryan. The Austro-Asiatic is represented by Monkhmer speaking Khasis and Jaintias of Meghalaya and Mundari speaking Munda Santal, Ho, Savara, Oraon etc. of the tea gardens of North-East India, Meitei, Barman, Baro Kachari, Deori, Hojai, Kachari, Tiwa, Mech, Mishing, Rabha of the plains, Dimasa, Karbi, Chakma, Garo, Hajong, Kukis, Hmar, Lakhar, Mizo, Rengma, Angami, Sema, Zemi, Tangkul, Konyak, Zou, Tangsa, Singhphu, Miju, Mishmi, Padam, Gallong, Tegin, Nishi, Sulung, Monpa etc. of the highlands of the North-East India belong to the tribes of the Tibeto-Burman linguistic groups. The Siamese-Chinese linguistic group consists of tribes like Aiton, Doania, Khamti, Khamyang, Phake, Turug of the upper part of the Brahmaputra valley and the Indo-Aryan group is represented by Assamese, Bengali, Nepali and Hindustani speakers of the region. These linguistic groups can be subdivided into six religious groups, namely Hindu, Muslim, Christian, Sikh, Buddhist and tribal religion.

An important variable of population of a region is its composition, in terms of race, language, religion, and nationality. Presence of sizeable number people speaking languages other than that of majority of groups preaching different religion etc., may pose some problems for a state's internal socio-political unity. The large area of North-East India with its variable landforms provide fertile ground for the germination of region diversities in the social milieu. The socio-cultural ethos of North-East India reflects such diversity. According to the social scientists India represents a unity in diversity which is the verdict of both geography and history. This unity in diversity is sybiotically linked and support and sustain each other. The present socio-cultural problems may be solved through an intelligent population planning aimed at integration of different groups of people of North-East India.

The degree of ethnic-cultural diversity and divisiveness of the region can be calculated by using an index of ethnic differentiation on the basis of Piasecki's formula of 1964[2].

$$S = 100 \sum_{i=1}^{k} n_i^2 / N^2$$

Where n is the size of ethnic group i, N is the total population of the region and k is the number of ethnic groups. The index of complete ethnic homogeneity is 100 and lower the resultant index, the higher will be the degree of ethnic differentiation. For example, the value of this index in Assam shows a higher degree of socio-religious differentiation.

Religionwise Population (1991 Census) in Assam

Total Population	Hindus	Muslims	Christians	Sikhs	Buddhists	Jains	Others
2241322	15047293	6373204	744367	16492	64008	20645	148313

It is mentioned that the essential feature of the social morphology of North-East India appears to be the symbiotic relationship between centripetal and centrifugal forces, producing a weak balance of unity in diversity. The stronger balance of the two forces may be created by the shift from subsistence agriculture to exchange economics[3], growth of social mobility within different groups of population and the growth of basic communication grids etc.

NOTES

1. Spate, O.H.K; Spate & Learmonth, A.T.A, (1972). *India and Pakistan,* Methuen & Co. Ltd., London, p. 6.
2. Piasecki, E. (1964). "Peoples of the World and an Attempt to Define Ethnic Differentiation of Territories" *Czasopismo Geograficzne,* Vol. 35, pp. 73-85.
3. Deutsch, Karl W. (1970) "The Growth of Nations : Some Recurrent Patterns of Political and Social Integration" in Kasperson, R.E. & Minghi, J.V. (Eds), *The Structure of Political Geography,* University of London Press Ltd., pp. 211-20.

6

ETHNIC ISSUES AND SECULARISM
Dialectical Approach for Conflict Resolution

RAMESH CHANDRA

In common parlance the term 'ethnic' refers to some particular group of people or a social-cultural conglomeration in limited sense of reference, being used at a particular time under specific situations of short endurance and limited context, as well as with long range objectives and interests of the group. The usage 'ethnic' derives its strength from the concept ethnicity–a concept which came into existence in social/cultural anthropology as method of analysis of social behaviour and events rather recently, say almost half a century ago as it was used first time in 1953 (*cf.* Glazeer *et al.*, 1975:1). Ethnicity is lucidly understood as an alternative identity of a person, group, state or sometimes even nation, based on physical characters giving to understanding of local and socio-cultural traits like categorisation of people into groups and geo-environmental habitat often referred as intake and such other attributes. Expression 'ethnic' seems to be accompanied by some sense of complex either 'superior' or 'inferior' depending upon the situation.

The term ethnicity has become popular among Social Scientists and also among those dealing with 'people' at different levels, viz. Nation, Region/State or even to interpret various social, economic processes and phenomena occurring to different ethnic groups, viz. cultural units. Fear of losing grip over resources, pinch on ethnocentric values and fanaticism including religious traits, cultural abrasion and linguistic perspective are also some usual phenomena culminating in the ethnic conflicts and segregation of people from one 'larger whole' to different smaller groups. Often such small groups take advantage of their being culturally different from 'others'. Issues related to ethnicity are by and large based on over reaction, exaggeration of facts and to some extent on the acts casting shadow on socio-cultural groups in terms of deprivation, frustration and bickering etc. Often ethnic issues erupt also as a result of treatment given by the social scientists to the concept itself in terms of their capability to interpret and elucidate the ethnicity and its ramifications in terms of ethnic issues notwithstanding the secular interest of the nation's integrity as their analytical approach leads to fragmentation of society into 'micro-isolates' with shifting identity. The treatment of ethnicity issues has so far been investigative in the interest of upholding micro-isolates and their values; ignoring or overlooking secularism while attempting to resolve such conflicts.

II

The roots of ethnic conflict, lie hidden beneath the concept of ethnicity since it is a system of categorization of people as 'we' and 'they' both at vertical and horizontal levels of identity having its sustaining force in the feeling of deprivation (*cf.* Danda, 1991:69). It works as structural reality as well as a processual tool in the society fragmenting 'people' into different groups–each solidifying its position as 'ethnic' group. For this, geo-ecological settings, economic pursuits and economy of the people, religious streams, linguistic traits and above all their physical make-up, all play a determining role in assigning some ethnic identity. Presently, 'planned development' has emerged as newly recognised dimension for reshaping the ethnic mosaic of the country. India, being a country having conglomerations of heterogeneous cultural patterns, people with strong sense of ethnocentrism nurturing feelings and emotions for their traditional values, perhaps cannot be dealt with by some jacket programmes and monolithic planning for development as these diversities are consciously kept alive because of endogenous as well as exogamous efforts (*cf.* Chowdhary, 1993).

As observed, some feeling of hidden unrest in suppressed form in the wake of controlling the natural resources and overpowering command over the same by so called 'outsiders' has led to ethnic conflicts in some parts of the country threatening the very existence of national unity and harmony. To understand the genesis of ethnic conflict one needs to comprehend the dynamic nature of ethnicity deriving its cause in inequality, imbalance, exploitation and deprivation and also creating cleavages among the people to take stride in protecting their interests. In a democracy like ours, ethnicity gives rise to the ethnic conflicts confronting both the major groups *vis-a-vis* minority groups, viz. the tribals, the religious, linguistic minority communities, the scheduled castes and the declared backward castes etc. on one pretext or the other. Religious and linguistic traits of ethnic group formation also do not lag behind in stimulating ethnic conflicts now and then. Also, conflicts arise out of sheer emotional reactions on the part of such groups to some unforeseen fear developing in their minds creating psychological stress on account of political thoughts, politicization of certain acts and misrepresentation of facts and events. How traditional values and religious beliefs can cause trauma of ethnic conflicts and mass violence has been witnessed in a ghastly incident that occurred in Rajasthan. The report stated :

> "In a shocking incident ... thousands of tribals armed with bows, arrows and axes attacked Jain temples, shops and houses. The reason –they were made to believe that Jain monks in the area had arrested the clouds and "stopped rain" (*baarish baandh*) in the drought hit region."

The incident led to destruction of two Jain temples and a number of shops and houses owned by the community in the town. The police had to open fire and 12 tribals received bullet injuries. In the recent past India has witnessed such a situation based on ethnicity and on call given for creation of a hill state in North-East, i.e. Mizoram. A memorandum submitted in 1970 to the then Prime Minister it was said

> "... frustration has overtaken the Mizo people largely in three ways : 1. The injustice done to them by dividing their homeland during the British *raj*; 2. The political instability brought about by the Government of Assam; 3. The economic instability as a result of mismanagement by the Government of Assam, ... It is very clear to everyone that it was due to gross mismanagement of affairs and a feeling of being dominated that a large section of people have revolted in 1966 in this peaceful land of Mizoram ..." (Goswami : 1979:205).

For ethnic conflicts and their resolution it can be taken as rather quick response to any situation weighing 'ethnic interest' at any level lesser than the desired/expected one for both the parties. Violence on this count once broken, does not focus the appropriateness of the action already being taken to create an atmosphere of disturbance, anarchy and feeble communal harmony. What essentially lacks in this situation is the effort from the beginning, to have dialectical approach to the problems. Some of the ethnic conflicts are based more often on flimsy, misleading, unreliable, twisted communicational messages which travel faster than the wind. That the role of mass media and oral communication if used in a distorted manner can spread mass violence cannot be undermined. Taking cue from this, a couple of years ago on the eve of Independence Day celebrations as a precautionary measure the then Chief Minister of Assam appealed to the Mass media (print) not to publish any news which may provoke ethnic/communal violence in the state. He made this appeal in view of prevailing terrorists activities/violence in the state or region (Doordarshan, 2:00 p.m. News Telecast, 14th August, 1999). Ethnicity is closely associated with egotism, ethnocentrism and issues relating to imposition, deprivation and devouring of the resources which are believed to be owned by the various ethnic groups themselves. India has experienced ethnic issues leading to mass violence on the issue of language in South, unequal development in the North-East, deprivation and exploitation in eastern states, fanaticism in northern states and witnessed situational ethnic conflicts turning into mass violence on pretext of inter-culturally unacceptable behaviour.

Yet, another dimension of ethnic conflict that remains embedded with social science in general and anthropology in particular is that of the capability to interpret 'ethnicity' itself with analytical approach and fragmenting society into micro-isolates with shifting identity. As discussed elsewhere "Anthropology also lays focus on 'small wholes' working on similar patterns ... yet the fact remains that it is a social science having commitment to humanity itself. ... The particularism crept in anthropological research does not aim towards synthesising vast 'small wholes' into some 'bigger whole' so as to represent similarities and generalities at the level ... to project anyone big homogeneous social/cultural group... where notion of 'oneness' and sharing of some commonness exists ... (Chandra, 1992). How redundant the ethnicity conceptualisation has become in contemporary times can well be seen in the research reported by Levine in terms "weakly theorised, lacking even an agreed definition, ethnicity has joined the list of deconstructed concepts in anthropology" ... The news is full of ethnic cleansing and genocide (mass violence) while the anthropologists stress that ethnicity is 'invented' and set to decentre the notion (e.g. Hanson, 1989). Further quoting Banks (1966) Levine in her research on 'Reconstructing Ethnicity' wrote "Banks notes that instead of confronting of problems of 'the parent concept', anthropologists interested in things formerly conceived as aspects of ethnicity are now writing about 'identity' and 'cultural politics'. This is an unequivocal instance of what D'Andrade (1995:4-5) calls 'agenda hopping'. When an area of research ceases to generate new ideas because its practitioners now understand how complex the phenomenon under investigation actually is, scholars begin to jump ship. ... In a sense ethnicity deserves what it gets. Afterall, stronger and more central building blocks of anthropological theory such as kinship, marriage, society and culture have been declared redundant 'so why not ethnicity'? It has been in a sorry state, nomothetically, for a long time" (Levine, H.R., 1999). With regard to ethnicity in an academic version of 'fiddling while Rome burns', post-modern anthropologists deconstruct while other commentators use our concepts to analyse contemporary events (Ahmed & Shore, 1995 in Levine, 1999).

III

Ethnic issues generally centre round the small micro-wholes of society, each highlighting some concern about pinch that the group has felt often blown beyond proportions to make the people sensitize about the 'occurrence' of smaller nature which could have been otherwise sorted out by amicable dialectical persuasion. While considering secularism as necessary overriding facet of ethnic conflict resolution by dialectical approach I cite views of our Prime Minister who emphasizing our country's commitment to secularism as basic tenet echoed this view recently in the Iranian Parliament (Majlis) that India would stay secular and even though 'there may be some occasional aberrations but neither the state nor civil society would ever weaken its bond with secular values inherent in our civilizational and cultural inheritance. He further added "our belief in secularism is rooted in a tradition which fundamentally respects man's spiritual quest and his freedom to pursue it in the manner in which he chooses to do so" (*Hindustan Times*, p. 1 April 12, 2001, Jaipur edition).

If ethnic conflicts are to be thwarted, remedy to this problem could be seen in changing the attitude, at condition level, towards other cultural/social groups, embracing them into a larger unit. This can be possible by weaving threads of commonality across the culture, empowerment and due share in controlling resources. Politicisation of ethnicity needs be refuted along with pampering of social groups with a view to have control over them for vested interests. Above all, such issues can be resolved by dialectical approach creating a congenial atmosphere of dialogue accommodating others' views in the interest of resolving such issues.

REFERENCES

Ang, Pen., (1999). 'Globalisation and the Politics of National Fear : Australia Confronts its 'Asian Future' in *The Eastern Anthropologist,* Vol. 51:3. Lucknow.

Ahmed, A. & C., Shore, (eds.) (1995). 'Is Anthropology relevant to the Contemporary World'? In *The Future of Anthropology*. London, Athlone.

Banks, M., (1996). Ethnicity : *Anthropological Constructions,* London, Routledge.

Berth, Fredrick, (1969). *Ethnicity Groups and Boundaries.* London, Allen & Unwin.

Chandra, Ramesh, (1992). Particularism and increasing Study Groups : Some observations' in *Man in India*, Vol. 72:1.

Chowdhry, S.K., (1993). *Myopic Development and Cultural Lens : An Evaluative Study of Tribal Development Programmes among Kondhs of Orissa.*

Danda, A.K., (1991). *Ethnicity in India.* New Delhi, Inter-India Publications.

D'Andrade, R., (1995). *The Development of Cognitive Anthropology.* Cambridge University Press.

Goswamy, B.B., (1979). *The Mizo Unrest.* Aalekh Publishers, Jaipur.

Glazeer N, *et al.*, (1975). *Ethnicity,* Massachusetts, Harvard University Press.

Levine, H.B., (1999). 'Reconstructing Ethnicity' in The Journal of the Royal Anthropological Institute. *Man*, Vol. 5:2.

7

SECULAR THOUGHTS AND COMMUNAL PRACTICES IN INDIA AND ITS NORTH-EAST

GORKY CHAKRABORTY

Secularism : Concept and Interpretation

The term secularism since it was first coined by George Jacob Holyoake in 1850[1] has been interpreted in a number of ways. Each group or sect whether political or social has conceptualised secularism in their own way and tried to place it within their restricted ideological framework. In the process the concept of secularism has gained enormous coverage both in spatial and temporal terms. It has become multidisciplinary in nature and ever encompassing in content over the years. A glimpse into the Encyclopaedia. Britannica in search of the term secularism will bear its testimony. It has been dealt with under various aspects ranging from Social Movement, Renaissance, Reformation, French Revolution, Mythology, Modernization etc. to name a few.

In terms of Social Movement[2], secularism indicates a movement in society directed away from other worldliness to life on earth. While in terms of Modernization[3], it reflects a move away from traditional ceremonial values towards values that are impersonal and utilitarian such as the amassing of scientific knowledge and its application to technology. Here Secularism manifests itself in social action. Again in terms of Supernaturalism[4], secularism has made the world a profane reality which is wholly isolated from both the sacred and supernatural. The interpretation of Secularism *vis-a-vis* Renaissance and Reformation[5] traces its growth since inception. It states that the professional class that grew up in the sixteenth century, however, was different in one respect from those that had gone before : it represented a predominantly secular culture – the product of Renaissance Humanism – and reflected the declining influence of church during the Reformation. While the section Myth and Mythology[6] which deals with secularism states that through its process of secularization, old myths are discarded and new myths are born. As a result of this fundamental questions about nature, universe and human being are increasingly answered or attempted to be answered in scientific and philosophical terms as opposed to mythical reasoning. Thus it is evident that the concept of secularism and its accompanying process of secularization deal with various aspects of human life and knowledge whether related to individual or the society as a whole. Our task in this chapter is 'therefore' to identify the areas of commonality among its various manifestations.

From the above interpretations it is clear that secularism and the process of secularization are an inseparable part of the concept of modernisation. So like modernisation the aspect of secularism has its political and social manifestations. Over the centuries, quite rightly or wrongly, economic modernization has been synonymous with industrialization while social and political modernization meant secularization. Thus the process of secularization in its course of action changed the social and political structures the seed for which germinated from a changed economic superstructure.

Broadly, in sociological terms the traits of secularism include (i) nature of social action, (ii) society's orientation towards change, and (iii) the degree of specialization and differentiation of institutions. While in terms of political norms it includes (i) nationalization of churches, (ii) the idea of sovereign government as a legitimate unit with rights to protect itself against sacred power, and (iii) equity and radicalisation of instumental values due to the growth of Protestanism[8]. These traits reflect the broad based nature of the concept of secularism and its process of secularization which has been largely common among various nations and nationalities in their journey for national reconstruction.

Nevertheless, a thin line of duality regarding the role of religion has always been evident in the concept of secularism which in other words creates the secular diaspora. Holyoake while coining the term secularism was always accommodative of religion while on the other hand Joseph Bradlaugh[9], another exponent of secularism, rejected religion and made science its deity. This difference between Holyoake and Bradlaugh regarding the form and content of secularism *vis-a-vis* religion constituted the basis of contemporary secular jurisprudence. Whether religion and secularism should co-exist together or should one be devoid of the other is still an ongoing debate.

This debate has undoubtedly placed secularism and religion into two different compartments. According to this division, secularism derives its reasoning from the state unfettered by theology whereas religion derives its utility and justification for God or some divine authority. So ideologically secularism claims to be based on scientific knowledge of things, political neutrality and human conscience and morality; and religion being anti-reason, averse to modernization and changes breeds social and religious antagonism and obscurantism against adversaries and unfaithful. In other words, secularism ignores or purposely excludes religion or religious considerations and evolves a system of social ethics based on humanism, whereas religion accepts or preaches a way of life where its followers subject themselves to the "Ultimate Reality"[10] or deity based on irrational and abstract assumptions.

The aspect of secular diaspora is evident in the process of national reconstruction in India too. The next section deals with the concept of secularism in India both in thought and in action in its pre- and post-independence phase.

Secular Thoughts in India

Secularism as a concept undoubtedly originated from the West and crystallized as a worldview under the influence of Renaissance, Reformations, Industrial Revolution and Democratic Transition[11]. However the ingredients which form the basis of secularism has been present and embedded for ages in Indian cultural traditions. The *Bhakti* and the *Sufi* movements are its living examples. Nonetheless secularism as a critique or reform process of religion gained momentum with the Western impact especially Western education. Western education helped the reformers to widen their mental framework which in turn provided impetus for rectifying and abolishing various social ills prevalent in the contemporary societies.

But the aspect of secular disapora (as mentioned in the earlier section regarding the role of religion) was not prominent during the late eighteenth and the nineteenth century. Except for a limited span of the Young Bengal movement under Derozio, the other social reformers used religion to rectify the ills of religion. One of the charges for the dismissal of Derozio from Hindu College was that he propagated atheistic ideas through his classroom lectures. Other than this, Raja Ram Mohun Roy came very close to an atheist stand. He later accepted God and the 'other world' for pragmatic reasons[12]. So starting from Brahmo Samaj (1827) in Calcutta, through the period of establishment of the Prarthana Samaj in Bombay (1867), the Arya Samaj in Punjab (1875), the Satyashodhak Samaj in Pune (1879) and the Indian Social Conference (1887), the necessity of social reforms was felt but it was focused on the reforms of religious beliefs and practices. Nevertheless this was inevitable as all the then existing social evils including *sati*, child marriage, caste discrimination, prohibition of widow remarriage etc. were found to be in the prevailing religious beliefs[13]. Therefore, the effort of the reformers was to reinterpret religion on liberal human lines.

So the nineteenth century reform movement due to its overwhelming focus on reinterpretation of religion did not give rise to a strong rationalist movement. Moreover the reform movements made no attempt at secularising social life in the sense of freeing social relationship from the sphere of religious regulations or asserting rationality as a basis of organising social life. Thus atheism or agnosticism which played an important role in European secularism due to the influence of scientific and rational ideas were largely absent in the Indian scene[14]. So the Bradlaugh version of secularism was absent in the nineteenth century Indian secular thought and the Holyoake version gained prominence.

This debate of whether to exclude religion or to reinterpret religion on modern lines became sharp during the twentieth century. While Gandhi pleaded for reinterpretation of religion, Nehru, M.N. Roy and others demarcated the sacred and profane activities. The religious world view of Gandhi and Nehru lead us to the most important phase of debate on secularism during pre-independent India. Gandhi was a devout Hindu and had strong religious orientation but his religious view were essentially personal in nature and he strongly pleaded against all forms of theocracy and fundamentalism. According to his words, "I swear by my religion. I will die for it. But it is my personal affair. The state has nothing to do with it."[15] Again he states, "I do not expect the India of my dreams to develop one religion, that is to be wholly Hindu or wholly Christian or wholly Musalman, but I want it to be wholly tolerant, with its religions working side by side with one another."[16] While separating personal religion with the secular state, Gandhi never hesitated to use religious symbols, myths, terms and images which appealed to the mass morality. His popular concept of *swaraj* was synonymous with *Ram Rajya* but this *Ram Rajya* was not Hindu *rashtra* it was the "establishment of the kingdom of righteousness on earth"[17]. Similarly resisting colonialism was upholding *dharma* and its resistance a *Dharma Yudha* for *Ram Rajya*. In other words Gandhi described *Ram Rajya* as "the sovereignty of the people based on pure moral authority."[18]

Nehru's approach to secularism was based on an uncompromising critique of religion. He may be described as the first Indian intellectual thinker who has not found it necessary to lean on religion. But his allegiance with Gandhi and involvement in peasant struggles helped him to appreciate and respect the moral values embedded in religion. So his ideals of secularism and deep respect for the spiritual and moral legacy of all major religions co-inhabited together. His understanding of history helped him to describe religion, specially organised religion as "blind belief and reactionary, dogmatic and bigoted, superstitious, and exploitative and preserver of vested interest."[19] In the same spirit he stated, "in a country like India, which has many faiths and religions, no real nationalism can be built except on the basis of secularity."[20] But unlike Gandhi, Nehru never used religious symbols or images to arouse the masses and led them into the freedom struggle. Nehru's design of promoting secularism was through a process of social transformation and economic development. While Gandhi dreamt of *Ram Rajya,* Nehru dreamt of a 'Just Society'.

The concept of secularism as defined by Gandhi and Nehru constituted the bulwark of Indian nationalism. This evolved through a process of national struggle and ultimately found its expression in the

Constitution of independent India. The Constitution guaranteed that the Indian state was not a theocratic one and simultaneously it guaranteed all individuals and minority communities the freedom to follow their own religion. Citizens could not only follow their individual faith but could also preach and propagate it. However, secularism in India did not mean freeing the life of an individual from religious dogma or from dominance and control by priesthood. The inherent contradictions of the secular diaspora 'therefore' remained embedded in the secular concept of the Indian state.

Indian Secularism in Practice

The secular India dreamt by the nation builders prior to independence has been put into practice in our tryst with destiny. We as concerned citizens have followed it in principle for over five decades in independent India. Where do we stand today? Has our secular experiment placed our nation at a higher pedestal in the global forum? Have we secularised the mind of the millions and helped them to stand against religious fundamentalism and bigotry? Have we been able to harmonise the relationship among various religions, ethnic, caste and linguistic communities? What are the achievements and drawbacks of our secular model and can we reformulate our secular model? These questions along with various others are disturbing the mind of all right thinking individuals in the country. A proper insight will 'therefore' lead us to a logical conclusion regarding the practice of secularism in independent India.

The biggest achievement of the Indian secular experiment has been that all moves towards a theocratic state has been defeated by the people. But the overall composition of the secular character of the state, the secular psyche, its mass appeal etc. bears the biggest question mark. India stands at crossroads today where the secular ideal of its Constitution has been under severe strain. The Parliament which has been regarded as the strong bulwark of Indian secularism has been transformed into an arena for trial of strength between secular and non-secular forces. In the name of a 'holy war' everything positive related with our democracy is being forfeited and the same 'war cry' of a two-nation theory is re-enacted. No doubt the actors have changed but the content remains the same. Therefore, the threat to secularism in

India is the biggest and gravest among all the challenges facing this nation today. The national fabric is torn apart in the name of religion and the age old cherished ideals of peace, amity, harmony and assimilation are forgotten. It is, therefore, high time now that we question our secular experiment and reformulate it identifying its shortcomings.

Indian secularism by means of a balance between true religiosity at personal level and secular ideals at the state level evolved a new dimension to this aspect. In a pre-industrial and petty-bourgeoisie socio-economic set-up religion seemed to play an important part and so without rejecting it, the state proposed to show equal respect to all its followers. This mystic balance, in practice somewhat created serious distortions. It kept religion in play and in turn enhanced religiosity, it preserved and projected religious identities and thereby increased the social distance between different religious communities. The Gandhian dichotomy between true religious at the personal life and secular in public life became futile in practice. It became unreal, for such a compartmentalisation does not really exist in actual life. "The personal belief may not interfere in public life all the time, but it surfaces quite easily when individual identities merge with the collective."[21] Thus we seemed to be fighting a monster without creating a positive belief against it.

Another inherent weakness of our secular experiment as highlighted by experts has been that the secular practitioners in India considered secularism as a 'spaceless' and 'timeless' concept. Secularism has been equated with an aggressive worldliness devoid of any moral outlook. To a great extent this process demystified religions but was unable to compliment it with an alternative way of life. So the Indian secular experiment while destroying the spiritual and moral values which were nurtured by religion for ages could not fill up the void. Amoral secular experiment resulted in a gap which in practice created further divisions in our society[22].

The secular vision in India has been devoid of the spiritual elements due to which the alternative moral outlook never developed nor moral order was given a proper shape. In a pre-industrial religious society the oral traditions of people's religion was not taken into consideration as a result of which the humanist traditions of Buddha, Kabir, Nanak or the Sufis remained outside the ambit of our secular thoughts. Our secular exponents due to their lopsided understanding of the Indian psyche created a void between the secular and the sacred and instead of harmonising them, placed each other as poles apart. The religiosity of the masses in a largely agrarian society like India contains a traditional and humanistic appeal, where religion and its myths and symbols are not only issues of faith and belief but a process of communication too. The rejection of these values has resulted in confrontation and dissociation of the masses from the secular experiment. Secularism remained confined within the confines of an "anglicized class" whereas the large majority of the Indian citizens remained aloof from this process of thought.

The cleavage has been further widened by an unbalanced pattern of socio-economic change. A class based economic development model further increased the hiatus between the haves and the have-nots. So on one hand the secular proponents in India couldn't understand the secular religiosity of the masses and on the other hand were unable to provide them with the fruits of economic development as were provided to the elite and anglicized section of the society. It created a perfect breeding ground for the fundamentalist forces to widen their reach among these sections of our population in order to fulfil their own political ambitions.

So in practice the Indian model of secularism neither could keep aside religion nor could blend the secular and sacred values together. Thus it became rootless, voiceless and directionless in its content and appeal remaining unconcerned about the vast majority for which it was dreamt as a tool of moral aggrandizement.

That India's North-East is no exception to this pattern may be seen from the following section.

Secular Diaspora in the North-East[23]

The Coupland Plan for a Crown Colony still haunts the mind of the people and psyche of the state in the north-eastern region of India. A buffer state in the bordering regions of India, Myanmar and Bangladesh was proposed to be set up by the British administrators. Their rationale was that since "the religion, language and culture of the hill tribes were alien to those of Hindus and Muslims, hence there was no point to drag the animist and Christians into a struggle between Hindus and

Muslims."[24] So a separate entity in the name of North-Eastern Frontier Province comprising Arakan, Chittagong Hill Tracts, Chin Hills, Sadiya and Balipara Frontier, Lakhimpur, Hill areas of Manipur and Tripura was supposed to be included in the proposed state. Surprisingly, after more than five decades of the proposed Crown Colony, the same areas are now the violent centres of ethnocentric conflicts and insurgency based secessionist movements.

Many of these upsurges and movements have a religious undertone and they fit into the ethno-religious framework. The religious under-current varies in degree which ultimately determines the political trend in the region. The minority tribes and communities along with the weaker sections are faced with a sort of imposition of the dominated caste/class Hindu-Hindi line in the name of integration. The Church and the Mosque are often symbolised as anti-national monuments which patronise secession although these religions have long been rooted in the soil of the North-East. So some amount of soul searching in these lines will help us to understand as to how these ethno-religious issues emerged and what has been the response of the Indian state? How has the Indian state dealt with these ethno-religious issues *vis-a-vis* its secular ideology? These issues, therefore, are a test case for the Indian model of secularism. In the next part we deal with these issues, their emergence and the role and response of the Indian state as a whole.

Succumbing to the protagonist of two nation theory the Indian state always rejected the concept of a Hindu *rashtra*. However during its birth as an independent nation, the Indian leaders betrayed the trust reposed on them by the Buddhist tribesmen of the Chittagong Hill Tracts. Although CHT had an overwhelming majority of more than 97 per cent of non-Muslim population, it was left with East Pakistan. The people and the public leaders along with the *Raja* expressed their willingness to stay with India but the Indian state responded by back stabbing the Chakma hill dwellers. This historic injustice to the Chakma population had serious ramifications on both sides of the border. In East Pakistan the state deliberately settled thousands of landless. Muslims in the CHT in order to change the demographic and religious pattern of the region. The result has been the birth of an insurgency movement by Chakmas in order to protect their homeland and identity.

On the other hand, those Chakma refugees who were settled in Arunachal Pradesh in 1964 happens to be treated as *persona non grata* by the government. It is almost 40 years that the hill dwellers are still a stateless person and are denied franchise and citizenship although the Indian law speaks otherwise. Thus secular India remained a passive onlooker regarding the plight of these Buddhist Chakma tribes and allowed its secular credentials to be diluted.

Secular India portrays a completely different posture in the Christian dominated states of Mizoram, Meghalaya and Nagaland where it allows the church to play an important role in matters concerning state policy and direction of politics in these concerned states. To quote the Nagaland Baptist Christian Council "it is not at all a question of taking party politics to the Church but rather of taking the spirit of Christ to the inspiration and upliftment of politics"[25]. Similarly it is "more or less obligatory for the candidates irrespective of Party affiliations to take pledge and sign their names to abide by the wishes of the Church."[26]

The religious connotations have not only played an important role in parliamentary process but also has been a contributing factor for split and disintegration of underground movements. NSCN, regarded as the mother of all insurgent groups in North-East India, was split into two during 1988 as religious differences played a key role in the underground organisation. To quote Mr. Isak Chishi and Mr. Muivah, "their old religion was animism. Perhaps the worst type was practised. They used human sacrifice; they are the only section of people among the Nagas who has this system to maintain their social status. In fact, he is not far from head hunting stage .... He and his men for a pretty long time objected to the incorporation of 'Nagaland for Christ' in the manifesto ... We felt called upon to preach the Gospel in that darkest part left behind by the world gone ahead of us. With missionary zeal we took the historic responsibility upon ourselves. Massive political mobilizations, social reforms and religious preaching were carried out side by side. Our Volunteer Gospel Teams, carrying babies, preached the Messiah everywhere with armed squads standing guard throughout, encountering many a time dangerous attacks. Thank God for the good time unfolded of NSCN to do His Will, the Will we ourselves have chosen, we could make a substantial progress in all the fields we undertook. Villagers now could realise the doom of the heathen world they had lived in. The persuasion over to the path of life brought a tremendous contrast. Besides, to redaunt to the glory of His Purpose in this part of the world healing powers began to work through some of His chosen women. Through prayers and the medicines of the Holy Spirit's revelation, a number of incurable diseases of years were healed in the full view of the people. Thousands were converted to Christian faith. Churches sprang up at villages and hymns chanted to His Name for the first time. By 1985, the converts reached around 40 thousand. Shattering of the old wrong world into a new one of hope really began. In the fullness of time His 'Amazing Grace' manifested itself. We are persuaded Christ surely remembered our little Nagaland, the darkest of all, at the time of His Crucifixion. Thanks, no part of Nagaland is left out of His salvation purpose"[27].

Again in Mizoram it is now well known how churches of different denominations disapproved MNF candidates *vis-a-vis* Congress (I) as the MNF snubbed the church leaders as not to interfere in temporal matters. With the blessings of the church, the Congress (I) election manifesto went on to define secularism in a new way. It stated "As Christians it is our bounden duty to proclaim the gospel. To fulfil this irreversible responsibility, we need secularism in letter and spirit. Congress (I) is the only party in the country which is committed to use secularism as a bedrock of unity. It is but reasonable that the Christian should lend support to Congress (I)"[28]. The results were vivid and clear as the church taught the MNF a lesson and paved the way for Congress (I) to capture power.

The character of the secular Indian state changes its colour in Arunachal Pradesh when compared with the Christian dominated state of Nagaland and Mizoram. In Arunachal there is a clandestine attempt to patronise the Hindu organisations to draw the tribesmen towards organised religion (read Hinduism) and prosecute the Christian missionaries by barring their entry into the state. As the Chakmas, the Christian converts are treated as *persona non grata* in Arunachal although the Constitution of India assures protection of religious and cultural minorities. The Arunachal Pradesh Freedom of Religion Act, 1978 although prohibits conversion from one religious faith to another by force, fraudulent means or inducement in reality, it has been applied to the Christian missionary work only. The Hindu line of our secular state is amply reflected here as its Christian line gets manifested in Nagaland, Mizoram or Meghalaya.

The religious undertone in Assam is much more camouflaging than any other states of the North-East. Here the underlying Hindu current is very much eminent and it gets manifested at times during critical junctures of various movements in the state. One such candid expression was made by then President of Assam Sahitya Sabha, Birendra Kumar Bhattacharji, “To some extent, it is true that Assam’s problem of identity has been enacted specifically by abnormal rise in population and a migration of lakhs of Bengali people over the years. Another fear expressed is regarding the rapid increase of Muslim immigrants in the state and their proliferation due to the practices of polygamy. Can ambition of Assam to remain a Hindu and Assamese state be fulfilled within the bounds of the secular Constitution of India? This is the real question”[29]. Similarly during the NAM Summit in New Delhi in March 1983, Deva Prasad Barooah, led an AASU team and presented a memorandum to the foreign dignitaries against the Government of India (which it meekly allowed) which stated “The government seems to be encouraging the entry and settlement of Hindu Bengalees from Bangladesh who will ultimately sweep the language, society and culture of the Assamese people. The Communist parties also seem to be interested to encourage these people as they have proved an easy vehicle to spread their ideology in this part of India”[30]. This clearly reflected the movement’s allergy and hatred towards the left ideology which of course got amply reflected during the prolonged movement.

The VHP supporting the AASU cause blessed them for their daunting task to save the motherland from the clutches of foreigners. The VHP organised huge Hindu congregations which were addressed by the AASU leaders as they upheld the banner of Hindu solidarity. Later the Hindu bias of the Assam Movement got amply reflect in the policies of the AGP government. The process of Hindu solidarity was openly manifested in the AGP-BJP alliance in the run-up to the state assembly election in 2001.

Therefore, the role of the ‘Secular’ Indian state has been in question in case of Assam too. On the one hand it knelt before the chauvinist false propaganda with Hindu communal undertones and on the other allowed the space and fuel to keep Muslim fundamentalism attain firm roots in the state. Exclusive problems faced by the Muslims have been ignored for long in Assam and the secular Indian state stood as a mute spectator regarding their humiliation and discrimination. The policy to brand all Muslims as Bangladeshis continue till today. The hype regarding the issue of infiltration from Bangladesh is still dominating the politics of Assam although the last two census reports project a different scenario. The inhuman approach of the state towards the issue of *char* and *char* dwellers continues till today. The state machinery and its secular counterparts used both these varieties sometimes in tandem and then against each other for serving its own purpose of bad governance, loot and exploitation of the region as a whole.

Epilogue

Unfortunately the Indian state due to its vacillating secular character and a strong communal undertone has been unable to respond to the issues concerning its citizens. The situation can be aptly expressed in the words of D.P. Mukherji, "Indian culture became less concerned with such affairs of the spirit as the person's soul and its discovery, and made instead a religion of politics, which culminated in transforming India into a mother-goddess, saints into political leaders and leaders into saints and heroes; patriotism became the 'religion' of the renascent India"[31]. The north-eastern scenario is nothing different as the policy of playing one religion against another has diluted our secular character. The secular cloak is unable to hide the ugly blood soaked religious dagger. As a result of which the ethno-religious issues have flared to unmanageable heights as the Indian secular state finds it almost impossible either to understand or to tackle it. The repressive state machinery adds fuel to further unrest and a fresh batch of insurgents responds to it. Thus the ethno-religious movements continue and a questionable secular Indian state falls far short of responding to it.

NOTES

1. S.N., Dhyani, (1996). *Secularism : Socio-Legal Issues* (Jaipur : Rawat Publication).
2. *The New Encyclopedia Britannica*, Vol. 10 (Chicago : Encyclopedia Britannica, 1988).
3. *The New Encyclopedia Britannica*, Vol. 8 (Chicago : Encyclopedia Britannica, 1988).
4. *The New Encyclopedia Britannica*, Vol. 11 (Chicago : Encyclopedia Britannica, 1988).
5. *The New Encyclopedia Britannica*, Vol. 19 (Chicago : Encyclopedia Britannica, 1988).

6. *The New Encyclopedia Britannica,* Vol. 24 (Chicago : Encyclopedia Britannica, 1988).
7. *The New Encyclopedia Britannica,* Vol. 24 (Chicago : Encyclopedia Britannica, 1988).
8. *International Encyclopedia of Social Science,* Vol. 6 (London : The Macmillan & Co. The Free Press, 1968).
9. S.N., Dhyani, (1996). *Secularism : Socio-Legal Issues (*Jaipur : Rawat Publication).
10. *Ibid.*
11. P.C., Joshi, (1995). *Secularism and Development : The Indian Experiment* (New Delhi : Vikas).
12. K.N., anikar, (1992). *Culture and Consciousness in Modern India* (New Delhi : P.P.H.).
13. M.S., Gore, (1991). Our Paradigm of Social Transformation in Kurien, C.T., Prabhakar, E.R., Gopal, S., *Economy, Society and Development* (New Delhi : Sage).
14. *Ibid.*
15. Quoted by P.C. Joshi, (1995). *Secularism and Development : The Indian Experiment* (New Delhi : Vikas).
16. *Ibid.*
17. *Ibid.*
18. *Ibid.*
19. Nehru, Jawaharlal, (1995). *An Autobiography* (London : The Bodley Head).
20. Gopal, S. (ed.), (1983). *Jawaharlal Nehru, An Anthology* (Delhi, Oxford University— Press).
21. K.N., Panikar, (1992). *Culture and Consciousness in Modern India* (New Delhi : P.P.H.).
22. For further details see Secularism Reconsidered : Some Reflections in Joshi, P.C., (1995). *Secularism and Development : The Indian Experiment* (New Delhi : Vikas).
23. This section is mainly based on Rabijit Choudhury, "Religious Undertone in Ethnic Issues in North East" in Datta, P.S. (ed.), (1995). *North East and the Indian State* (New Delhi : Vikas).
24. *Ibid.*
25. *Ibid.*
26. *Ibid.*
27. *Ibid.*
28. *Ibid.*
29. Rabijit Choudhury, "Minority Movements : Emergence of the United Minority Front" in Datta. P.S. (ed.), (1990). *Ethnic Movements in Poly-Cultural Assam* (New Delhi : Vikas).
30. Aabijit Choudhury, "Religious Undertones in Ethnic Issue in North-East" in Datta, P.S. (ed.), (1995). *North-East and the Indian State* (New Delhi : Vikas).
31. D.P., Mukherji, (1958). *Diversities* (New Delhi : P.P.H.).

8

EQUALITY, FRATERNITY AND DEVELOPMENT
Resolving Ethnic Conflict

AMALESH BANERJEE

Ethnic conflicts have occupied a considerable length of history of different nations, both developed and developing. Contemporary ethnic conflicts of Yugoslavia and Sri Lanka and in other parts of the world are no better than the American Civil War and British reformation movement of medieval period or the strikes of Patricians and Plebeians of Greek history. Ethnic conflicts in India in recent history have religious, economic and sociological and political character. In this chapter we take up the community and ethnic conflict in the broader perspective of India. The story of North-Eastern states is hardly different from that. The causes of ethnic unrest and the measures to be taken for resolving that are also analysed.

Nature of India : Ethnic Language and Culture

India has a long history of ethnic conflict. But her innate strength of openness and tolerance has largely assimilated different communities. Traditionally, different ethnic groups have been living harmoniously over centuries. However, there had been spurts and conflicts engineered by interested groups and individuals. With the growth of population, persistence of illiteracy, and scarcity of land and other resources, the distribution of economic benefits have become more unequal. In recent history ethnic conflicts grew up along these lines.

India has, according to 1971 census, as many as 1600 languages and mother tongues of which 18 languages are Schedule VIII languages and cover about 96 per cent of the total population of the country. Most of these Schedule VIII languages are state languages. Each of these major languages has a number of sub-groups and variations. These regional variations of the same language are associated with ethno-cultural traditions. Besides these major languages, other languages are mostly spoken by minor ethnic groups localised or dispersed and do not have even organised dialect. With the development of politico-economic conditions in different regions there is a process of assertion of identity as well as affiliation and assimilation with dominant language groups. The assimilation of Bhojpuri, Magadhi and Maithili in Hindi is a gradual process of assimilation. Some ethnic groups and their languages are coming up and evolving in a full form. Languages such as Santhali, Dogri (of JK), Tulu (of Karnataka) and such others are developing and claiming for recognition as the Schedule VIII language. Hundreds of ethnic groups having diverse customs, culture and language are existing in different parts of the country's hill and plain areas.

Before coming to other complexion of Indian ethnicity, we indulge in a little more digression on the linguistic genesis of Indian ethnic composition.

Broadly speaking the languages of India can be divided in four families which comprise all other sub-streams of languages. Dravidian, Indo-Iranian, Austro-Asiatic and Sino-Tibetan. The major groups of Dravidian languages are spoken in south India. Indo-Aryan is a sub-group of Indo-Iranian language family which is itself a part of the Indo-European language family (to which Latin, Greek, German, Slavic, Roman and other European languages belong). Another sub-group of Indo-European language family is the Iranian sub-group of languages which are spoken in Iraq, Iran, Afghanistan and also in parts of Soviet Union.

The roots of Indo-Aryan group is to be found in Sanskrit, the classical language. Pali, Prakrit and Hindi are the descendants of Sanskrit. Indian ethnic character and language and culture got a strong contact with Persian, the Iranian language as a result of Muslim invasion of India time and again. The development of Hindustani is a result of this intermix of Persian and Indian people.

Two major languages following from that are Hindi and Urdu. Hindi has two groups – Kosali or eastern and western Hindi and the Magadhan group. Western Magadhan group comprises Bhojpuri and Sadani, central Magadhan group comprises Maithili (North Bihar) and Magadhi (in South Bihar). Eastern Magadhan language family comprises

Bengali, Assamese and Oriya. Austro-Asian languages are broadly spoken by tribal population like Munda and Kolari group. Khasi is one of the Austro-Asian language spoken in Meghalaya. Sino-Tibetan languages are represented by various offshoots of the Thai and Chinese language groups. The Khampti is spoken by small tribes in the eastern frontier of India. Manipuri or Meithei has Tibetan Burma dialect. Nepali uses Devanagri Hindi script and Lepcha is a branch of Tibeto Burman dialects.

Ethno-Religious Position

Ethno-religious scenario of India is another dimension of ethnic complexities. India is the home of some great religions and the birth place of some other religions. Although India has no state religion, vast majority of the people are Hindus and are spread over all states. Hundreds of ethnic groups of tribals have had animistic religious practices. Almost thousand years of Muslim rule and three hundred years of British colonial rule also resulted in large scale religious conversion. In many areas religion and language have undergone change. As a result of these new ethno-religious groups emerged.

Hinduism has been a great unifying force and has the pre-Aryan link with Dravidian elements. The *Vedas* of Aryans and Dravidian scripts have made a fusion in Hinduism. Shak, Huns and Muslim, Christian and Zorastrian came from outside India. Jainism and Buddhism, two offshoots of Hinduism, are spread over to other countries. Mauryan emperor preached Buddhism in many parts of Asian countries. Thus the ancient story of ethno-religious transformation is a pointer to the dynamics of ethnic and religious changes.

Ethnic Population

If we look to the states of India this will also provide lessons as to how hundreds of ethnic groups are living and working together towards a harmonious living with distinct identity of culture and faith. Entho-religious composition found an ideal existence in Indian states of which Jammu and Kashmir is the best example and Kerala and West Bengal are good examples. In spite of having different ethnic and religious groups, ethnic harmony exists and cultures of different ethnic groups are flourishing. Earlier we have seen ethnolinguistic classification and Bihar's three major language dialects coming closer to the state language

Hindi. Maithili which is a distinct dialect is also assimilating itself with state language. Various complex ethnic composition exists in Jharkhand. According to 1991 census there are as many as 49 tribes and semi-tribes in Jharkhand and not all of them are classified as scheduled castes, scheduled tribes and backward communities.

Large tribal groups such as Kurmis, Santhals, Mundas, Oraons, Kharian and Hos are distinct groups with lakhs of people spread over different areas having distinct dialect, tradition and culture. Many of them are victims of upper caste terrorisation, militant oppression, racial and cultural discrimination and driven from their possession of natural resources. Ethnic composition of Orissa is also revealing. In 1971 census tribals constituted 23 per cent of the state's population and declined to 22.2 per cent in 1991 census as stated in Table 8.1.

Table 8.1: Tribal Population in India, 1991

States	Population in Lakhs	Per cent to the State's Population
Andhra Pradesh	42.00	6.31
Assam	26.74	12.82
Bihar	66.17	7.66
Gujarat	61.62	14.92
Himachal Pradesh	2.18	4.22
Karnataka	19.16	4.26
Kerala	3.21	1.10
Madhya Pradesh	153.99	23.27
Maharashtra	73.18	9.27
Orissa	70.32	22.21
Rajasthan	54.75	12.44
Tamil Nadu	5.74	1.03
Uttar Pradesh	2.88	0.21
West Bengal	38.09	5.59
India	677.58	8.08

Source : Census of India 1991.

In Orissa there are 62 tribal communities of which 25 communities speak their own languages. Kondh, Santhal, Soura and Kolha have their own scripts and comprise one-third of total tribal people in Orissa. Another group of tribes (8) do not have their written language but each has more than one lakh population. (Oraon, Kisan, Khadia, Gond,

Paraja, Bhumija, Munda, Lodha, Sabar belong to this category); 13 other minor communities have their own spoken language; then there are about 37 other tribal communities who do not have spoken languages and speak languages of their neighbouring tribes. For development purposes tribes are classified as (a) Primitive living in inaccessible hill areas; (b) Tribes in transition living in foothills and forest areas; (c) Assimilated tribes who have integrated themselves in non-tribal cultural system; and (d) Aristocratic tribes who are by origin tribes but are now indistinguishable from other non-tribals.

In the North-East region, according to 1991 census Arunachal Pradesh has 111 tribes and sub-tribes. Most of these people live on shifting cultivation. Due to lack of communication most of the tribal people living in hill areas are in isolation and are, therefore, devoid of full benefits of development. Actual cultivation is done by non-tribals and immigrants, including Nepalis, Bangladeshis and plain tribals on lease basis and this has led to considerable complication. The other North-Eastern states also have dominant tribal population. About 90 per cent of Meghalaya's total population of 18 lakhs are tribals of various complexions. Nagaland has been plunged into violence since 1950 when A.Z. Phizo took to arms for a sovereign state of Nagaland. Recent history indicates that Naga underground tribes are divided and some are still maintaining a lingering hope of independent state while other are fighting for a Nagalim (greater Nagaland consisting some territories of Assam, Manipur and Burma). Different Naga tribes are spread over different neighbouring states. Manipur has a sizeable group in Ukhrul area. Now a constant tussle is on between two states; while Nagas claim Ukhrul as their land, the Meiteis, the valley people of Manipur are not to allow the separation. Thus Nagaland has two types of strife : one for their unified land, and, second for retaining their identity in an independent state in the great Indian subcontinent.

Language and cultural homogeneity and purity often lead to tribal strife. Manipur Meiteis do not allow Bishnupria community to live in their land. They consider Manipur Bishnupria as the language of alien land; hence they drive out the Manipuri Bishnupria tribals. Manipur is inhabited by various communities including Meiteis, the dominant group, Tangkhuls, Maos, Kukis, Muslims and others.

Ethnic cleansing led to violence between the Nagas and the Kukis. Another example is provided by Santhals and Boros in Kokrajhar area of Assam. Bodos are driving out the Santhals from their houses they have been living from centuries.

Ethnic composition of the population of West Bengal is no less complex. As we have seen above that around six per cent of population of West Bengal are tribal. Most of the tribal population came in the state in different connection – either driven by natural or human forces or due to pull of occupation and urbanisation. Western districts, Midnapore, Bankura, Birbhum, Burdwan as well as northern districts, Darjeeling, Jalpaiguri, Coochbehar and Dinajpur are the major concentration of tribal population. There are three groups of tribal population in West Bengal namely the pre-Dravidian, Dravidian and Mongoloid. The first two groups comprise Santhal, Munda, Korah, Mohali, Lodha, Kheria. A sizeable number among these tribal groups were driven from other neighbouring states by zamindars, caste repression and natural calamities. Also rapid urbanisation and mining development had drawn a considerable number of indigenous and tribal people as labour in those areas. Similarly in North Bengal, Mongoloid tribes like Bhutia, Chakma, Lepcha, Sherpa, Toto, Metch, Rabha etc. comprising only three per cent of the tribal population of the state live near the foothills of Himalayas. Although small in group some of them have distinct socio-cultural heritage.

Conflict and Causes

Having examined the extensive phenomenon of ethnic development in different parts of our country, we can now briefly discuss the nature of conflicts and causes of conflicts. (a) Ethnic conflict may break out of sheer hatred and one ethnic group may raid the area of another driving out the latter; (b) Ethnic conflict may take the form of driving out one group by another group in order to grab the land.

Causes of Conflicts

Ethnic relation examined historically in different countries and India indicate that it is a complicated problem and multiplicity of reason may be identified. In our country, over centuries different flows of migration, invasion and forced settlement took place. Old and new settlements got mixed up leaving a legacy of heterogeneous components of religions and cultural remnants. This had developed into conflict of identity and crises for preserving secluded virtues of primitive egotism. Nationalism in Indian freedom movement could hardly change that total fabric except some splinter excitements here and there.

As stated above, ethnic composition in India reveals profound diversities in race, religion and culture. This has been further accentuated by unplanned trickle down process of centralised planning and economic development. We can classify a few reasons for the ongoing conflicts arising out of this diversities and divisive trends. (a) First is the subjective and the normative set of factors which comprise religious, linguistic and cultural issues; (b) Secondly, economic status, inequality, dispossession of land, denial of economic advantages, oppression and exploitation are also important reasons for ethnic conflict; (c) Ethnic conflict is also interpreted as a legacy of colonial expansion and policies. During the colonial period American Indians were used as slaves and millions of Negroes were imported as slaves in Mexico, Argentina, Brazil and USA. These colonial settlers exploited the slaves and immigrants in the merchant interest. This is the phenomenon in our number of states; and (d) Thirdly, political and administrative suppression and denial of freedom in decision making process is also a strong reason for ethnic conflict. If we look at the ethnic conflicts in different parts of the country it will appear that many of these factors combined together hastening explosive expression of unrealised aspirations.

Resolving Ethnic Conflict

History is replete with instances of ethno-religious conflicts. In the global context the religious conflicts have been resolved by continuous assimilation and new perceptions. Great religious preachers emerged whenever there were conflicts in the established religions like Christianity, Buddhism, Hinduism. Deformation and Reformation of Christianity is a great historical event (Mac 15/547) as Luther launched Ninety-five of theses as the catalyst of the Reformation (Mac 15/549). Jainism and Buddhism also witnessed similar reformation. Evolution of Hindu civilization is even more pervasive. It is a convergence of divergent faiths assimilating with the mainstream practices. It is the selective and synthetic practices of Hindu system that has made Hinduism both a civilization and a conglomerate of religions, with neither a beginning, a founder, nor a central authority, hierarchy, or organisation. It is the belief of eternal march of human beings in the fuller perfection and the process of integration with the divinity that has made the Hindu religion most assimilative, tolerant and all-embracing of the divergent flows and practices, (Mac 8/888). Many practices and components of other faiths i.e., Jainism, Buddhism have gradually contributed to the greater composing strength of Hinduism. Under the vast umbrella of all-pervasive existence of eternal soul, Hinduism has accommodated indigenous beliefs, pre-Aryan sects, *ahimsa* of Jainism and Buddhism. Indian National Flag, is a an assertion of this great assimilative strength of Indian civilization. From the time of Sankara to Ramakrishna many saints, organisations have emerged and contributed to the eclectic excellence of Indian integrated faith. From Brahminism, Sakti, Bhakti cult and more recent, Kabir, Nanak, Ramakrishna, Brahmosamaj, Arya Samaj there have been a continuous exploration of eternal spirit and universality of existences, animate and inanimate form, in the universe. Thus ethno-religious conflict resolution is essentially the inner strength of Indian civilization. Those who instigate ethnoreligious conflicts should take lesson from history of Indian civilization which is antithetical to conversion, cleansing and killing (Macro 8/906).

Ethno-religious differences are in a constant process of transformation with the march of science and technology and enlightenment and understanding among the people through greater mobility and awareness. Not only the established religions but also the tribal religions are undergoing transformation. Tribal religions beliefs are based on natural phenomenon, ignorance and charisma. With the coming in contact with stronger culture, the two cultures synthesise together to give rise to a new religion. This new type of religious movements of tribals is found in North America, South Africa, Rhodesia, New Zealand and other parts of the world (Mac 18/698-705).

Conflicts and Culture

Culture is the composite expression of human behaviour and is the style and mode of perception of life. It is conditioned by bounds of natural topography in which the people live, the history of language, literatures, the faith and religion and the influence of other countries. Since indigenous and tribal people live in a difficult geographical setting their faiths, customs, traditions are conditioned by limited knowledge and limited perceptions of the natural phenomena.

On cultural front, conflict arises due to suppression of culture or language which is already developed. In recent history of Indian sub-continent, violent explosion of cultural and language suppression has resulted in the formation of Bangladesh.

In our country linguistic state formation has been as administrative step to resolve the conflict and to develop the languages. But that was not exhaustive enough to contain the cultural conflict. Languages which are not state languages, but are included in the Schedule VIII, receive special attention for development. Urdu which is not a state language but included in the schedule is prevalent across the state. Similarly the languages which have developed substantially and have large following should be included in the schedule. As mentioned above Dogri, Santhali, Nepali, have large following and developed literature; hence they should be included in the schedule.

However, hundreds of other mother tongues and dialects should have the proper opportunity of use and expression upto a certain level. Finally, minor dialects of hundreds of ethnic groups and tribals have to be developed in a common dialect and assimilated with the developed languages. Even a fairly developed sub-group language, Maithili has been assimilated with state language Hindi. While developed Bodo language deserves equal treatment with other developed languages, it has to expand and include other sub-dialects of the region so as to develop into a widely similar language with common dialect.

Strength of dynamic development of language and culture lies in the open society and co-existence of other minor languages, dialects and customs of ethnic groups. Mutual cross-fertilization of culture, language and religion is a historical process and a step towards advancement.

Education

For resolving ethnic conflict, education has to be universal among the different ethnic groups. Education opens the door to enlightenment which in turn, will transform the people to be tolerant and accommodating.

All steps should be taken to develop and preserve the colourful culture of the nationalities and the ethnic groups. Promotion of mass culture and traditional qualities of the tribals is an important step to resolve the ethnic conflict. Promotion of Kok Barak language of Tripura and Santhali language in West Bengal are cases in point.

Kala Sanmilani

All ethnic groups have a very lively and natural expression of art, dance and music. The folk dance and music of north-eastern states are very lively and natural which appeals to human feelings universally. Connoisseurs of music and dance and the government must come forward to enrich the people-oriented traditional dance, music and art of the hundreds of ethnic groups in this area. There has been attempt individually in the past to develop the tribal culture of the regions. Maharaja Bir Chandra was an illustration of individual effort. But in the present democratic set-up people's organisations should come up in the North-East with larger initiative and interaction to develop the latent potentiality of tribal art and culture.

Administrative Steps

Major steps to resolve the ethnic conflict have to be taken at the administrative front. Besides encouraging the culture and language of the tribals, states have been formed to satisfy subnationalities. Autonomous Councils have been formed. Considerable progress has been achieved in Tripura.

Land

One very acute problem of ethnic conflict is the sharing of natural resources. Tribals are hundred per cent in the lap of nature, born and brought up in nature, cultivating stretches of land on hill side and shifting from place to place. Tribals should not be pushed out of their land and forest area. Settled cultivation with ownership of land and input support from the government is the main passage to prosperity. But with population growth among tribal themselves, there should be gradual process of rehabilitation of the tribal people from their limited area to the extended area outside. Alternative income opportunities have to be developed in the tribal area. Land reform and redistribution of surplus land to a great extent benefit the landless tribals. Land ownership will encourage higher productivity and income. Much of the anger of small tribal groups is due to deprivation of their settlement.

West Bengal

West Bengal has made considerable success in this field. Almost one-fourth population of the country are scheduled castes, scheduled tribes and other categories. Even with the formation of separate states in the North-East, poverty could not be eliminated. In West Bengal, as we have seen above, there are 6 per cent scheduled tribes of India. But in all-India perspective about 80 per cent of these people who received land are in W.B. Minority Development and Welfare Corporation of West Bengal has done commendable work in extending loans to the tribals for taking up self-help projects. Around ten thousand men and women tribal people received financial assistance for such self-help activities.

IRDP and other central projects for housing settlement are being utilised throughout the country. However, there is more importance for cluster approach rather than individual approach.

Micro Project and Regional Plan

Micro project for combined ethnic group in a particular small sector is essential for development. Health education, sanitation, cultivation by minor ethnic groups in a microscopic area is of primary importance.

However, regional plan is essential for development of natural resources and for greater production and employment opportunity of the ethnic groups. While panchayat can take up the micro projects, a regional plan comprising districts and panchayats are essential for agricultural, irrigation, drought and flood reduction.

Recently regional plan has been given due importance in West Bengal. The North Bengal development plan and Western District development plan are important steps in the direction. In Orissa also very recently the chronic drought-hit tribal settled western districts are brought under a development council. Ladhak in Jammu and Kashmir, Surat and Kutch in Gujarat are now having regional planning which will vastly improve the tribal people.

China

China has made a successful development of the ethnic groups. Larger ethnic minorities have been given autonomous areas and development projects are implemented in those autonomous areas according to the needs of those regions. There are 53 minority groups spreading over about 60 per cent of the total area of the country with only 6 per cent population or 35 million. Large minority groups have some kind of autonomy or government, autonomous areas of several sorts have been formulated on the basis of geographical distribution of nationalities (Mac 4/270-4).

Thus, ethnic conflict resolution requires great imagination, tolerance, catholicity and administrative and economic strategy. India has a great history of absorbing the diverse ethnic groups. However, in modern times the rights, justice and equality of the people have to be ensured. Minor ethnic groups and tribals were historically oppressed and deprived of justice and freedom. They were under subjugation of either landlords, traders or high caste people. Time now has come to eliminate this social gap for harmony and progress.

People's Forum

Social scientists have not neglected the importance of pressure groups in the development process. Sen has specifically pointed out that when the people are neglected and oppressed they must rise in self-righteousness; they must rise in fury. Social and political form is an important bargaining instrument in the socio-political structure of our country. Democracy is a very powerful platform where people can exercise their freedom for alleviation of grievances and injustices.

However decimation, cleansing and annihilation is a negative process. A vicious cycle of hatred and violence will entail further retaliation and resultant slow growth and accentuation of poverty. Hence development and social justice require participation, deliberation, cooperation and interaction – all the democratic means to resolving the conflict.

Conclusion

Ethnic conflicts arise out of socio-economic conditions within political economic structure of the country.

If land, labour, capital, culture and religion are the major sources of conflict among the human race then liberty, equality, fraternity and economic development are the effective means for resolving the conflict. This is true with the blacks and Indians in America. Irish and Scotch in UK, Bavarians and Jews in Germany, Slovaks and Czechs in former Czechoslovakia and minorities in the eastern states of our country.

Conflicts arising out of diversities and divisive trends may be classified as (a) originating from religions and cultural set of factors; (b) denial of freedom and suppression of rights; (c) poverty, inequality, dispossession of land, oppression and exploitation. Many factors combine together for explosive expression of unrealised aspirations. During the post-independence period inter-linkage of caste-class, economic and political factors degenerated the ethnic conflicts into violence and displacement of people from their homes and cleansing their areas by terrorist activities.

The democratic Constitution of India has made enough provision for resolving the ethnic conflict. Upliftment of Tribal people, their empowerment of democratic rights, and equality are important measures for resolving the conflict. Development of capability and freedom from oppression through economic and administrative reform are the two-pronged strategy to resolve the ethnic conflict generated through socio-economic inequality and oppression.

REFERENCES

Agarwal, A.C.; Maniklal Bose; A. Janaiah (2000). Poverty and Income Distribution. (Chattisgarh), *E.P.W.*, December 30.

Bardhan, Pranab (2001). Social Justice in the Global Economy, *Economic and Political Weekly*, February 3-10.

Borpujari, H.K. (1970). *Problems of the Hill Tribes of North-East Frontier.*

Dass, G. (1995). *Tribes of Arunachal Pradesh in Transition.*

Ekka, Alexus (2000). Jharkhand Tribals : Are they Really a Minority, *E.P.W.*, December 30.

Encyclopaedia Britannica (1982). Several Volumes. Micropedia and Macropedia.

Guha Thakurta, S.N. (1986). *Tripura,* National Book Trust, New Delhi.

Geetha, V. (2001). Who is the Third that Walks Behind You? *E.P.W.*, January 13.

Hussain, Monirul (2000). State Identity Movements and Internal Displacement in the North-East. *E.P.W.*, December 16.

Janaiah, A. Mahabub Hossain, M.L.Bose; Jawahar Thakur (2000). Rural Income Distribution and Poverty in Hinar, *E.P.W.*, December 30.

Kaul, Rekha (2001). Accessing Primary Education, *E.P.W.* January 13.

Kissku, Upen (2001). Pashchimbonga : Prasanga Adibasi Unnayan (Bengali), *Nandan*, March 2001.

Kamat, A.R. (1980). Ethno-Linguistic Issues in Indian Federal Context, *E.P.W.*, June 21-24.

Pantham, Thomas (2001). 'Liberal Multiculturalism Reconsidered' review article in *Economic and Political Weekly,* Feb. 3-10.

Parekh, Bhikhu (2000). *Rethinking Multiculturalism; Cultural Diversity and Political Theory.* Macmillan Press, London.

Roy Burman, J.J. (2001). Shivaji's Myth and Maharashtra's Syncretise Traditions, *E.P.W.*, April 14.

Sen, A.K. (1999). *Development as Freedom.* Oxford University Press, New Delhi.

Sen, A.K. and Jean Dreze (1997). *India : Economic Development and Social Opportunity.* Oxford University Press, New Delhi.

Vidyarthi, L.P. (1997). *Tribal Culture of India.* Concept Publishing Company, New Delhi.

9

ETHNO-CULTURAL PARANOIA AND POLITICAL DESIGN
Some Reflections

ABHIJIT CHOUDHURY

The Dilemma of World Community *Vs.* Exclusive Communities

Years ago, I came across an interesting title, *The World My Village*. So far as I remember, it was authored by Mrs. Ellen Roy — the American wife of the Indian Marxist revolutionary, M.N. Roy. What struck my imagination was its title! In this work the world-view of on individual, committed to Roy's 'Radical Humanism', was reflected. Her views about the human problems verged on cosmopolitanism. Since then, decades have passed. We are now witnessing worldwide historic transitions beginning in the late nineteen-seventies. Keeping track of these developments, we may discern two main trends in our community/group behaviour patterns. On the one hand, we are trying to visualise the world as our home. And on the other, we are, under most of the circumstances, trying to rationalise that *our homes* should remain our exclusive *worlds* barred to the 'outsiders'!

The first trend is closely connected with the contemporary historical developments which have built up a global market economic nexus that no political system can ignore any more. Despite the fact of the US dictations, which is of course unwelcome, to the Third World, we have to agree that the *Perestroika* in the erstwhile Soviet Union, the Fifth Modernization bringing about socialist market economy in China and India's current economic reform programmes are all, a reflection of opening up of the locally protected systems to the new necessities of our times. The pressures of global changes were manifested in the Cuban election held in 1992-93. The Khomeini-led Iranian system, though anti-West in its bearings, has been unable to withstand the need for readjustment of its economic relation with some Western countries, say Germany. Of late, the movement towards the European Union has been a case at hand.[1]

Yet, the world has not become 'unipolar'; since in spite of a general process of 'westernisation' continuing to mould and shape our material and ideological existence, we within our respective ethnic folds are constantly being guided by the considerations of 'we' and 'they' in our inter-ethnic and cultural transactions. That way, our group behaviour reflect our communal exclusiveness. Parochial though, it is the reality of human nature. Perhaps it would be difficult to avoid this question. Is communal exclusiveness ingrained in human nature? For, we may easily identify the operation of the dialectics in human nature. While on the one hand, we exhibit from time to time our tremendous potentials to act in unison to help and co-operate with fellow human beings cutting across geographical and ethno-cultural borders and even emotionally feel for them in the event of a catastrophe; on the other, we also behave in the ugliest possible manner *vis-a-vis* our other ethnic neighbours as it so happened in Bosnia or nearer home in Manipur. This second aspect of group behaviour may compel one to seriously ponder on the views of certain social biologists like Desmond Morris and Edmund Wilson about, territoriality and antipathy towards the 'outgroups.' At this point I may hazard a poser: *Are such aspects as the above in our group behaviour genetically transmitted through an emotional build up through several generations; or, is it that we carry potential genes guiding such reaction after they are activated by our social traditions emotionally and by environmental influences!*[2]

In this context, the happenings in the post-USSR Commonwealth of Independent States (CIS) and in some East-European countries including the erstwhile Yugoslavia may come to our mind. Events in the former Yugoslavia involving the mutually embittered ethnic groups may happen elsewhere. The KOSSOVO crisis continues. Czechoslovakia has already broken apart.[3] Even though one may agree that the Marxist-Leninist experiments with the 'nationality question' in the former USSR and elsewhere in the Socialist World assisted the process of development and articulation of the backward 'nationalities'; one has to acknowledge the fact that the inter-ethnic contradictions and rivalries could never be eradicated. They only remained subterranean in a centralised command system of political economy.

The whims of a leader like Stalin who would, for example, transplant the Muskerite Turks from the Caucasus region onto the Tadjik homeland in Central Asia on suspicion of collaboration with the German invaders, exacerbated the ethnic divides which led to riots in Tadjikistan in 1990-91. It appears that dealing with the 'nationality question', neither Lenin nor Stalin could really fathom the depth of man's basic instincts like competitiveness and acquisitiveness guiding and rationalising his personal equations as well as his 'in group' loyalties. The unification of Vietnam and, later, of Germany illustrate the fact that ethno-cultural homogeneity within a more or less territorially integrated area can break the ideological and other barriers. Politico-economic problems like stagnation and readjustment usually act as some of the catalysts in the process.

Extremes of ethno-cultural paranoia had surfaced in the civil war in former Yugoslavia, in Nagomo-Karabakh region and elsewhere in the bygone Soviet Union. The indigenous 'native' demonstrations throughout the two Americas – North and South – during the quincentennial celebrations of Columbus' discovery confirmed that the Amerindian irredentism has taken a firm hold on the psyche of the indigenous people there. Indirectly, the award of 1992 Nobel Peace Prize to Ms. Rigoberta Menchu served as a recognition of the Amerindian assertion of identity. The current controversies in New Zealand and Australia involving the Maori and the Australian aboriginals demands on their lands and their rights have the same tenor. They rightly demand the correction to the wrongs done to them. The very recent "Sorry", the Australian State was compelled to say, to the Aboriginals for the "Stolen Generation" is a straight pointer to the fact that the 'mischievous West' could not claim to be the sole keepers of human conscience! The Irish, Welsh and Scottish contradictions *vis-a-vis* the English cannot be wished away.

Another interesting negation of the concept of 'unipolarity' is the alignment of the Islamic Nations *vis-a-vis* the West. Polarisation continues with the changing power equations. The Islamic antagonism to the West, it may be remembered, is the product of western colonial domination both in politico-economic and cultural terms. The West viewed Islamic dominance over a major chunk of Afro-Asia as symbol of medieval backwardness – a view still continues to be articulated circuitously by many western writers like Samuel Huntington.[4] The close connections between colonialism and associated anthropo-historical practices had accentuated the conflict between the world views of the Christian West and the Islamic world which have found a newer expression in Huntington. However, from historical point of view, the domino effect of colonialism on the countries like India, led to withdrawal on the part of the Muslim elites. Similar situations could be seen in many Islamic societies, for instance, in West Asia and North Africa. This initial reaction paved the foundation for some modernist movements like those of Sir Sayyid Ahmed Khan in India, of Mustafa Kemal Ataturk in Turkey, or Jaglul Pasha in Egypt. The continuing antagonism was sought to be either compromised or reduced by these movements, although they could not eradicate them. So, we find a revival of Islamic movements in Turkey, Egypt and Albania now! The formation of an Islamic Economic Union of some Central Asian states with Iran serves as an end product of this continuing antagonism. Politically, it is expressed through an Organisation of Islamic states. Taking India and China as other Unique Civilisational/Culture Zones, one can take notice of a 'multi-polar' world instead of the 'unipolar'.[5] That is why the current opening up processes are accompanied by growing ethno-cultural paranoia. At the root of this paranoia we can trace the fear of economic dominance by the technologically advanced West at the macro-level of international relation. At the micro-level of local zones again, the inter-ethnic relations are shadowed by a fear of losing one's identity with the ongoing market processes and the question of sharing the available resources.

A note of caution may be sounded at this point, that the observations above should not be construed as my subscription to the concept of 'cultural assimilation' of different ethnic groups (I prefer the use of 'ethnos' for them). It is to the contrary. In fact, history demonstrates that one of the hardest tasks before us – as members of our respective groups – is how to overcome, as yet, the limitations set by our cultural geographic backgrounds. Our mindsets are largely moulded by our habitats and the environs they offer as well as by our emotional 'in-group' loyalties. Despite the westernising processes our group loyalties cannot die altogether. This is particularly true with regard to cultural traditions of which the Japanese experience is one of the classic instances. A human world without socio-cultural diversity is bound to be a monolith. Cultural unipolarity should, therefore, always be unwelcome! Thinkers like Nehru and Verrier Elwin, within their own limitations, rightly sought to encourage the tribals of India to develop according to their own genius. Seen from this angle, the very idea of 'assimilation' is against purity and democratic principles. A *cultural* interpretation of, say the Indian history, based on the idea of assimilation must be avoided. In Canada, the French Canadians could partake of the evolution of the Canadian political economy without being 'English' Canadians. They would naturally reject Mr. Mulrony's proposals of a 'unitary' Constitution. In the Indian context, debates on the Centre-State relations assume historic proportions in the light of these experiences.

Here, one may pause to ponder if plurality is rooted in the problems of centrifugal tendencies in ethno-cultural terms. Plurality, by itself need not be treated as the root of all such problems. Theoretically speaking, liberalism provides enough room for plural articulation of ideals and aspirations. Nor pluralism is entirely negated in socialism.[6] Consensus, dissent as well as an adjustment of class antagonism (as in West Bengal or Kerala) constitute its political foundation.[7] The Marxist-Leninist system believes that the individual is capable of transforming himself within the socialist context. The works of George Thompson (*The Human Essence*) or Adam Schaff (*Marxism and the Human Individual*) demonstrate this belief. However, Marxism and Leninism does not encourage *pluralism* in ethno-political terms; though it provides for an alternative outlet for dissent and consensus through the working of "democratic centralism" within the party and power structure of a basically 'unitary' nature. Because ethnic-politics and ethno-nationalism eat into the attempts at eradicating a class-structured society—the long term goal of Marxism and Leninism. However, recent happenings in the Socialist world have necessitated a rethinking on the actual functioning of "democratic centralism" in tackling dormant ethno-nationalism. My contention is that though plurality is not at the root of centrifugalism, it very often faces the clash of interest among the ethnic groups constituting it.

Ethnicity essentially represents cultural articulation of identity. Often symbolisms, apart from norms and practices, drawn from customs, beliefs, values and vehicles of articulation provide for ethnic specificity. Dress and food habits and certain articulatory vehicles of emotion like dance forms also carry the aura of ethnic identity. Though 'nationality' emerges partly from the ground reality of historic group cohesiveness, it is also essentially a product of the realm of consciousness of that ground situation. Ethnicity represents an articulation of 'nationality' which can be both cultural and political at the same time in the sense that political mobilisation of ethno-cultural symbols attempts at consolidating ethno-nationalism. Therefore, 'ethnicity' and 'nationality', are collateral. The Laskian concept of 'nationality' as a special corporate unity "emanating from a spiritual sentiment or principle" due to sharing of common history and traditions by a territorially well defined culture group signifies homogeneity, which guides inter-ethnic relations in a plural political-economy. It is natural, therefore, that the 'in-group out-group' contradictions are often sharp in a 'heterogeneous' plural system. To illustrate this contention a few historical examples may be drawn.

Take, for instance, the case of the Roman world. As the empire spread across the known world, the ethnic contradictions involving the pagan Romans, Christians, Jews, Blacks and the so-called 'barbarian' tribes grew sharper. There were not only *class* contradiction as manifested in the slave revolts supported by the 'coloni' (free peasants); but also ethnic struggles in different parts of the empire (e.g., the Gaul, Germania, Britain, North Africa, Danubian frontier and Israel/Palestine). Passing over, if we look into the subsequent history of Europe, the jew-Christian antagonism becomes evident. In spite of many an internal contradiction due to varying degrees of historical and culture-geographical backgrounds of the Jews from different parts of Europe and the world, the Jewish nationality was cemented by Judaism with its Yiddish vehicle. Judaic norms and practices serve to symbolise their ethnic articulation *vis-a-vis* the Christians. Both of them remained mutually exclusive and paranoid. The Fascist anti-Semitism was only a climactic aspect of what had been going on for centuries.[8] Albeit in its most extreme form.

A plural state and society is, in Lord Acton's views a "necessary condition" of civilised life. It presupposes that 'inferior' or 'exhausted and decaying' ethnic groups revive and progress in political union with races 'intellectually superior' or by their contact with a 'younger' vitality. This is primarily a liberal justification for a plural system. But the condition necessary to Lord Acton's 'ideal situation' are seldom to be found. Today's technological civilisation with a growing global population problem associated with economic recessionist trends and unemployment, environmental degradations and socio-economic disparity (due to governmental failures and other factors) among the various global regions is witnessing sharper competition for resources. It, in turn, leads to paranoid inter-ethnic reactions which are increasingly surfacing in their bitter forms. What had happened in, say Georgia involving the Abkhazia region or still happening in the former Yugoslavia between the Serbs and the others like the Croats, Bosnian Muslims and Kossovan minorities go to revive the older principle of "one nationality one state" along the Brycean definition of *nation* that : "A nation is a nationality which has organised itself into a political body either independent or desiring" to be so. The aftermath of the break up of the USSR appears to fulfil the Hayesian notion that : "A nationality by acquiring unity and sovereign independence becomes a nation". The erstwhile Soviet Union ultimately came to serve as the cradle of several new nations. That the attempts at adjusting the antagonistic interests in a multi-national/multi-ethnic political-economy like the USSR have failed due to *human* and other reasons exposed the fact that a centralised command system of power structure cannot hold a heterogeneous system together for long.

In the multi-ethnic American politico-economy, the context of plurality assumes an interesting dimension in view of the talk of "American dream" and "Americanism". Already since the seventeenth and eighteenth centuries, the concept of "Americanism" was emerging. A French observer Crevecoeur made a point in saying that :

> A European, when he first arrives, seems limited in his intentions as well as in his views; but he suddenly alters his scale. He no sooner breathes our air then he forms new schemes, and embarks on designs he never would have thought of in his own country ... He begins to feel the effects of a sort of resurrection; hitherto he had not lived, but simply vegetated; he now feels himself a man, because he is treated as such ... He begins to forget his former servitude and dependence, his heart involuntarily dilates and glows, and his first swell inspires him with those new thoughts which mark an American."[9]

In the literary scene of the USA — from Fennymoor Cooper and

Mark Twain to Robert Frost and John Steinbeck — the American psyche has been tuned to that quest. But, culturally, it represents an attempt to consolidate their federal structure *vis-a-vis* various undercurrents of ethnic identities in the shape of Asian-American, Black-American, Euro-American and the native-American lobbies. In the Presidential Election Campaigns, Bill Clinton often spoke of an "American dream". A clearer vision of this 'dream' is yet to emerge. Is it merely consolidation and spread of democratic values as it is understood there; or is it to be achieved through the American domination in world affairs? The recent American policies directed towards "unipolarity" indicate the second option more than the first. At least, this American 'megalothymia' is betrayed in the Economic Espionage Act passed in 1996.[10] Moreover, Crevecoeur's "Americanism" was not meant for the American natives, who were ruthlessly deprived of their rights by the Federal Government.

Similarly, the confederal structure of the Canadian political economy manifests its ethnic history. The Latin American Literature with its bedrock of nativism has been, in essence, a quest for a Latin American identity bereft of its European past. Given these backdrops, delineated above, how do we make an attempt at minimising the perplexing dilemma of choice between the World Community and the mutually exclusive communities! In the present capitalist crisis of the world, due to the faulty Western methods, the struggle for economic survival has assumed a 'Darwinian' proportion. These problems are compounded by vulgar consumerism of market economy, demographic imbalances and disparities in different parts of the world. I doubt if the trans/multi- national business lobbies can help our struggle against these problems. Under the circumstances, the Gandhian view that the Earth has got enough resources to satisfy our need but not our greed assumes new relevance. It does not require to reiterate that the principle of equitable distribution and sharing of resources may assist in finding a way to minimise the aforesaid dilemma. I emphatically hold that the current American ways of dealing with these problems and its attitude to the rest of the world will take us further away from the resolution of this dilemma. Our experiences of the controversies surrounding the recent questions of international relations around the Maastricht Treaty and the Euro Parliament etcetera, have shown that it would not be easy to overcome the claims of national interests. Meanwhile, the USA would do well to remember that even the haughty Athenian and Roman empires could not survive the ravages of time!

The Context of the Indian Transition

If the Indian situation is studied within the general framework attempted above, then certain insights would emerge. Two things are to be borne in mind. One, that India is an entity with continental characteristics in every respect; and two, that the process of India's transition to modernity since the nineteenth century are not yet over. On a localised scale of the South Asia, the two types of mind-sets – we are tracing – are also working in our multi-ethnic political-economy (I call it a meta-ethnos or meta-ethnic entity). One is that there is a general pan-Indian frame available as a result of long cultural process in history, the freedom struggle, and the post-Independence Indian state knitting together a more or less common politico-economic programmes. The other is that regional and local aspirations as increasingly articulated *vis-a-vis* the centre often accompanied by ethno-cultural assertions. Both of them are intertwined with the issues of our resilient caste, tribal, and religious norms and practices. Though it is argued by Nirmal Kumar Bose that the caste structure of our society provided a certain degree of social stability for centuries due to the security it afforded within one's own caste and because of mutual economic interdependence of the caste; it is also true that caste provided a closed social structure where caste antagonism was inbuilt. Because, mere bringing about institutional changes at political, economic and cultural levels (including education) in the colonial times would not have generated enough force to bring about those social conflicts, as we know in context, to the fore.

The so-called Aryanisation process, which has been actually a *two-way* traffic of forging the Aryan-non-Aryan worldviews, value systems and practices together accompanied by the justificatory interpretations, brought a semblance of social stability. As centrifugalism emerged in a heterogeneous system, the feudal social formation used the tactics of 'carrot and stick' to hold the system together wherever it could. But adjustments were achieved over the centuries at popular level due to the *bhakti* and the *sufi* movements. Just as the medieval Hindu states could not adhere to the *dharmashastras* in their entirety in pursuance of their state policy due to the changed circumstances; so the Islamic regimes of even Firoze Shah Tughluq and Aurangzeb could not always follow the injunctions of the *Shariat*. The orthodox Islamic theory of state had undergone modifications upholding the necessity of *Jahandari* (Secular practical considerations) from the days of Iltutmish to Aurangzeb and his successors. Numerous records, including the *farmans* and correspondences, provide the evidence. In North-Eastern India, the Ahom state tried practical adjustments of interests with the neighbouring peoples like the Nagas and the Khasis. However, all conflicts could not be resolved (for example, the Sikh-Mughal contradiction in the Mughal State; or the Bamunia/Ahom-Sankaria contradiction in the Ahom State).

The colonial political-economy, primarily geared to exploitation, not only exacerbated many dormant elements of conflict but also added new problems to the already existing ones. The Western world-views and morality were often sought to be imposed on the Indian milieus to serve colonial purposes. This point was poignantly brought out by Verrier Elwin during his controversies with the Church of India in as late as 1935-38 leading to his relinquishing priesthood. The context was the question of tribal development in Central India.[11] What is important is that with the resultant disorientations new tensions surfaced. The electoral system introduced through the periodic constitutional doses, social legislations, propagation of Christianity, a basically elitist education – all these innovations among others, opened up new power equations. Over and above these, the most significant development of the colonial era was the linkages established between an improverished and dependant economy and the world colonial economic order which contributed towards regional disparities within the subcontinent. However, this nexus gave rise to the local capitalist and other interests. It is interesting to note that Indian capitalists and farm-workers' interests could not overcome the characteristically high religiosity marking India's freedom struggle. Even Gandhi used certain symbols, including that of *Ramrajya*, with religious and obscurantist overtone. While enabling mass mobilisation on the political front, it also served to invite ethno-cultural alienations which was the ultimate weakness of freedom struggle. So, why blame only the British *divide et impera* or the Aligarh movement alone for its indirect contributions towards the 'two nation' theory. Bankim Chandra Chattopadhya's nationalism was essentially Hindu in content and Sir Amir Ali's Islamic. However, in his essay, *Bangadesher Krishak* (The Cultivators/Ryots of Bengal), he was critical of the British land tenure adversely effecting the interests of the farmers — be they Hindu or Muslim. He was also conscious of the negative sides of the Hindu traditions in different epochs of history. Sir Amir Ali, too, perceived that all progressive developments in the sub-continent should bless the Hindus and the Muslims alike.

The emerging power equations, nevertheless, disrupted the traditional structure of hierarchy along caste and other lines resulting in clash of interests. Ambedkar's neo-Buddhist movement represented an attempt at countering caste based hegemony which was a logical conclusion of a long process of building up of social tension. The colonial legacy of playing the religion card along with other ethnic symbolisms has been retained in independent India. The religion based partition of India, by itself, had jeopardised further the operation of secularism in India in real sense of the term. We are practising a secularism which has been already weakened by the cross-currents of caste and religious orientations during the freedom struggle. Another important factor of ethnicity associated with what the Nationalist and the Marxist thinkers preferred to call the 'Nation-in-the-making' process in modern India in evolution, has been the language issues.[12] Thus ethno-cultural paranoia in the Indian context has precisely been intensified by our caste, religion, and language based politics.[13] *Caste* is included, as within the Hindu fold caste oriented distantiations also have assumed an ethnic proportion, say in the Kamma-Reddy-Brahmin, Mahar-Maratha-Brahmin, Lingayat-Vokkaliga-Brahmin, Brahmin-other-non-Brahmin, Yadava-Thakur-Rajput, etcetera antagonisms in the state-politics of Andhra, Maharashtra, Karnataka, Tamil Nadu, Bihar and Uttar Pradesh respectively. The very recent Thevar-Dalit clashes in Tamil Nadu merely expanded the horizon of potential conflicts.

Historically speaking, the processes of build up of social and political tensions were accentuated by the politico-administrative categorisation of some ethnic groups into scheduled castes and scheduled tribes. This was done following the Census of 1931 and the Government of India Act of 1935. Apart from this, the systems of the 'Partially Excluded' and 'Excluded' Areas were also introduced. There were administrative justifications for doing so.[14] Ironically, however, these processes accelerated the tendency towards communal exclusiveness and latent ethnocentrism surfaced openly, complicating the course of our contemporary history. The reason is that though such measures were rightly taken for the uplift to the socio-economically backward ethnic groups, who so far played only a marginal role in the Sub-continental life, the politicisation of these processes since 1919 gave rise to ethnic contradictions in the emerging Indian political-economy. Its legacy was manifested later in the frequent caste-wars and in the caste rivalries exposed during the Mandal Report controversies. Today, India is operating as a multi-ethnic system under much more trying circumstances. From demographic, economic and political angles the mutually contradictory interests of the different ethnic groups have grown much more competitive since 1947. Politico-economic lobbying are being increasingly coloured by ethno-cultural considerations. Even within a particular pan-India lobby, say the business interests this element surfaces more often than not. Guha has shown, for instance, that in the tangled politics of Assam, in 1979-84, the northern and western Indian business interests clashed with that of the Bengali.[15] I made private inquiries, while at Aligarh in 1991, on the Aligarh riot of 1990-91. I found that this riot was partly produced by the attempt of the Hindu Big Business to dislodge the small lock manufacturers who were mostly Muslims.

The attempt at imposition of Hindi as our *lingua franca* created a divide between the Hindi and the non-Hindi speaking areas, especially North and South India. The concept of Indian 'Nation' was wrongly based on this attempt as it indirectly demanded linguistic assimilation of the other ethnic groups in the long run. That the attempts at linguistic domination can turn dangerous may be gauged from our experience in Assam. The language agitation of Assam since 1948 actually shattered the processes of building up of a composite Assamese society involving the various tribal as well as the other non-Assamese ethnic groups. The periodic Census related language politics was viewed as an expression of Assamese chauvinism by the neighbouring Khasi-Pnar, Mizo and, later, Bodo peoples. The division of Assam into four states of Nagaland, Meghalaya, Mizoram and Assam was partly the result of the language policies pursued by successive governments of Assam. The question of dominance by the regional 'mainstream' of Assamese people was also related to this issue.[16] At present, in the context of Eastern India the Bodoland, Gorkhaland and Jharkhand movements articulate the identity crisis leading to ethno-nationalist upsurges. In recent decades mutual ethnic distantiations have emerged as a powerful force eating into the fabric of our corporate life. The Indian political-economy is acquiring a fragmentary character along linguistic, religious, caste and tribal-non-tribal lines. Earlier it was thought that the linguistic re-organisation of the states and the creation of safeguards for all categories of minorities in our Constitution would hold in balance these mutually contradictory interests. I am afraid that these hopes have been belied not because of our federal structure, but due to the numerous political designs suited to the politicians' personal calculations utilising local aspirations. The current happenings in the erstwhile socialist countries demand a deeper analysis as these are not irrelevant for the Indian experiments with a "nation-in-the-making".

The system of representation in the Lok Sabha and the Rajya Sabha mainly on the basis of population structures has led to disproportionate dominance by the Hindi Belt followed by South India. For the last fifty-one years of Indian independence, the highest positions of the President, Vice President and Prime Minister in the Indian Executive continued to be filled up from these dominant lobbies, only with rare exception. The candidature of Prof. G.G. Swell of North-Eastern India for Presidentship, in one of the recent Presidential elections, was supported by the opposition BJP. But the motive was general electoral considerations more than anything else! The support of the scheduled castes and scheduled tribes was sought through this move. Though on Constitutional principles the elections to these highest posts of the state should be above caste, tribal and zonal considerations, it has been seen that in practice such factors are given undue importance in nominating a candidate even when such persons may or may not have capability. The experience of a Serb-dominated Yugoslav political-economy must be borne in mind.

Politics of Ethnic Lobbying and Ad-hoc Arrangements

The stresses built up due to the inter-lobby bickerings between the Sikh and the North and Western Indian Hindi/Hindu interests had, to some extent, to do with insurgency in Punjab. The Sikh ethno-cultural paranoia found its expression through the 'Khalistan' movement; which in turn could be traced back to the Sikh reform movement of the late nineteenth and twentieth centuries as it also represented their cultural assertions. Later, some of the first steps were taken to give political shape to such assertions by making Gurmukhi-Punjabi as the official language of Punjab and by dividing Haryana from the former. The concept of Khalistan has a 'cultural' context since its main inspiration is drawn from a reference to the Sikh history especially that of their struggle from the *periphery* against a Mughal Centre. Sikh symbolism was, in fact, highlighted by the institutionalisation of the *Akal Takht* by Guru Hargovind (1606-1644) and the *Khalsa* by Guru Govind Singh (1666-1708) with strong political tone.

In Kashmir, the problem is complicated one. Like North-Eastern India, the location of Kashmir in a very sensitive international zone with Pakistan, Afghanistan, China and Tibet on its three sides has rendered the situation of insurgency piquant. The Maharaja's signing of the Instrument of Accession was forced by the circumstances imposed by Pakistan. The questions of plebiscite and special safeguards under Article 370 are still surrounded with controversies. The current happenings in Central Asia and Afghanistan have added to this situation. Pakistan has systematically organised an anti-India campaign to inform the local minds. But what is peculiar is that the state not only did *not* counter these activities, but also did nothing to remove the causes of popular disillusionment – rampant corruption and backwardness. Under such circumstances the Article 370 remained meaningless. It is unfortunate that the centuries-old works of Kashmir *sufism* in building up of a *Kashmiriyat* have been completely negated. This situation is further confounded by an interesting case that in the Pak-Occupied Kashmir (POK), the Muslim Hunjas and their Balti neighbours are hostile towards Pakistan. Will they accept predominance of the Valley Muslim in the hypothetical event of Kashmiri independence? What will be the reactions in Ladakh and Jammu? The lessons of the clan and tribal tangles in Afghanistan with the ramifications of the Pushtu/ Tadjik/ Uzbek ethnic contradictions cannot be ignored in the Kashmir context.

In recent time, the North-Indian Muslim lobby has emerged as the most assertive 'minority' lobby championing the cause of Urdu. Besides, the centre's vacillation, since 1986, regarding the Ram Janambhumi-Babri Masjid issue became glaring when it refused to declare the complex as our archaeological heritage and a national monument (which was suggested by the Indian History Congress). The promise of reconstructing the Mosque had only served to reflect the *ad-hocist* attitude of our policy makers. The Ayodhya episode has confirmed the lack of our political 'will' of ever acknowledging that "prevention is better than cure". Similarly, the series of dismissal of the state governments since 1959 reflected upon the *ad-hocist* political games rather than actually solving the related problems politically. In my lay perception, anyone can take advantage of these tactics. When we talk of value-based politics, we have to uphold certain political principles and morality for a better functioning of our plural system.

Practically, all sorts of ethno-cultural paranoia are being exploited by our so-called popular representatives. The reports on, for example, the Bhagalpur, Delhi and Bombay riots provide ample evidence. The present Hindu-Muslim polarisation is a natural sequel to these processes. The *ad-hocist* policies are responsible for the postponement of a firm decision at political level. However, this policy-type is the end-product of our politics with its 'vote banks' unofficially defined along caste, religious, linguistic, tribal and other lines. Though it is not unique to the Indian system as such, and though democratic operations demand such adjustments; this pattern has *two* "negative" aspects about it. These are :

(i) it negates the political 'will to act in time due to 'myriad' considerations; and
(ii) the unscrupulous elements get a scope to manipulate the human paranoid tendencies.

But political 'will' also demands the courage to tackle the roots of the problems like insurgency. For instance, the insurgency of Kashmir, Tripura, Manipur and Assam type have been mainly the product of political corruptions and economic grievances. As yet, political 'will to deal with these problems is not visible. Periodic declaration of packages does not go to ameliorate these grievances, because a lion's share is always pocketed by the local ruling elites.

The unenviable political culture of this type acts as the breeding ground for ethno-cultural paranoia. Such paranoia work at the levels of various pressure/interest groups even within a given ethnic group, that is, at the micro-level of a society and polity. For instance, among the Khasi-Pnars such groups involved in mutual rivalries are represented by the Catholics, Protestants and Seng Khasis. The Khasi-Pnar politics do show the cross-currents of power equations and bickering among them. However, a general trend is also noticed in the overall electoral processes in North-Eastern India through the last few decades. It is the impact of the goings-on at the pan-Indian level at the centre that is reflected in the state politics. Political cross-currents cutting across ethnic lines do occur. For instance, a good number of Khasi-Pnar Christian elites think that the BJP style of politics is the natural consequence of growing Islamic militancy all over the world. Some of them do not mind forging an alliance with them or other similar elements. But we have to remember that such tendencies are usually temporary in nature. They rise with particular political waves and issues and go with them. What has been more pertinent, from time to time, at the macro-level of pan-Indian politics is the wider North-South divide. It has been expressed, for example, in the rejection of the popular mandates of North India by the electorates in South India, voting in opposite direction. I can recall that as a post-graduate student I was told by the late Vice Chancellor of NEHU, Dr. C.D.S. Devanasen, after the South rejected the Janata Party in the 1977 general elections, that the North-South divide in 'our policy' was open. Subsequent electoral results continue to exhibit more or less similar tendency. This type of regional political assertions are becoming widespread with specific regional/provincial agenda forcing stage of condition regimes at the Centre to reckon with them.

In the context of the above observations, the almost century-old ethnic problems in Assam comes to our mind. The Assam crisis reached a state when the ULFA extremism emerged as a natural sequel to the AASU led anti-foreigner movement since 1979. It had a historical connection with the Assamese-Bengali contradiction. Delhi's *ad-hocist* attitude in its policy towards a peripheral state like Assam finally contributed into the growth of a general feeling among the Assamese – especially among the elites – that they were being exploited economically. Such feelings of the Assamese were strengthened by the unforgivable statement of Pt. Nehru on the eve of the Indian debacle in the China war (1962) that he felt for the "people of Assam", as if they were to be left to their fate! Later, the fear of their being politically and culturally dominated by the non-Assamese was added. The Assamese-Bengali contradictions, which constituted essentially a middle class phenomenon, now turned into a mass movement directed against all non-Assamese in general. The ULFA ideologies refuse to align the Assamese with the rest of India. In this connection, it may be said that it would be naive to think that just because many members of the AASU could not get a share of the cake during the AGP interlude in Assam politics (1980s), they initiated the formation of the ULFA. This phenomenon was rather the climactic point of a historical process. The AASU movement and the ULFA represented ethno-nationalist forces.

On the other hand, these forces served as an eye opener to the non-Assamese, especially the Bengalis. Those among them who were aware of a long standing historical connections between Assam and East Bengal, and were born here, began to visualise themselves as the Bengali speaking Assamese and accept Assam as their homeland. I observed this attitude during that painful phase of the movement when ethnic paranoia reached its height. Though this fact has been a positive gain for the ethnic processes in Assam; the post-movement developments, as is seen today, have not carried these processes further due to continued paranoia. However, the movement effectively challenged Delhi's discriminatory attitudes on the question of oil and coal royalty to Assam, as compared to that of Gujarat or Bihar. I happened to read a pamphlet on this issue written by the late Chief Secretary of Assam, Dharmananda Das, which poignantly brought out the facts. This royalty was subsequently raised. Unfortunately, however, the problem of corruption, so endemic in Assam, was never taken up either by the ASSU or the other forces.

Rajiv Gandhi's Assam did not succeed in removing the irritants particularly that of the 'foreigners' from Bangladesh who would, it seems, never really be identified and ousted. There are two factors, namely :

(i) The ULFA's use of Bangladesh every now and then; and
(ii) The powerful 'Muslim' vote bank in the Assam valley.

The Assam Accord thus remains an *ad-hocist* measure with the absence of necessary 'will' to fulfil it on the part of all concerned. The illusory success of the Hiteshwar Saikia Government with the ULFA menace was exposed with the resurfacing of this outfit in the later day AGP regime. The unresolved Bodo-non-Bodo, Karbi-Assamese-Nepali and Ahom-caste Assamese ethnic contradiction still remain complicated. The Bodoland crisis continues as a vexed problem already costing in terms of lives and properties. In Mizoram, the Hmar militancy – along with the Chakma and the Reang problems – point to the political manipulations of the Centre's Accord with the late Laldenga.

The ethno-political affairs of Meghalaya, Tripura, Nagaland and Arunachal Pradesh are no exception. Ethno-cultural paranoia is manifested in varying degrees. In Meghalaya, for instance, Khasi-Pnar and Khasi-Garo contradictions verge on this paranoia. Some Pnar intellectuals have asserted, at times, that the Pnars were a separate ethnic group from the Khasis. With political corruption rampant, constantly shifting power equations have built up stresses under which the ideological basis of the Khasi-Pnar cultural identity – as provided by the concept of Ka-Hynniew-Trep – is being tested. Whereas the Khasi Student Union is talking of "Zaitkynrew" or well-being of the Khasi-Pnars, which forms part of their programmes. Meanwhile, the Garos remain largely alienated with some Garo organisations demanding a separate Garo state. The recurrent tribal-non-tribal disturbances in and around Shillong since 1979 have confounded the communal divide further. In the case of Arunachal Pradesh, the Inner Line System, operating since 1874, has almost acquired the symbolic status of protective barrier meant for preserving tribal identity *vis-a-vis* the 'outsiders'; while among the various tribes mutual clash of interest are slowly emerging. The other tribes are becoming apprehensive of domination by the Adis.

Nagaland may afford an interesting case study where the attempts at a lingua-franca through the use of the so-called 'Nagamese' has not succeeded much in forging a really 'common' ethnic symbol. Christianity though minimised the open inter-tribal feuds, could not eliminate them altogether as some recent events have demonstrated. Perhaps the long-sustained 'social memory' of inter-tribal antagonism does not die so easily. This fact is reflected in the chequered history of Nagas insurgency culminating in the present divide between the Isaac Swu-Muivah and the Khaplang factions of the NSCN. Therefore, like Laldenga's dream of a Greater Mizoram, the Naga dream of Greater Nagaland comprising the Indian and Burmese Nagas may remain distant if not unattainable! In Manipur, the Thangkul Naga-Kuki, Kuki-Paite, Meitei-Pangal and Naga-Meitei (on the question of Sadar Hills) contradictions are clearly visible in the state politics. Even for the pre-colonial days we have the instance of Kuki rebellion against the Manipuri ruling elites. Exploitation at economic level found their expressions in ethno-nationalist outbursts and even in inter-ethnic conflicts. The questions of the control of resources and economic subservience resulted in the violent Naga-Kuki and Kuki-Paite clashes making rounds. The peace agreements are proving illusory. The Tripura politics, on other hand, is moving round the tribal-Bengali contradictions. The population inversions, leading to the Bengali dominance in Tripura, have mainly been due to four factors, viz.

(i) Proximity of Tripura with the Bengal plains[17];
(ii) Hinduisation of the local ruling elites;
(iii) Policy of the Tripura Raja to settle the Bengalis for economic purposes (e.g., agricultural and commercial pursuits and revenue settlements); and
(iv) Partition of Bengal in 1947 and the resultant refugee influx.

Economic backwardness of the Tripura tribes coupled with these factors, besides the habitual political games of the parties concerned, led to insurgency involving the various outfits (which are an expression of crisis of ethnic identity).

Historically, this region (NE) served as an area of tremendous interactions among the immigrating human groups. Gradually, within their specific environmental zones they evolved as 'exclusive' ethnic groups. Despite the evidence of their mutual dependence they remained as 'exclusive' as they could which moulded their psyche. They played a restricted/localised role *vis-a-vis* the so-called Indian 'mainstream'. Only later on, under the forces released by colonial processes their interaction with the others began to grow. One instance is that of the tea-garden labourers brought from outside and then implanted on, say the Bodo habitat. With the participation of the formerly exclusive ethnic groups in the democratic processes in post-independence India, their transactions with the outsiders are bound to be complicated. However, as experiences elsewhere would show, compared to the tribes in, say Gujarat-Maharashtra or Bihar, the North-Eastern tribes in general are provided better safeguards for their identity. The Sixth Schedule gives them a larger degree of political autonomy and cultural safeguards. Unlike in Andhra Pradesh, Madhya Pradesh (where now, of course, the Chhatisgarh State has come up) and Gujarat they have not been exposed to ruthless exploitation. With the exception of the Tripura tribes (e.g., the Reangs) or the Kachharis and the Karbis in Assam, many of the North-Eastern tribes were effectively protected since the days of the colonial regime.[18] In contrast, the Dang tribes in Gujarat are severely exploited by the vested interests within and outside the government. Similarly, the sugar barons of Maharashtra are exploiting the tribal in certain belts.[19] In their case, the paranoia towards the 'outsiders' may be justifiable. But, in certain protected states of the North-East – where various institutional arrangements operate as "states within the state" to provide safeguards – such paranoia are not always understandable and which are often cleverly manipulated by the politicians.

At the same time, westernisation processes have largely corroded the traditional bases of their identity leading to the emergence of numerous contradictions. Another development is that most of the tribes in the North-East have acquired Roman script while taking to writing from oral tradition; and then they began to use language as a symbol of ethnic assertion. In some cases, an ethnic group, say the Meiteis, were demanding a change of script from Bengali to Roman and finally adopted their original script; or the Bodos gave up the use of Assamese. Of late, the demands for inclusion of the Meitei-Manipuri and of the Khasi into the Eighth Schedule are an outcome of ethnic resurgence. The Santhali movement for the Alchiki script in West Bengal and Bihar is more or less on analogous development, though in a different historical context. Interestingly, a generally 'westernised' elite within the North-Eastern tribal milieu articulate their concern for identity. Here lies the basic contradiction. Coupled with the paranoia regarding the 'outsiders', it has created a situation which resulted in the lack of political 'will', locally for industrialisation. Does it go to show that the *locals* do not have enough faith on their own state governments supposed to ensure their protection from exploitation? As experiences in Central India and elsewhere have shown, protection must, of course, be given to them *vis-a-vis* the unscrupulous business interests.

An Exercise at Suggestions

Perhaps due to colonial hangovers the Indian political-economy today often behaves as a backward looking system. Otherwise, how can one explain the secondary importance given to the larger socio-economic and political issues like the dangers of the Dunkel Proposals, the Stock Exchange Scam, and the need for free universal elementary education, or the right to work! The system seems to be more interested in making an 'issue' out of a 'non-issue' like the Mandir-Masjid controversy. Given this state to affairs almost throughout India, we cannot expect the North-Eastern region to remain exceptional in ethnic and political terms. Therefore, the first requirement for an efficient and equitable functioning of our 'federal' structure is : a firm political will both at central and state levels to act on full utilisation of our resource potentials, industrialisation and control of increasing ministerial and bureaucratic corruption and wastage. It has been seen that in spite of the planning processes at least forty-eight per cent of our population remained illiterate, sanitation is still wanting in more than *sixty* per cent of the villages, and forty-five per cent of Indian population are living below poverty line. The work of a few voluntary organisations in literacy and self-employment programmes, for example, in the Burdwan and Bankura districts of West Bengal and in Ernakulam district of Kerala are encouraging for one to suggest that the developmental administration in the North-Eastern region may encourage the voluntary agencies to participate. It would reduce the dependence on bureaucratic management. However, minimum state supervision of the activities of such agencies would be necessary in view of misuse of resources by such agencies.[20]

As for the North-Eastern region, its location on an international frontier zone of strategic importance has confounded its already complicated political and ethnic processes. India's cool and hostile international surroundings in this region account for this situation. In addition, the ambivalence in our policy towards the Chakma issue, the happenings in Bhutan, the crisis of democracy in Burma, and the Tibetan issue has highlighted the lack of a firm foreign policy resolve on our part. Definite foreign policy formulations, in these directions, are necessary.

Last Few Words

The reflections on the issues raised above are based on experiences and understanding of events spanning over more than thirty-five years. It is a welcome feature of democracy that is a mechanism of mutual adjustments of contradictory aspirations and claims of the ethnic and the interest groups participating in it. It is a continuous process. But it can succeed only when a political ideal and vision are held above the cult of personal and private gains. Paranoid tendencies come naturally to the comparatively smaller ethnic groups. But this can effectively be tackled through value based politics dispensing equity and justice. We have seen that in rural Meghalaya sometimes the calculations of an erring politicians is upset by popular common sense approach of the voters in his constituency. This type of electoral reaction can be seen elsewhere in India too. Lastly, whether we continue to remain a multi-ethnic political economy or finally emerge from the "nation-in-the-making" process successfully is only to be seen in future. Mere sermonising 'national integration' may not help us.

NOTES

1. This point has been discussed in some details in my paper, "Future of the Present of a Frontier : India's North-East in the Age of Libertarian Market". In Das, G. and Purkayashtha, R.K. (eds.), *Liberalisation and India's North East*, New Delhi : Commonwealth Publishers, 1998:105-122, pointing out the compulsions.
2. The works of Desmond Morris and Edmund Wilson, though considered vulgar by some Marxist thinkers, do signify an attempt at understanding animal and human behaviour which hint at genetic factors. A UNI Report, dated February 10, 1994, from Udaipur (Rajasthan) says that in his study, Mr. Raja Tehsin, a wild life expert, has indicated some species of birds and animals, including the deer, seem to inherit the knowledge of topography for which genes could be responsible.
3. When I met a Slovak tourist in New Delhi, in December 1996, he told me that though a separate Slovak State had been setup, there was no bitterness between them and the Czechs.
4. See his *The Clash of Civilisations and the Remaking of World Order*. New Delhi : Penguin Books India (P) Ltd., 1996. See the chapters on "Civilisation in History and Today", "Economic Demography and the Challenger of Civilisations", and "The Cultural Reconfiguration on Global Politics". Making a distinction between the 'Asians' and the 'Muslims', he says that Islamic Resurgence along with Asian (East Asians?) affirmation have been the sources of "greatest resistance to Western democratising efforts" (p. 193).
5. In 1997, Russia and China signed a treaty declaring that they would uphold 'multipolarity'.

6. This point is raised only in restricted sense, since in a socialist system no institutionalised 'Political' opposition is allowed.
7. Normally the Dictatorship of Proletariat acts as a means of class struggle until a socialist society is consolidated and conducted through tribulations of class antagonism. Looking at the state of affairs in China, West Bengal and Kerala, I am constrained to observe that under changing circumstances, the Marxist governments there, have tried to adjust class antagonism by means of legislation (e.g., land reforms in West Bengal under the very able guidance of Binoy Choudhary) rather than having recourse of class war.
8. Ben Macintype in a report, "Rattling the lost Skeleton in the Closet", in *The Statesman*, 12 October, 1998. The Roman Catholic Church in France have apologised for what was done in France during the Vichy regime with regard to the Jews. However, there were exceptions too. The programs in Russia directed at the Jews both before and after 1917 are well known.
9. Quoted in B.P. Dalal, *Glimpses of American History*... Bombay: Vora & Co., 1990 : 13.
10. Discussed in my paper, Das & Purkayastha, *op. cit.*, : 121-122.
11. See Verrier Elwin. *The Tribal World of Verrier Elwin : An Autobiography*. New Delhi : OUP, 1988:86-99. His Link with Gandhi and the Congress was questioned.
12. See S.K. Chaube. *Hill Politics in North-East India*. Calcutta : Orient Longman, 1973, for this context, too, of the Hill State Movement. For a detailed study for the first few decades of independent India, see Selig S. Harrison, *India : The Most Dangerous Decades*, New Delhi : OUP, 1968 Reprint.
13. *Ibid.* The situation have not changed much since then.
14. See W.V. Grigson. *The Aboriginal Problem in the Central Provinces and Berar*. Nagpur : Govt. Printing C.P. and Berar, 1944 (Reprinted by Vanya Prakashan, Bhopal), on the conditions of the tribes in that province. He ably argued for the policy of 'exclusion' and 'partial exclusion'. His data on exploitation of these tribes by the money lenders and intermediary landlords from outside seems to be convincing. *See* Para 476 to 484, pp. 424-429.
15. Amalendu Guha, "Little Nationalism Turned Chauvinist : Assam's Antiforeigner Upsurge, 1979-80", in *EPW*, XV (41, 42 and 43), 1980 : 1699-1720.
16. *See* Chaube. *op. cit.*
17. See J.B. Bhattacharjee, *Social and Polity Formations in Pre-Colonial North-East India*. New Delhi : Har-Anand Publications, 1991: 65-78, for details on the first–three factors cited above.
18. Though the Karbis were put under the system of partial exclusion and later, after independence, granted the benefits of the Sixth Schedule their poverty facilitated the transfer of their land to the others. Extreme poverty among the Kachharis led to similar situation.
19. I had the first hand experiences of social activists involved with their cause at my disposal, after I met one of the activists, Dr. Jaganath Pathy of the South Gujarat University, at Surat in 1991. I got the details from him and from Dr. Sajal Nag then at the Centre for Social Studies, Surat.
20. Recently many NGOs have been accused of mishandling the funds. The Naga Students' Federation, for instance, raised this issue in context of Nagaland. Many even suspect that some NGOs could be involved in the western acts of bio-piracy in india.

10

UPHOLDING THE VALUE OF SECULARISM IN NORTH-EAST INDIA

J. B. GANGULY

The basic philosophy of our Constitution was spelt out in historic Objective Resolution propounded by Jawaharlal Nehru which was adopted by the Constituent Assembly on 22 January, 1947. This resolution, which inspired the framing of the Constitution, was a solemn resolve of the founding fathers of the post-colonial Indian nation-state to proclaim India as an Independent sovereign Republic 'wherein shall be guaranteed and secured to all people, *inter alia*, freedom of thought, expression, belief, faith and worship'. It was also emphasized that safeguards would be provided for minorities, backward and tribal areas, and depressed and other backward classes[1].

Referring to this resolution Nehru declared that it was something more than a resolution. It was "a declaration, a firm resolve, a pledge, an undertaking and for all of us a dedication"[2]. Such a pledge was made in order to remove apprehensions and forebodings in the minds of the religious, linguistic and ethnic minorities, as well as the people of the fringe and tribal areas regarding their future in the free Indian Republic. And without earning such confidence of all minority groups the Indian nationhood could not be shaped on a sound footing.

The essence of the Objective Resolution found expression in the Preamble to our Constitution, which as amended in 1976, underlined the solemn resolve of the people of India "to constitute India into a Sovereign Socialist Secular Democratic Republic and to secure to all its citizens : Justice, social, economic and political; Liberty of thought, expression belief, faith and worship; Equality of status and of opportunity, and to promote among them all; Fraternity assuring the dignity of the individual and the unity and intergrity of the Nation."[3]

The constitutional and legal importance of the Preamble has been confirmed by the Supreme Court in several of its decisions, and the Preamble unambiguously enshrines the ideal of secularism. The secular state of India is constitutionally obliged to protect all religions equally and the state itself does not profess any religion as the state religion. Each citizen accordingly enjoys the fundamental freedom of religion, that is, to profess and practice any religion of his choice. The state and its institutions are also required to practice strict impartiality towards all religions.[4]

In post-Independence India, the special and urgent problems of the people of North-East India were addressed by the Government by making special provisions in the Constitution for removing the people's apprehensions and respecting their aspirations and for ensuring people's involvement in the process of decision-making, formulation of programme and their implementation. The NEI's social and economic development was given special importance. The approach to tribal development was laid down by Nehru. One of the leading national dailies of the country, normally. *The Statesman* (Kolkata) has argued that values are not necessarily religious, rather, "some of the most essential values of our times are non-religious values – objectivity, rationally and freedom, to name the three most important."[5] Agreeing with him we may also assert that it is not necessary to be religious to learn and imbibe the core religious values of love, compassion and charity. In today's world those values have actually become secular values. Tolerance of, and respect for, the opposition's views on political, cultural, religious and economic affairs, etc. is the most basic value that need to be nurtured in a democracy.

The core traditional values of the people of NEI manifest egalitarianism, social equality, fellow-feeling, honesty, altruism, absence of gender-violence, etc. Some of these values are being compromised and diluted, particularly in the urban areas, in the wake of the economic, political, and social development processes set in motion in the region since the 1950s. Even the bane of corruption in public life has been growing and spreading. Moreover, many parts of NEI has become the scenes of movements highlighting ethnic separatism and the right of secession from the Indian Union resulting in acts of terrorist violence as also armed intervention by the Government to suppress such activities. In fact the region has been witnessing widespread turmoil. The then Prime Minister of India, enunciated a fundamental principle of tribal development stating.

> "People should develop along the lines of their own genius and we should avoid imposing anything on them. We should try to encourage in every way their own traditional arts and culture."[6]

From these historical documents, it should be amply clear what profound importance must be attached to the upholding of the ideal of secularism in NEI by all means so that there would be no apprehension or suspicion in the minds of the people that there might be any possibility of imposition of the exclusive religious or cultural identity of the central ruling elite on them in any form. Unfortunately, of late, the concept and the national ethos of secularism has been under severe assault as the tenets of religious fundamentalism, communalism and cultural chauvinism have been in the ascendancy in the country. Even the secular character of our educational system may be jeopardized if the newly framed national curriculum framework for school education is implemented in order to include education about religion as a subject for the school children. Preparations are also afoot to include astrology, the art of priesthood, etc. as teaching subjects at certain levels of the undergraduate and post-graduate courses of studies.

The changes are being proposed arguing the case for value education so that the growing menace of corruption, crimes, violence etc., in inter-personal relations can be checked. In a befitting critique of such ideas, the Editor highlights loss of lives and infringement of individual liberty in many respects.

In such a situation, if any direct or indirect attempt is made at tampering with the value of secularism and the rights of the peoples of the region to preserve their respective ethnic, cultural and traditional identities, it will cause further estrangement of tribal-non-tribal, and regional-central relations which will seriously jeopardize the on-going process of negotiations and parleys with the different secessionist groups for peaceful solution of the region's problems. Therefore, for the sake of restoring peace and amity in the region, all official and non-official agencies and the civil society should unequivocally uphold the objective of secularism by all means. People of the North-East must be guaranteed their right of developing along the lines of their own genius.

NOTES

1. Durga Das Basu (1983). *Introduction to the Constitution of India*. Prentice – Hall of India Pvt. Ltd., New Delhi, p. 20.
2. *Ibid.*
3. Government of India. *The Constitution of India* (as modified up to the 15th January 1980), p. 1.
4. Durga Das Basu, *op. cit.,* p. 26.
5. *The Statesman*, Kolkata, 8 January, 2002, Editorial entitled, Who Needs Religion?
6. Verrior Elwin (1988), *A Philosophy for NEFA*, Government of Arunachal Pradesh, Itanagar.

11

SECULARISM IN INDIA
Problems and Perspectives

R. N. PRASAD

I

Since the study is concerned with Secularism in India, it is necessary, at the outset, to know of the concept of secularism. The word 'secular' is derived from the Latin word *seculum* which means 'Temporal world'. George Jacob Holyoake is credited with the coinage of the word 'Secularism' used the term to denote social ethics based on natural morality, but independent of revealed religion and supernaturalism. Secularism according to the Oxford English Dictionary, means "concern with the affairs of this world, worldly, not sacred, not monastic, not ecclesiastical or sceptical of religious truth". According to G.G. Hackman, Secularism signifies the kind of life that is lived in complete indifference to God and to religious values. In other words, secularism is neither anti-religious, nor non-religious. Secularism is neither anti-God nor pro-God. It treats alike the devout, the antagonistic and the atheist. It eliminates God from the matters of the state and ensures that no one shall be discriminated against on the ground of religion. To clarify further, it is better to mention that secularism promotes understanding, harmony and cooperation between different religious groups for national unity, entails the supremacy of state and its laws equally for all citizens, helps liberation of the civic policy from religion dominated groups and parties, and enforcement of the principle of fraternity of the citizens and not members of primordial groups–religious, linguistic, ethnic or regional. Secularism as a phenomenon in India represents a struggle for building an integrated political community in a multi-religious situation and also against the process of fragmentation of our integrity and community as a sovereign people.

Secularism is the refutation of any form of theocratic culture and religious separatism and it is opposed to the domination of any church, priest or any form of organised religious authority in its political culture. But it does not mean opposition to religion. It also does not mean appeasement of the minority, and it certainly, also does not mean religious dictatorship of the majority. It is simply a code of behaviour in relation to man's social and political activities independent of religion. Thus secularism with all the rationalist and humanistic values triumphs only by relegating man's religion to his personal life. Secularism cannot and does not exclude minority religions from its purview. That is to say, the concept of secularism applies universally and without making an exception of any religion. Secularism requires that the citizens themselves keep to their religion separate from the rights and obligations of citizenship. It, thus, stands for secular attitude in the common man. Briefly, secularism, rightly understood, embodies a broader vision, greater inspiration and more progressive outlook than that provided by traditional religions whether of the majority or the minority. It greatly concerns for culture, social progress, improvement of the material conditions of man and economic justice to society. Secularism also envisages a political structure in which individual is not subject to any social inequities imposed by the religious sanction.

In fact, secularism is a principle of policy which aims to extricate from the traditional nets of religion everything in which the state has a vital interest from the point of political, economic and social progress.

II

The secular state is one where the concept of secularism should be the accepted policy. A secular state treats religion as an individual enterprise and individual action lying outside the true and legitimate province of government. It should observe scrupulous neutrality among religions and confine itself to secular objectives clearly dissociating itself from religion. Secularism is not so much a matter of state policy but an attitude, a way of life which leaves no room for intolerance and leaves each individual to develop his inner life in his own way. It is not merely the peaceful coexistence of different faiths but an affirmation of the duty of the state and its citizens to look at each individual citizen, not as a part of a group but a free normal person with his own rights.

The foundations of India are based on the democratic principles and the secular provisions in the Constitution. India is a secular state. So the state guarantees individual and corporate freedom of religion dealing with individual as a citizen irrespective of his religion. It does not promote any religion. It does not also interfere with any religion. There are people of different faiths living in India. Although there have been intermittent religious conflicts, India is secularly established as a secular state. As regards secular provisions in the Constitution for the promotion of a secular state, the liberty of worship proclaimed in the Preamble to the Indian Constitution is ensured by recognising it as a Fundamental Right. There are detailed provisions in the Chapter III of the Constitution on Fundamental Rights for securing the freedom of religion.

Articles 25-29 guarantee every individual the freedom of religion to profess, practise and propagate his own religion without interference and at the same time assume strict impartiality of the state and its institutions towards all religions. The secular nature of the state has been further emphasised by inserting the word in the Preamble to the Constitution by the Forty Second Amendment. Article 25 further adds that all persons within the jurisdiction of the Republic, whether national or foreigners, are equally entitled to freedom of conscience and the right to freely profess, practise and propagate religion. But this right is subject to two limitations. This right cannot be misused to contravene public order, morality, health, and other provisions of the Fundamental Rights. This right does not prevent the state from making any law regulating or restricting any economic, financial or political or other secular activity which may be associated with the practice of that religion. Nor does it restrict the right of the state to legislate for social welfare and reform or for throwing open Hindu, Sikh, Jain institutions of a public character to all classes and sections of the people professing these religions. The court has the right to determine whether a particular right or observance is regarded as essential by the tenets of a particular religion.

Article 26 of the Constitution also guarantees to each person and every section the right to establish and maintain institutions for religious purposes, to conduct his or its own affairs in religious matters, to own and acquire movable and immovable property and to administer such property in accordance with the law. Religious property enjoys tax concessions. To Article 28, no religious instructions shall be imparted in any educational institution other than those under an endowment. It further restricts the right of the state to religious instructions and lays down that no student attending any educational institution recognised by the state or receiving monetary aid from the states shall take part in any religious instructions or attend any religious worship without his/her consent.

Thus every person has the right to hold any faith of his choice. Every group has also the right to preach the aims of its religion. But the Supreme Court has held that the right to spread does not give any one the right to convert people of other faiths by such means, fraud, inducement or allurement.

III

The freedom of conscience and religion enshrined in the Constitution prohibits discrimination by the state on ground of religion, caste, sex and place of birth. But this right does not prevent state from making any special provision for the advancement of any socially and educationally backward classes of citizens or for the scheduled castes and scheduled tribes. Article 16 further guarantees every individual the freedom of equal opportunity in the matter of employment or office under the state. So the state is prohibited to discriminate on grounds of religion, race, caste, sex and place of birth in the matter of employment. But clause (3) of Article 16 does not prevent the state from making any provision to reserve appointment or posts for any backward class of citizens, who are not represented adequately in the state services. This provision may be called protective discrimination to correct the traditional inequalities. Thus according to Nehru and Constitutional law experts like Prof. Alaxandrowicz, the discrimination is meant to protect the interests of certain backward and depressed classes. Further no individual is discriminated to have access to public places, places of worship and admission to any educational institution maintained or aided by the state and the right to vote. Article 17 forbids the practice of untouchability in any form, to give effect to this fundamental right. The enactment of the Untouchability (Offences) Act, 1955 under Article 17 of the Constitution is the greatest achievement in abolishing the age-long practice of Hindu religious custom of untouchability which is against the fundamental rights of the citizens that all are equal and also is against the principle of welfare state. Secularism is, thus, essentially a practical approach for maintaining social stability and harmony.

The Constitution also protects the cultural and educational rights of religious and other minorities. Articles 29 and 30 safeguard the right of the religious and other minorities to have a distinct language, script and culture of their own, and to establish and administer educational institutions of their choice. But the state cannot impose on them any culture other than the communities' own culture. Also no individual can be denied admission to state maintained and aided educational institution on the basis of religion, caste, sex and language. The state in granting aid, shall not discriminate against any educational institution managed by a minority whether based on religion or language. To Article 30(1), if the state acquires the property of a minority educational institution, full compensation has to be paid.

The commitment of the secular state has to provide secular law to the citizens as well as to play active role in secularising society. While the idea of the secular state implies secular law, it also contains a conception of freedom of religion which for many present day Hindus and Muslims has a direct bearing on the continuance of their respective religious laws. But this obligation of Indian Secular State has been served by Article 44 of the Directive Principles of State Policy and accordingly, the state must endeavour to secure for the citizens a uniform civil code throughout the territory of India. In fact, important areas of civil law, including marriage, divorce, inheritance, succession, all remain under the religious personal laws. But India is committed by its Constitution (Article 44) to the elimination of this system of personal law for the sake of promoting secularism and democracy to an extent. But in this context, the enactment of the Muslim Women (Protection of Rights on Divorce) Bill to override the Supreme Court judgement in the *Shah Bano case* by the Rajiv Gandhi government in 1986 was a severe setback to secularism and democracy.

Since India has a multi-religious society, the country provides for each citizen the fullest freedom in religious faith and worship, and ensures good relations among various religious minority groups and promotes not only religious tolerance, mutual respect and accommodation of dissent but also reverence for all religions so that the people understand each other better and live amicably together. Indian Secularism opposing the narrow orthodox and fanatical religious views also encourages people to stress on truth, goodness, justice, fair play, and moral uplift because, there is no religion higher than truth and righteousness. The secularist policy of the government also means that all individuals in political, economic and social matters irrespective of their religious beliefs and other distinctions, enjoy equality of rights.

IV

Seeing the happenings caused by a decline of democracy in the country today, it is almost impossible to be very optimistic about the future of secularism in the country. Despite the Constitutional safeguards in favour of secular commitment, fundamentalist and militant communalism, casteism and ethnicism generated by the old British game of 'divide and rule' continue to raise their ugly heads from time to time, trying to fragment the national identity as well as plague the political system. There are also some aberrations in the Indian Political System, namely, populism, parochialism, and the breakdown of the national consensus, which stand out as severe impediments in the process of socio-economic transformation and secularisation. Politics has become the handmaid of hooligans, musclemen, money power, flattery, blackmail, cheating, bribing, pandering to the beast of communalism and ethnicism. To grab and retain power in their hands and in the hands of their families and friends have become the supreme consideration of politicians. Hence, the politics of vote, with all its corollary, determine all policies and actions. What better method, can there be to monopolise power than to nurture the divisions of society into various castes, and ethnic communities on a mutually fighting posture and then exploit their fears and susceptibilities to the misfortune of secularisation in the country. The vested interests in all the communities and the politicians of all hues, who better in power-politics of the country, indulge in these nefarious games and fissiparous tendencies, in varying degrees. They play dual role marked by public promises and private betrayals to retain themselves in power. Thus politics divorced from morality neither implements the secular provisions of the Constitution of India for secularising the Indian society nor finds solutions for national unity. As a result, the secular civic culture has not been fully internalised by all sections of the Indian society.

The existing socio-economic structure based on the capitalist path of modernisation/development that the country has adopted after independence, has sharpened not only the caste, religious, linguistic, cultural and ethnic distinctions and communal tensions, it has also increased/widened regional economic imbalances, disparities frustration, estrangement, feeling of deprivation, socio-economic injustice, negligence and insecurity coupled with the instinct of preserving the distinct cultures and traditions among various nationalities, sub-national groups and ethnic tribal groups. The market economy framework has only helped to create a new propertied dominant caste-*cum*-class forces, bereft of values which thrive on castes opportunism, patronage, nepotism and corruption, keeping the lower classes and classes outside the pale of the beneficial effect of national development and the range of national prosperity. In a situation of unequal advantage, every increase in the GNP and in national standards of living would continue to give unequal benefits to the entrenched 'haves' at the expense of the disinherited and dislocated 'have-nots', notwithstanding the slogans about democratisation, distributive justice and socialism. The fruits of economic development should reach the common poor man. Because the common masses prefer economic advancement to political emancipation. This has not happened because the government has been highjacked by the politician-bureaucrat-contractor lobby, middlemen and the powerful economic strata of society. The hold of middlemen or contractors or dominant class over the government can be broken, if developmental works are transferred to local institutions. Involvement of local people in federal nation-building through local institutions is essential to deepen the concept of both secularism and national identity. Besides, if the common poor people from the background of oppression, deprivation, exploitation, socio-economic injustice, land alienation and dependency are to be liberated, the present socio-economic structure, which increases/permits inequality/disparity, exploitation, injustices of all sorts, oppression and emergence of propertied dominant class, has to be radically restructured/transformed. It may be also mentioned that a narrow economic approach or bureaucratic approach must give place to a new enlightened and progressive policies for bringing about the basic socio-economic changes, which will certainly contribute to secularisation, modernisation and political integration at a rapid rate. Also the ills of social injustice and economic inequality, poverty, want, unemployment, deprivation and alienation must end fast to promote secular civic culture and national solidarity.

V

Adherence to religion and religious system is not communalism. Exploitation of religion is communalism. Attachment to a religious community is not communalism. Using religious community against other communities and against the nation is communalism. A true believer in religion, is also expected to be a good human being. But it is wrong to assume that communalists are religious people, in the real sense of the word. Communalism is perversion of religion from a moral order to a temporal arrangement of contemporary convenience, from a faith into a constituency, from a strategy of living into tactics of politics, from an end to means. Communalism exploits parts of religious dogma for expedient political purpose. It is promoted by a real or an imaginary fear of other communities. Communalism is the enemy of progress, revolution, democracy, federal nation state building, and non-religious state structure building.

Communalism is basically an ideology of political allegiance to a religious community as a primary and decisive group in the polity and for political action. It is a sectarian, restrictive and negative response to the process of modernisation, and modern-nation-building. Communalism, thus, is a political strategy opposed to nationalism as an aggregation of multi-ethnic, multi-religious and multi-lingual communities. Communalism is also opposed to secularism as a pattern of socio-cultural coexistence and political integration. Communalism is opposed to a rational civic basis of party formation and political system. Communalism perceives majorities and minorities as segments and divisions within a polity and a nation, based essentially on religious communities and not even on any other ascriptive basis (like that of family, clan, tribe, caste, language, region or domicile), and certainly not on the basis of political, ideological, party, class interests or state consideration, which is the hallmark of a modern political system. Politicisation of religious community opposed to other communities and the nation is the main plank of communalism. To attack and murder a human being in frengy or riot, only because he belongs to another community is the worst form of communalism. To incite communal animosity and hatred by word of mouth or publication, particularly by using one's privileged position in profession and society especially the media, is wicked and manifest communalism. Communalism, today, is a multi-pronged challenge which seeks to disrupt India's multi-religious fraternity. It is also an affront to India's nationalist identity, and tragic setback to evolving secular culture. It is subversive of our political stability, economic development and secularism.

VI

The neglect in providing education for the children and youth leaving their minds devoid of the ideal of secularism, equality and humanism and the failures of development plans have facilitated the spread of the reactionary and divisive influences of communalism and religious fundamentalism among the people. Thus in an emerging highly technical society, neglect of education and development may promote mediocrity among the youth thereby exposing them to the reactionary forces waiting for an opportunity to spread their influence. Can any development programme hope to succeed without universalising and democratising education and decentralising the planning process? Briefly, it may be said that communal violence is an expression of the failure of the process of nation-building. The problem of the future of secularism in India is not just a social problem of achieving a changed pattern of thought and behaviour of different people of India. It is mainly an economic problem of removing the obstacles in the path of the development of the people so that they can develop according to their own genius and culture. The perspective has to be of involving the people in the solution of their own problems. But this can be possible only by implementing land reforms. Because, giving land to landless means transferring assets to the assetless. So removing inequality in landholdings is also necessary precondition for meaningful decentralised planning.

Besides, the government, the political parties and the voluntary organisations, wedded to secularism must come together forgetting their personal bias and prejudices to work out a common agenda for action to fight the forces of communalism and fundamentalism.

Education plays a vital role in promoting democratic secular values and ensuring the unity of the people and their loyalty to the nation.

So it needs to adopt an educational system bereft of all communal, religious and regional negative influences. A plan to revamp the educational system and recast it with a thrust towards unity, secularism and democracy should be drawn out by educationists, Vice Chancellors of Universities and heads of national educational institutes of standing. They should examine education at all levels as to impart a pronounced emphasis on democratic secular values, both in class work as well as field practices. Such an emphasis can be promoted through various social, cultural and recreational activities of the N.S.S., N.C.C., sports and culture, youth camps and inter-University meets. All sectarian and communal organisations should be disaffiliated from students' and teachers' union. The U.G.C. should play a vital role in this regard.

The Ministry of Human Resource Development should gear all its activities to the principal role of promoting democratic secularism in the educational institutions to fight the communal and religious forces. Education policy must aim at not only inculcating scientific temperament, it must develop a sense of tolerance and feeling of oneness and nationalism in students. Short crash courses in promoting the values of secular democracy, objectivity and rationality should be organised in all institutions of learning and training.

Similarly, all non-governmental youth and welfare organisations, getting support from the government, should also relate their activities to fight the communal and sectarian forces influencing the youth in the country.

Political parties wedded to secular values should come together to fight the emerging influence of communalism/fundamentalism in the country. There is an urgent need in India today to create a national front of democratic and secular forces in order to restore to the Indian state the authentic secular image, and help it to play the catalytic role as an instrument of socio-economic change, in order to change a traditional society into a modern polity.

An emphasis on the humanist tradition in all religions should be made. Because it lays stress on individual moral code, propagates the values of love and compassion in human life, and bridges understanding between diverse religious traditions, by identifying similarities of images and values, despite divergences in nomenclature. It projects the basic values of life and happiness for all, adherence to truth, goodness, fairplay, toleration, mutual respect and accommodation of dissent. It speaks of God as a universal God, of religion as a humanistic endeavour of society as a common responsibility. It points out to the futility of doctrinaire disputation and dogmatic fights, and extols the lasting benefit of the values of 'live and let live', of plurality of perception but unification of human goodness and concern for all.

Besides, the democratic and socialist appeal must have had a positive content in respect of peoples' sense of loyalty to their language and history. On such approach, a sense of loyalty to the Indian nation can be built up and her secular character guaranteed.

In brief, Indian democracy and secularism must aim at the process of incorporating various parts of the society into a functioning whole towards the reduction of barriers between various parts of the whole, opening up of communications and ultimately for tolerance of ethnic differences within the unity, and the emergence of shared values and perspectives or consensus.

At the same time, as we enter the new millennium, we the citizens of India, irrespective of caste, community, religion, politics and region have a responsibility to come together to keep this nation secular. Our task is to root out the communal cancer. India cannot prosper, if the country is divided on the basis of ethnicity, caste, creed, beliefs or religions. Ours is a country of diverse cultures and people. Each of the groups — regional, linguistic, religious and social — in the country has made its unique contributions to the rich legacy of India. Differences in ethnic origin, creeds, cultures, religions and beliefs do not have to divide us. They can enrich and promote. It is the politician of the kind we have in the country who have divided us to further their own interests. The need today is to go beyond such divisions and fight for a secular and pluralist nation by uniting ourselves. We cannot progress if we allow our leaders to flout laws, appoint criminals as ministers and allow them to engage in communal politics by destroying churches, mosques, people and institutions. We need to make a conscious choice to come together in spite of all differences to save India. We have a duty and a responsibility to protect the rich pluralistic and secular heritage of the country. Let our determination be as we have to work for the protection of the pluralistic cultural heritage of India by defeating opportunistic ethnic militancy and communal forces and their leaders.

Despite all this, as a conclusion, it may be noted that it appears difficult to establish secular society based on civilized, humane and just civil order without giving any reference to the existing social structure and class character of the state power in India. The capitalist state of India based on class, caste and religious divisions cannot have a secular society/spirit of fraternity and assure the vulnerable and the very poor sections of the Indian society liberty, equality and dignity. Briefly, a multi-religious society cannot have a democratic and federal state without secularism. Secularism cannot be possible, if secular politicians and bureaucrats are not managing it. It is only democracy based on secularism which will keep India united and the other road will lead to violence and disintegration of the country. So, re-ordering human relations in the economic sphere between the rich and the poor to eliminate the exploitation of the disadvantaged/deprived sections of the Indian society has to be made. Besides, to construct a new federal balance in India, the present centralised federation may be changed into a co-operative and federal polity.

REFERENCES

Balasubramanian, M. (1980). *Nehru : A Study in Secularism,* New Delhi, Uppal Publishing House.

Bhargava, G.S. Secularism and Democracy, *Mainstream,* January 30, 1993.

Gajendragadkar, P.B. (1969). Concept of Secularism, *India and Foreign Review,* 1 April.

Gupta, Shrinivasa. (1991). Nehru and Secularism, *Link*, November 17.

Glasner, Peter. F. (1977). *The Sociology of Secularisation : A Critique of a Concept,* New Delhi, Ambika Publications.

Khan, Rasheeduddin (1993). Secularism and Social Transformation in India, I, II, III *Mainstream*, April 24, 1993, May 1, 1993 and May 8.

Mustafa, Seema (1992). Taking Secularism to the Masses, *Mainstream*, January, 25.

Nandy, Ashis (1992). Secularism, *Seminar*, June.

Patwardhan, Achyut (1992). Secularism and the Religious Mind, *Mainstream*, August 15.

Prasad, R.N. (1998), National Agenda of the New Government : Administrative Dimensions – An Appraisal (in) *Administrative Review*, An annual Journal of the Indian Institute of Public Administration, Mizoram Regional Branch, Aizawl, 1996-97 (Two Issues).

Prasad, R.N. (1989). Jawaharlal Nehru and Problem of National Integration : A Study (in) *Teaching Politics, The Journal of the Delhi Political Science Association,* Vol. XV No. 1, (Deptt. of Political Science, University of Delhi).

Rahman, A. (1992). Science and Secularism, *Mainstream*, November 17.

Seshadri, K. (1991). Nehru and Decline of Democracy, *Link*, November 17.

Uniyal, Lalit (1991). Lalit. On Secularism, *Mainstream,* October 26.

12

ETHNICITY, ETHNIC CONFLICT AND CONFLICT RESOLUTION IN NORTH-EAST INDIA

SUSMITA PRIYADARSHINI

Ethnicity is the term used by the people to identify themselves. It may be defined as an organizing principle by a group of people in order to differentiate themselves from other groups in terms of race, kinship, language, customary mode of livelihood, culture and religion. An ethnic issue is always an emotional one and it may take violent turn at any time.

The ethnic issues before the North-East states are as follows :

1. Bodo-non-Bodo conflict in Bodo dominated areas in Assam.
2. Anti-Chakma movement in Arunachal Pradesh.
3. Anti-outsider movement in Meghalaya.
4. Naga-Kuki conflict, Kuki-Paite clashes in Manipur.
5. Tripuri tribal-Bengali settlers conflict in Tripura.

The ethnic conflicts have already taken serious turn in the states of Assam, Manipur and Tripura giving rise to several insurgent groups. Conflicts among these linguistic and religious ethnic groups tend to centre round issues of local power, economic deprivation, educational opportunities etc. It is seen that ethnic conflicts take violent turn in N.E. when the tribal people feel that they have been exploited or deprived by the non-tribals or outsiders or think that other tribal groups are responsible for their lot. Actually the roots of the problem are economic, political and emotional and not ideological.

In order to end these conflicts steps should be taken to ensure economic upliftment of the deprived ethnic groups as well as emotional and psychological integration. In this chapter, an attempt has been made to find out the main causes of ethnic conflicts in N.E. Region and to make an assessment of steps taken by the government to resolve the conflict.

Naga-Kuki Conflict

The Kuki-Naga strife has a long history. But the process of reclamation of territory was intensified after 1963, when the former Naga hill district of Assam, gained statehood. The Kuki leaders also aspired for Kuki-land comprising the districts of Churchandpur, Chandel, Senapati, Tamenglong and parts of Manipur and Nagaland, Assam and Myanmar. Kuki militant organisations such as the KNA, KNO and KNF have time and again asserted their claim to the areas which would constitute Kuki-land.

But Kuki demand has been opposed by the NSCN(IM) which is at the fore-front of the confrontation with the Kukis.

Ethnic violence escalated in May 1992, when the Kuki militants asked the Nagas to leave Moreh, a town near Indo-Myanmar border. Moreh being the centre of smuggling activities, unspecified quantity of purified heroin is smuggled out of Moreh into Manipur and from there to the rest of India everyday. Violence began when the Kukis refused to pay the loyalty tax to the NSCN(IM) stating that Moreh is included within their territory, but population-wise, the Nagas outnumber them by a thin margin.

The Naga-Kuki conflict demanding their self-proclaimed territory is a threat to the territorial integrity of the state. Rumours like consent for greater Nagaland or Bhutan type arrangement time and again provided fuel to the fire.

Actually, there are two governments functioning in Manipur. One at night and other at day. Again the condition of internally displaced people in Manipur due to the ongoing ethnic clashes between them is pathetic. Some of the poverty ridden women affected by ethnic clashes are taking shelter in Imphal and indulging in flesh trade while some others are in the drugs trade.

There are two main economic factors intensifying the conflict between the Nagas and Kukis.

(i) Notice served by the UNC to the Kukis on 22 October, 1992 asking them to vacate the Naga-inhabited areas within December 1992. But the Kukis of Manipur are also owners of the land. So, the Kukis showed strong resistance and determination to oppose the Naga move.

(ii) Another economic factor related to the township of Moreh. Both the Naga and Kuki groups want to control the business activities of Moreh town as it has been a source of revenue for the so-called underground activities.

Bodo Movement or Bodo-non-Bodo Conflict

Bodo-non-Bodo conflict is not a very old problem. A section of the youth of this ethnic group has been trying to regain their lost vintage since the 70s of last century. Bodos are seen more concentrated in an area lying between the river Sonkosh of Dhubri and Kokrajhar districts and Orang river of Darrang district. The area lying in between comprises either wholly or partly the district of Kokrajhar, Bongaigaon, Borpeta and Nalbari Districts, Rangia sub-division of Kamrup district and Darrang District. Arising out of relative deprivation, the Bodo movement was led by a student body. Of course, the Bod did not want to secede from India but sought a separate state by the name of Bodo Land. But the movement did not remain non-violent due to the formation of BPAC. ABSU leadership presented a number of documentation to the Government in justification of their demands for a separate state with status of Union territory under the provision of Articles 2 and 3 of the Indian Constitution for the plan tribals of Assam in the Northern valley of Brahmaputra along with the foothills of Bhutan and Arunachal Pradesh for all-round security and development. They also claimed to divide Assam on fifty-fifty basis and detailed explanatory document was submitted on 10 November, 1987 to the President, Prime Minister and Home Minister of India. Although initially a separate state with the status of Union territory was demanded, later on it was declared that the ultimate aim was full statehood. However, after the death of U.N. Brahma, the leadership agreed to sign the memorandum of settlement for maximum autonomy within the framework of the Constitution of India for social, economic, educational, ethnic and cultural advancement of Bodos. But the irony is that boundary demarcation controversy has become more and more curious with every passing day.

Of course, recently the officials of the Ministry of Home Affairs have been given to understand that the Assam Government and BLT have arrived at some understanding on the demarcation of boundary. The new Bodo agreement involving the Bodo Liberation Tiger is expected to be signed soon at the initiative of the State Government.

Observations

1. The integration of the people of the North-Eastern Region into the Indian nation, pacifying all the ongoing ethnic conflicts is not an easy task. National, strategic and humanistic considerations alike demand that peace, tranquillity, contentment and orderly progress should be fostered in this vital and vulnerable region which has been historically the route of foreign invasions from the east. There are many obstacles in the way of integration of this border with the rest of India. But the most important of them all is the general ignorance and lack of knowledge about the area and the people of this region. This gross ignorance and outdated knowledge about the people of North-Eastern region are largely responsible for much of the administrative bungling and mismanagement and consequent wrong decision on the part of the policy makers in distant Delhi and the executioner on the spot.

2. Sometimes, even the role of the government comes under suspicion. Some tribal people complain that the Kuki-Naga conflict is the result of appeasement policy towards the Nagas. According to them the Kukis are considered as the only obstacle in the design of greater Nagaland and hence the Nagas served quit notices to the Kukis in 1992 leading to the unprecedented violence. Whereas the Nagas feel that the Kukis are allegedly joining hands with the Government of India to neutralise the Naga movement. In 1992, the necessary ground for agreement between the Government of India and the Kukis was planned in this direction. They believe that the said agreement was signed in 1992 and under this agreement the Government of India supplied arms and military training to KNF with their base at Moreh to neutralise the Naga insurgents and as a reaction to this development the Nagas attacked the Kukis. It will be possible to arrive at a fruitful solution if different ethnic groups become ready to discuss freely the differences and points of conflicts among themselves.

3. Again, while discussing the underlying causes of the Bodo-non-Bodo conflict, the immediate occasion was provided by the example of Assam movement and its obvious success. The Assam Accord promised a series of safeguards for protecting the distinctive identity of the people of Assam. We can think that if proper safeguards for different communities were actually worked out, the Bodo-land movement might not have assumed the proportion it did. Clause 6 of the Assam

Accord said "Constitutional, Legislative and Administrative safeguards, as may be appropriate, shall be provided to protect, preserve and promote the cultural social, linguistic identity and heritage of the Assamese people". Clause 10 provided "It will be ensured that relevant laws for prevention of encroachment of Government lands and lands in tribal belts and blocks are strictly enforced and unauthorised encroachers evicted as laid down under such laws." Thus the failure of Assam Accord in particular also contributed to the gathering storm in the Bodo dominated areas of Assam.

4. The so-called maximum autonomy as mentioned in the Bodo accord was however a delusion. Under the constitutional provision, states do not enjoy autonomy. It is hardly possible to find any real trace of autonomy in power sharing in a meaningful way in the Bodo Accord or for that matter, in the Bodoland Autonomous Council Act, 1993.

5. After independence or slightly before that different sets of people particularly the migrants from the then East Pakistan and now Bangladesh used to occupy the vacant lands, either Khas-lands or V.G.R. or P.G.R. or Forest land and settled there. People of other parts of the state also migrated to the land despite the introduction of tribal belts and other legislations.

Rather, covertly or overtly the migrants used to own land in the belts and blocks, whereas the tribals who used to cultivate land and settle in the forest villages, have been not only denied the right of ownership of the land but also some of them have been evicted. All these have made the Bodos to feel unsafe and insecurity threatened their very existence. In fact, conflict between Bodo and Bengalis and Bodo and Jharkhandis have the origin in this trend.

6. The question of ethnic identity is too real in Tripura as the state has been overwhelmed by the influx of immigrants from Bangladesh especially after partition of India and merger of the state with the Union of India. There are many economic and emotional factors that have made the people ethnicity concerned. They are,

(i) Alienation of tribals from their lands by the non-tribals or Bangladeshis.
(ii) Restrictions in the movement of hill-dwellers to the plains.
(iii) Restriction in the process of taking ploughs by the Jhumias.
(iv) Increase in the exploitation of tribesmen by a section of wicked traders, mahajans and money-lenders.

7. The recent decision of the Central Government to extend the Ceasefire with NSCN(IM) without territorial limit is a blunder on the part of the Central Government. It has chance to affect both the territorial integrity and ongoing ethnic conflict in the North-East Region. This decision of the Central Government caused apprehensions in other states like Assam and Arunachal Pradesh as the outfit has been demanding major portions of these states for inclusion in the proposed Nagalim. As per map of the proposed Nagalim, which has been projected by the NSCN(IM) through its website the outfit claimed that areas like the Dibang Valley, Lohit district and Tirap of Arunachal Pradesh should be included in Nagaland. The map of Nagalim includes Karbi Anglong and North Cachar Hills District of Assam. The map also includes parts of Golaghat, Sivasagar, Dibrugarh, Tinsukia, Nagaon and Cachar districts of the state and most parts of the state at Manipur.

According to the NSCN, Nagalim without the knowledge and consent of the Naga people was apportioned between India and Burma after their declaration of Independence. The part, which falls in India is subdivided and placed under four different administrative units — Assam, Arunachal Pradesh, Manipur and Nagaland state. The eastern part which Burma claims is placed under two administrative units — Kachin State and Sagaing Division. So, the extension of the Ceasefire has given rise to apprehension in the neighbouring states about the possibility of the NSCN setting up camps to stake claim over the area later on. There is certain possibility that it will further intensify the ongoing ethnic conflicts in the NE, particularly in Manipur. In Manipur the population of Naga group of tribes is more than the Kuki group of tribes. From the widespread arson and destruction arising after the declaration of ceasefire, we can easily guess that it will further aggravate Kuki-Naga and Naga-Meitei conflicts.

REFERENCES

Baruah, Girish and Borpuzari, Hira, *The Process of National Integration in the N.E.*

Hussain, M. *The Assam Movement.*

Misra, Udayan. *Quest For Identity.*

Magazine "*Prantik*", February 1995 Issue.

Phukan, Girin. *Political Dynamics of N.E. India,* Essay in honour of Prof. Barrister Pakem.

Sen Deka, Kanak. *Asomar Gosthi Danda Aru Samagic Vivartanar Dhara.*

13

ETHNICITY IN TRIPURA
A Conceptual Framework

MAHADEV CHAKRAVARTI

The question of 'ethnicity' has perhaps never been so important for the social scientists at the global level as at present. No doubt, the unmistakable disinctness of a particular social group with its own identity mark generates social distance between itself and others, but because of the ethnic consciousness for self-determination, the entire structure of the present 'nation-state' system has been threatened in various parts of the world. Ethnicity claims a 'space' and fragment in a plural society. Ethnic conflicts since the early sixties of the twentieth century. Particularly after the distintegration of socialist states in Europe in the last decade, have assumed compelling significance for the researchers of social sciences throughout the globe. Nobody can deny that it is the manifestation of a deeper problem, that of unfulfilled aspirations of a social group, and the ethnic question in Tripura is no exception to this general rule. One cannot take an exclusive view of ethnic consciousness being either linguistic or cultural or religious, as there may be various factors responsible for such outlook, but everywhere the elite in that social group usually takes the lead to take the advantages of the forces of modernisation in the political, social and economic fields. Sometimes it leads to clash of interests between different forces and violence. Although violence is more an aberration than the norm in the past days of Tripura, still since 1980s ethnic violence and insurgency have become an important feature of the social fabric. One more important and interesting aspect of the present trend may also be pointed out in this context. Today in the age of globalisation when the tendency everywhere seemed to be more towards homogenisation, we are to see the opposite tendency in the case of ethnicity. Instead of being at loggerheads with each other, the two opposite forces, i.e. globalisation and localisation (ethnonationalism)

– sometimes reinforce each other. This is true in the case of Tripura and many other places also.

It is sometimes said that ethnicity results in a kind of 'defence mechanism' against the domination by the relatively advanced section of the society. Tripura is the only state in India where the tribals – who once constituted the majority – had been reduced to a minority position by the successive waves of immigration of non-tribal people before and after 1947. Through *jungle-abadi* and other systems the Manikya rulers of Tripura had once openly invited the non-tribal peasants of his Chakla Roshnabad Zamindary (now in Bangladesh) for a change for the age-old *jhum* system to settled cultivation and for having more revenues. The non-tribal peasants also played a leading role in transforming the jungles into fertile land and in pushing forward the state formation process and economic growth of the state. Due to the changed demographic profile, particularly after the division of India in 1947 when hundreds of non-tribal refugees took shelter, the ethnic balance became very delicate and fragile. According to 1991 census, out of a total population of 27,57,205, only about 31 per cent are tribals. The percentage of tribal population, according to 2001 census, is yet to be published. The fear of submergence of tribal culture within the dominant Bengali culture has become apparent. There was a "deep sense of historical injustice" in the tribal mind. The fear-psychosis in tribal mind had ultimately helped the emergence of ethnocentrism (i.e. in-group feeling), a sense of tribalism, revivalism, insurgency and the slogan of deportation of 'foreigners' (a fall-out of the Assam movement) through violent means. True, ethnic insurgencies are directly related to unemployment, under-employment, economic backwardness, rising expectation due to growth of literacy (Tripura had the tradition of 'people's education movement' since 1949 in spite of economic backwardness) and simultaneous frustration. The demands of the ethnic groups deserve greater understanding as fear and frustration provide a breeding ground for ethnic insurgency. The psychological distances between tribals and non-tribals – the 'we' and 'they' divide (as used in the theory of alienation) – are again widened due to the insurgent activities and guntrotting terrorists of both the groups.

The growth of elite and middle class in tribal society gave fillip to the ethnic forces which particularly pointed out the unequal power relations in every sphere of life. Since the days of the Manikyas, and particularly after the merger of Tripura with the Indian Union in 1949, the non-tribals took front seats in the polity, society, bureaucracy, judiciary and other state apparatus. Naturally the new elites in the tribal society felt excluded either from the state formation process or nation-building. The situation became more acute after the farewell to monarchy as the Manikya rulers belonged to the tribal group. The root of ethnic consciousness is to be searched in this historical context. The tribal ethnic leaders are not ready to take into cognizance the contributions of non-tribals in any field. This trail of bitterness and attitude of 'they' and 'foreigners' are reflections of deeper malice which pervades the whole society. According to one assessment, ... the politics of identity.... is basically the politics of philistines, trapped in the world of appearances, fighting imaginary enemies. It draws its strength from prejudices and misconceptions of groups about themselves and others. Its ideology masquerades class exploitation and ignores the material structures and forces responsible for their problems. Feeding on the fear of the 'other' it pits one community against the other and mobilises the people along ethnic lines. Trying to project itself as hapless victim of the 'other' every group tends to interpret history to suit its convenience and necessities.

Thus we have a new interpretation of history of Tripura to suit the purpose of the ethnic leaders. The class formation or class exploitation in the society does not find any place in such history. The glorious struggles of the past – where tribals and non-tribals were equal partners – are not to be mentioned in it. We have here the constructionist approach – to ethnicity. Ethnic ideas, terms and identities are constantly constructed and re-constructed by the emerging middle class and entrepreneurial elites of the tribal society to suit their gains. Sometimes the agenda of identity politics has nothing to do with the interest of the people to whom it claims to serve. The demand for Roman Script in place of the prevalent Bengali script for Kak-Barak language, reconstruction of the age-old calendar of Tripura, i.e. 'Tripurabda' by obliterating the traditional Bengali names of months and days, disbandment of traditional social and religious festivals having an iota of Bengali Hindu influence and even to discard the wearing of *sarees* by women etc. have already raised a lot of controversies in the society. All these loud campaigns have drowned the voice and urge for economic development which is at the root of the problem. Some particular symbols or codes or idioms of ritual or ideas of kinship or customary laws or patrimony or marriage system etc. have sometimes been "invoked and reworked by people in their strategies aimed at producing active political collectivities" for political ends.

S.J. Tambiah in his framework of ethno-nationalist conflicts in South Asia has argued that whatever the historical root and antecedent, contemporary ethnic conflicts are largely the products of interests rooted in the representative or participatory democratic system of today; and ethnic violences are particularly noticeable during election time when political parties seek to take advantage of the vote-bank revolving round caste, community, tribe and religion. The recent election of Tripura Tribal Areas Autonomous District Council (TTAADC) is a pointer in this respect. In a plural and fractured society, electoral politics and struggle for power sometimes consolidate ethnic identities and loyalties and Tripura is not an exception. Not that all members of a particular social group subscribe the same sentiment, but ethnic feeling sometimes becomes so overpowering that even if a member of any particular group wishes to escape it, he/she is not allowed to do so even at the point of gun. There are a number of recent case studies in Tripura in this respect.

Recently, the term 'indigenous' is coined in the politics of ethnicity; although identification of indigenous people is indeed problematic and there are controversies regarding this identity being conceptualised at different levels. The U.N. declaration of the year 1993 as the international year of the indigenous people has only sharpened this controversy. To evoke a sense of "self-esteem and pride rather than a sense of lowly and inferior society that often goes with terms like tribe or tribal", to construct a new myth and to valourise the past by glorifying the traditional culture and representing it as unchanging and timeless – all attempts are now being made. In fact, a new political party 'Indigenous People's Front of Tripura' (IPFT) now not only dominates TTAADC, but wants to dominate all spheres of tribal life. But the controversy regarding indigenous and non-indigenous tribe still remains. Again, the use of term 'Barak' to denote tribal culture of Tripura may not be equally applicable in the case of all the nineteen tribal groups of the state. The Reangs call themselves as 'Bru' with a different tradition. Similarly, the Chakmas, Mogs, Lushais etc. have their own interpretations. Thus there are difficulties to use a single term to denote all the tribes of the state. The inter- and intra-tribe conflict on the use of the term 'Barak' or 'Borok' nation is another feature of the society today.

Geographical location is an important factor in shaping the attitude of the people towards one another. Tripura today is a land-locked state surrounded on three sides by Bangladesh and the geographical continuity of Tripura with the rest of India is only on the northern side with Assam and Mizoram as neighbours. Topographic seclusion, economic backwardness and ethnicity are inter-twined. The hills and forests of Tripura not only provide the tribal people protection from outside forces, but help them to maintain their identity. The location gives stimulus to the growth-retarding systems and taboos to continue. The 'radiating influence' of the Indian National Movement and essence of the freedom struggle did not fully reach Tripura as it was a princely state from time immemorial with age-old feudal structure and was "not psychologically prepared for various changes" in the entire country even after integration in 1949. The roots of ethnic problem are to be searched in this geo-political and psychological context.

In 1949, i.e. at the time of merger of Tripura with the Indian Union, an organ named 'Sengkrak' or 'Chengcrak' was formed with some associates of Tripura palace aiming to merge Tripura with Pakistan; but the conspiracy was foiled and 'Sengkrak' was dissolved for the time being. In 1967 the same organisation again emerged and gave a call for deportation of Bengali refugees from Tripura. Although the tone was some what militant, but it subsided subsequently. That the ethnic idea was in the air, would be evident from the aims and objectives and activities of a lot of organisations since the fifties of the twentieth century. Paharia Union (1951), Adivasi Samity (1952), Tripura Rajya Adivasi Sangha (1953), Adivasi Samsad (1954), Eastern India Tribal Union (1956), Tripura Upajati Juba Samity (1967) and finally, Tripura Upajati Gana-Mukti Parishad which was born as Mukti Parishad in 1949 – all were equally concerned with the demographic revolution and the plight of the tribal people. The leaders of all these organisations were influenced by ethnic feelings, but that was a period of 'soft ethnicity', to use Milton Yinger's concept, which with the passage of time and the change of guard gradually changed itself into 'hard ethnicity'. Thus the gradual transformation of the ethnic concept is another important feature and the time factor is also equally important. Recently, some Bengali racist outfits also have raised their heads in some parts of Tripura to face the situation.

REFERENCES

Chakravarti, Mahadev, (2000), 'Tripura ADC Election, 2000 : Terror Tactics win' in *EPW*, Vol. XXXV, No. 30, July 22-28, pp. 2615-17.

Guha, Amalendu, (1984), 'Pan-Indian and Regional Nationalism : The case of North-Eastern States' in *Social Science Probings*, New Delhi, Vol. 1, No. 1 March , p. 121.

Jodhka, Surinder S., (1999), 'Community and Identities : Interrogating Contemporary Discourses on India' in *EPW*, Mumbai, Vol. XXXIV, No. 41, October 9-15, p. 2958.

Jawaharlal Nehru's, remarks while addressing the S.C. & S.T. Conference in New Delhi in 1952.

Srikanth, H., (2000), 'Militancy and Identity Politics in *Economic and Political Weekly*, Assam' in Mumbai, Vol. XXXV, No. 47, November, 18-24, p. 4124.

Tambiah, S.J., (1997), *Levelling Crowds, Ethnonationalist Conflicts and Collective Violence in South Asia*, Sage Pub., Delhi, p. 8.

Xaxa, Virginius, (1999), 'Tribes as Indigenous People of India' in *EPW*, Vol. XXXIV, No. 51, December, 18-24, p. 3595.

Yinger, Milton, (1994), *Ethnicity : Sources of Strength? Sources of Conflict?* State University of New York Press, New York, 1994, p. 3.

14

ETHNIC IDENTITY ISSUE OF ARUNACHAL PRADESH

R. P. BHATTACHARJEE

Introduction

Arunachal Pradesh is the largest state in North-Eastern region of India with a population of 10,91,117 and population density of 13 persons per square kilometre (Census, 2001). The state has over 110 tribes and sub-tribes while 26 are major tribes.

The state remained almost unknown before the advent of the British in Assam (1826). Very scanty information were available about the region. Knowledge regarding socio-politico economic conditions of the people were limited.

This sparsely populated state is a tribal state. The tribal people formed 88.76 per cent of total population during 1961 which fell down to 63.66 per cent during 1991. The indigenous tribes-men of Arunachal Pradesh belong to the linguistic family of the Tibeto-Burman group. This is the generic name. They are commonly known as the people of Mongoloid origin and have been referred to in the scriptures as the Kiratas. They are the first settlers of the region, who because of geographical and historic reasons remained isolated from the national mainstream for a very long time and the process of opening up is still on (Bhattacharjee, 2000 : 19).

More interestingly, the different tribes within the region, broadly speaking remained cut-off from each other, being situated in narrow valleys, separated from each other by high hills. Earlier, owing to lack of communications, mobility was very limited, tribes were knowing only their immediate neighbours. The trading and social relations were either with the southern plains or with Tibet in the north depending on the location of villages. There was hardly any east-west communication. The result was that tribes in Lohit and Tirap districts, were complete strangers to Monpas in the present West Kamang district or to Apatanis and Myishis in present Lower Subansari and Papumpare district culturally, linguistically or even ethnically (NCAER, 1967 : 11). The state was earlier known as hidden land which is no more so today with the advent of modern administration after the attainment of independence in 1947 and gradual expansion of administration till today specially under the impact of recent political, administrative and other changes. The majority of the tribes of the state were in isolation earlier but after independence, the gap is narrowed down specially in geographical and communication constraints. Today people are more aware of each other specially with the introduction of advance communication media both print and electronic.

As stated earlier, this is a tribal state. According to mother tongue (1991), 19.9 per cent of people were speaking Myishi language, 17.9 per cent were speaking Adi, 5.0 per cent Monpa, 4.6 per cent Wancho, 3.5 per cent Nocte, 3.3 per cent Mishmi, 2.9 per cent Tangsa and 1.0 per cent Miri/Mishing (Census, 2001). Thus, according to language, each of the tribes is one ethnic group. Let us now discuss what is ethnicity.

Ethnicity

Ethnicity is a new concept in Social Science. It was first used by David Rieaman in 1953 as referred to in the 1972 Supplement of the Oxford English Dictionary and subsequently by Cynthia H. Enloe and in India by J. Dasgupta. Before 1953, other terms like 'ethnic communities' by Caroline F. Ware in the Encyclopaedia of Social Science, 'ethnocentrian' by Edward Ryron Reuter in a modern Handbook of Sociology were used. Since 1953, the terms used were 'ethnic-groups' by H.S. Morris in the International Encyclopaedia of Social Sciences (1968), "Primordial (group) attachments" by Clifford Geetz; "communal group" by Daniel Dell; and "minority groups" by Preston Valien. All these terms aim at identifying a particular social group (Datta Ray, 1989 : 1-3). There is, thus, a divergence of opinion as to what is really meant by ethnicity. It becomes all the more difficult if we are to apply the term to the tribal communities of North-East India in general and Arunachal Pradesh in particular.

There is likely to be a never ending debate on the term ethnicity. It can be viewed in terms of socio-cultural or physical characteristics or in tems of religions, racial, national linguistic and so on. Here if the learned scholars agree, we may define ethnicity as *disadvantaged minority groups*. To make it more clear, it should be noted that Parsis in Mumbai are a minority group but they are not termed as ethnic-group because they are well-off. Some scholars opine that under the special variant of Indian pluralism, the majority-minority syndrome does not apply to ethnic groups. In states like Nagaland, Arunachal Pradesh, Meghalaya, for instance, the tribal population are in majority but for that reason, they cannot lose their ethnic group status (Kashyap, 1998:32).

The same person may belong both to a majority and a minority, e.g. one may be in majority by religion and in minority by language or *vice versa*. What divides, also unites. Religious affinity would unite co-religionists in various linguistic groups while at the same time divide each of the linguistic groups.

The Identity Issues

In the case of Arunachal Pradesh, we have seen earlier that in terms of language no groups are in a majority. Now let us find the groups in terms of religion or believers in different faiths. Here, the majority of the people are of Tani-groups who worship Donyi (the Sun) and Polo (the moon), these two objects become the living god and goddess for the people of Arunachal Pradesh. Then these two cosmic objects conjugated into one Donyipolo. It becomes a divine entity for the people of Tani-group. Therefore, Donyipolo as a crude form of religion was there in Arunachal Pradesh from time immemorial. According to Apatani's belief, it was the goddess Sun (Aayo Donyi) who saved the life of Apatani, the first man on the earth when he was in a difficult situation. Henceforth, the Sun was considered as the saviour of mankind on the earth. Therefore, from time to time, the Apatanis worship the sun and the moon for health and longevity. The Adis consider the Donyi and Polo as the two divine eyes of Sedi-Melo, the supreme authority in the universe. The conjugation of Donyi and Polo has something philosophical and deeper meaning. The sun with its rays sustains the lives on the earth and also transmits the message of divinity to the human beings. The moon by reflecting soft light comforts human beings and infuses the feeling of serenity in human mind (Kaning : 2000). The Donyipoloism, hitherto, crude form of religion of the Tanis, has gradually and slowly being shaped by Rev. Talom Rukbo who has been working tirelessly to spread the spiritual message of Donyipoloism for the last several years. Since 1990, this is recognised internationally by the International Association for Religious Freedom (IARF). In the Congress of 1993 (Bangalore) and 1996 (Seol), the priests and religious leaders of major religions of the world had appreciated a lot on the steps taken by Arunachalees to preserve their own religious practices (Kaning; *ibid.*).

Recently, the conversion of the indigenous ethnic group into different faiths has become a serious ethnic issue of identity for Arunachal Tribes. The identity of the tribes reflects in participation of different festivals like Nyokum Yullo (Nyishi), Mopin (Adi, Gallong), Solung (Adi, Padam, Minyong), Dree (Apatani), Chaloloku (Nocte), Sangken (Khamti), Moh or Mol (Tangsa), Losar (Monpa) etc. (Kani, 1995:10-19).

It is observed that all the believers of different converted faith do not participate in different indigenous festivals similar to old days and even there is erosion in traditional social and community services.

The distribution of population by religion in Arunachal Pradesh in percentage is shown below (Bhattacharjee, 2000:60-61).

Table 14.1: Distribution of Population by Religion in Arunachal Pradesh (%)

Religion	1971	1981	1991
Hindus	21.99	29.24	37.04
Buddhists	13.13	13.69	12.88
Christians	0.79	4.32	10.29
Muslims	0.18	0.80	1.38
Sikhs, Jains and other Religions and persuasion and religion not stated	63.91	51.95	38.41

Source : Census of India, 1971, 1981, 1991.

The indigenous faith is included in the last row where we find that there is erosion in their beliefs. According to National Family Health Survey (NFHS-2) 1998-99, religion of household head in percentage in this state was Hindu (37.5), Muslim (1.3), Christian (13.0), Sikh (0.1), Buddhist/Neo-Buddhist (11.0), other (36.0) and no religion (1.1) (EPS : 2001; 511). This shows further erosion in the indigenous faith due to conversion of local tribes into organised external faiths. According to above stated census reports, we find that the percentage of both Hindu and Christian is increasing while percentage of other religious faith of indigenous ethnic groups is decreasing. This issue of conversion is causing threat to ethnic indentities and cultural heritage of Arunachal Pradesh and making conflict situation which should be resolved within ethnic framework. The indigenous faith and cultural society of Arunachal Pradesh (IFSCAS), Nyishi Indigenous faith and cultural society (NIFCS), Donyipolo Mission, and other organisations are spearheading the movement to preserve the identity of the state's indigenous people. Awareness is created in the mind of the youth to protect and preserve the age old cultural and religious practices. Arunachal Pradesh is regarded as island of peace. This should not be disturbed through proselytization.

REFERENCES

A Brief on preparatory work for Census of India, 2001 (for mother tongue data, 1991).

Bhattacharjce, R.P. (2000). *Economic Development of Arunachal Pradesh.* Himalayan Publishers, Itanagar, pp. 1-19.

Bhattacharjee, *ibid.*, pp. 60-61.

Census of India, (2001), Series 13, Arunachal Pradesh, p. ii, Provisional Population Totals.

Datta Ray, B. (1989). *Tribal Identity and Tension in North East India*, Omsons Publications, New Delhi, pp. 1-3.

Economic and Political Weekly. Vol. XXXVI, No. 7, Feb. 17-23, 2001, p. 511.

Kashyap, Subhas C. (1998). "Ethnicity and constitutional reform in India" in *Ethnicity and Constitutional Reform in South-Asia* Ed. by Iftekharuzzaman, Regional Centre for Strategic Studies (RCSS), Colombo, p. 32.

Kaning, Mihin, "Donyipoloism – A Glimpse – I" *The Arunachal Times,* dt. 30.12.2000.

Kani, Take (1995). "Agricultural Festivals of Arunachal Pradesh", Institute for Preservation of Art, Culture and Literature (IPACL), Itanagar, pp. 10-19.

NCAER (1967). *Techno-Economic Survey Report of NEFA*, New Delhi, p. ii.

15

ETHNIC ISSUES IN NAGALAND AND NORTH-EAST INDIA

SUKHENDU MAZUMDAR

We notice typical ethnic issues in Nagaland which requires indepth study and a very close understanding of the problem and *vis-a-vis* an open mind to accommodate everything in its totality. Nagaland created on the 1st December, 1963 with its capital at Kohima has an area of 16,579 km. and the state has been divided into 8 districts. "In Nagaland, it was this wisdom of our former Prime Minister, coupled with the desire of a vast majority of the Naga people to live in peace and with dignity that eventually led to the signing of an historic 16-Point Agreement between the Government of India and the Naga People's Convention in the year 1960. The grant of statehood in 1963 was but a natural culmination of this agreement. Since then, despite missing out on the benefit of nearly three Five-Year Plans, Nagaland as the 16th state of the Indian Union, has proudly marched ahead on the road to progress and prosperity" (excerpts from the speech of Shri S.C. Jamir on 22nd August, 1998 at New Delhi while receiving the National Integration Award). The religion practised is of course Christianity and the practice of animism is no more heard of, may be one or two stray cases here and there exist which we need not take into account. The official language followed is English and the common *lingua franca* is 'Nagamese' a raw blend of Assamese, Hindi, Bengali and English which is understood and spoken.

Ethnicity, as we see it today, in the context of twenty-first century is obviously a configuration of some factors where culture, religion, racial feature, language and historical bondages and symbols and their distinctive features etc. play a vital role. But it should be kept in mind that no configuration is of static nature since dynamic variables are always there which gradually take root in the system and give it a permanent colour and shape. Regarding the advent of Christianity Dr. V.C. Kanite Sema feels, "Tribal religions are among those uninstitutionalised religions sacked by Christianity". The waning of tribal religion by the organised religion is crystal clear. The poverty ridden tribal people really accepted Christianity when they were made to understand that God as postulated in Christianity is the most powerful and supreme over spirits and demons. Thus, it is clear that the tribal religions that had no access to script and scriptures and so their established systems have had to accept the same. Though it is a fact that where the culture is too strong and there is a strong background of established system and philosophy, it could resist the foreign religion to overpower them. "Most of the schools that were opened during the late nineteenth century in the North-East were run by the missionaries. Obviously, Christian education was taught. However, in the process of christianising the tribal people, especially the Nagas, the Assamese converts and Assamese language were the most important instruments for reason of familiarity and custom" (Dr. Kanite). Dr. Jasbir Singh Ahluwalia, V.C., Punjabi University, in his presidential address at the International Conference of Ethnicity observed, "In the twenty-first century society ethnic, ethno-religious, ethno-social, ethno-political consciousness would play significant role—both positive and negative. Positively, ethnic consciousness, in general would be a significant constituent factor in evolving multifocal, pluralist dispensation of the future. Negatively, if suppressed by unitarian-totalitarian trends and forces, ethnic, and in particular ethno-religious, consciousness would assume sharper militancy and even more acute violent forms, threatening peace, harmony and amity."

Thus, no nation-state can be composed of a uniform classification of people, but the remarkable classification is the ethnic one which plays a vital role in determining the socio-political umbrella of ethnicity in a large group of people or even a smaller group of people confined to a particular geographic parameter and environment. The North-East is a typical example to be studied where many a ethnic group exist in a close proximity with varied colours and a distinct division of their own. Their ethnic consciousness is the need of the time towards multi-focal, pluralist arrangement along with the keen desire to belong to the members of the contemporary communities. Ethnicity, thus has played a role in injecting the group values and the realisation of the value of existence. Though from time to time we have witnessed tremendous uproar and conflict in the different ethnic groups for their supremacy over others and also autonomy and other issues which demand political solution at the state level. We can take a few cases to mention, e.g. Bodos are demanding Bodoland, Karbis are asking for their autonomous state, autonomous districts are demanded for Rabha-Hajong, Missings and Tiwas and then the Nagas stand for their greater Nagaland.

The state of Nagaland is a unique combination of many tribes and their languages. Some of the major tribes and their festivals I would like to mention are :

Tribe	Festival	Tribe	Festival
Angami	Sekrenyi	Ao	Moatsu
Sumi	Tuluni	Lotha	Tokhu Emong
Chang	Naknyulum	Phom	Monyu
Konyak	Aoling	Sangtam	Amongmong
Yimchunger	Metemneo	Rengma	Ngada
Khiamniungan	Tsokum	Zeliang	Chega Gadi/Hega

The Naga people are gradually coming together and sorting out their group clashes and heading for the issue of a greater Nagaland even. Still there are lots of conflicts among themselves which virtually weakened this race. In the words of Shri S.C. Jamir, the Chief Minister of Nagaland, "The last decade of the twentieth century has been particularly a painful and violent period for the Naga people. It has now culminated in fratricide amongst Naga brethren which is of the greatest concern. On the one hand, there is the deep pain of bloodshed and the loss of precious lives. On the other hand there is the greater peril that the Nagas of the future will be divided on tribal, village and clan lines leading us back to the dark head hunting past, instead of looking to the future with hopes and confidence. Along with it, in the name of Naga Sovereignty, the social and economic systems of the land have been systematically torn down and crippled. Our work culture is dying and replaced by gun culture. In the name of freedom, the Naga values of discipline, honesty and hard work are being lost sight of. There now exists the spectre of a generation of youth whole philosophy is steeped in mindless violence and easy money. In fact the Nagas who were a free people are now in chains socially, economically and politically. Can we then call it a "righteous cause" or "holy cause" when everything is being destroyed." (excerpts from Independence Day speech, 1999). This clearly sounds the concern of the person who has been leading the state of Nagaland for a long time.

But the trouble begins when the mad race for such issues gain momentum. Truly speaking, we do not see any end of such conflicts and rivalries and really find it very tough to handle since they require careful and delicate handling with broadness and political wisdom. Things really appear out of gear when we confront such separatist movement gaining momentum and when law and order comes to a halt. Sometimes, it is the politicians who play pivotal role where either make or mar is the outcome. The wall between the majority and the minority and the game of politicians with their vested interest and along with the classification of language, territory, occupation, cultural differences and physical attributes matter a lot. One such typical case-study can be cited from the state of Tripura which reveals such power-game of one over the other. The situation of Tripura is today not what it was a few decades back. There the tribals and the Bengalees always have had a mutual understanding of co-operation and trust and feeling for oneness; but the gradual influx of refugees from Bangladesh has changed the scenario and chemistry of the two groups and virtually led to an imbalance between the tribal people and the Bengalee population. Thus we witness an attempt on the part of the minority tribal people to launch brutal attacks on the majority to bring things to an equilibrium and create an atmosphere conducive to a separate home-land of their own.

16

CONFLICT RESOLUTION IN NAGA SOCIETY
Past and Present

S. D. NANDI

Conflict between individuals and groups is social phenomenon. Pursuit of self-interest or of group objectives are socially acceptable behaviour in all cultures. Conflicts arise when interests clash, rights are asserted, claims and counter-claims are made. Every society must address itself to resolving conflicts within the system of values it cherishes.

A wide range of alternative methods are available to society at any point of time for resolving conflicts. Short of violence, the method that is socially sanctioned in any culture reveals the basic values and ideas of the people. It also reveals their own perceptions about themselves as parts of the society and also their relationship with others like themselves in the society. Their preference for a particular method also communicates whether to use coercive means to suppress or resolve conflicts amicably within the given framework of value system.

All pre-modern societies adopted non-formal methods to settle disputes. They viewed conflicts as a form of social behaviour and sought to obtain a solution through what is understood as community approach. This was done to contain conflicts within their social boundaries. They drew upon custom, traditions and precedents to settle disputes through mediation and arbitration.

The non-formal methods adopted by early societies are processes which are still found convenient. Associations based on religion, profession interest groups and even political parties still prefer to contain and resolve conflicts within their own boundaries. Any dissent is suppressed through coercive methods. If, however, these methods fail to resolve the conflict, factions fall apart and splits take place.

On the other end of the spectrum are available the formal legal methods with codified laws, courts and services of lawyers. Litigation is a preferred alternative which modern societies go for. Over time, a gradual shift takes place from traditional to modern ways. Process of conflict resolution also shifts from non-formal to formal method. Many modern governments, in order to preserve and sustain the traditional societies incorporate the customary practices into formal law. Increasingly customary practices are being codified and law courts take cognizance of these practices.

Community approach to dispute settlement perhaps, found its best expression in pre-modern Naga villages. A totally illiterate people without any script, handed down through oral traditions their shared visions and values to succeeding generations uninterruptedly through millennia. For them it was not the nature of the conflict *per se* but the nature of their resolution that spoke of the kind of society they lived in. They also left for us a model of harmonious and stable society in which individuals lived in close proximity, sharing each other's happiness and sorrows and living in amity.

A Naga village is inhabited by several exogamous clans. A clan is the basic social unit of Naga society. Each family within a clan is believed to have descended from a common ancestor and as such is related to others within the clan through blood. A clan council looks after the affairs of the clan. The clan chief happens to be the oldest surviving member of the clan. In the past he was a great partiarch. In the past the chief was assisted by family heads or clan elders. Intra-clan dispute were settled in a spirit of accommodation like those within a family. Clan bonds being very rigid, disputes among clan members were not allowed to disrupt the bond. The overwhelming consideration in any settlement was to ensure harmony and unity among the members. Often coercive methods were adopted to ensure compliance.

The highest forum to adjudicate dispute within a village was the village council headed by its chief. He was assisted by clan chiefs and some important family heads. Complaints of serious nature were referred to it. The chief, on receiving the complaints, fixed a date for hearing. The disputants were asked to present themselves along with their supporters before the council on the date of hearing. Members of the public could also be present during the hearing. The council heard both the parties, examined witnesses and assessed the evidence. A decision was arrived at in keeping with the "general feeling" of the village community. In arriving at a decision customs, conventions, traditions social norms and values were kept in view. Any decision of the village council was binding on disputing parties and any dissent was punished.

The nature of dispute settlement to a large extent depended upon the nature of relationship the disputants had with one another. In a village, each individual's status and role were strictly defined. He existed on a co-ordinate of vertical clan and horizontal kin relationship. Such relationships were intimate, mutual and sharing. The nature of dispute settlement, therefore, aimed at preserving that relationship and not destroying it. The entire adjudication process had the overwhelming aim of preserving social harmony and unity among the members of the village community.

Introduction of British rule and subsequent independence of the country altered, among other things, the method of dispute settlement. The customary and non-formal methods of the Nagas, as practised through centuries and in isolation that helped them to maintain cohesiveness of the society, came under threat and gradually gave way to formal method of the "due process of law." Once the rigid traditional order degenerated, clan and kin bonds were loosened. Society still retained the outer shell but internally the age old social values were radically changed. The dominant shift was towards individualism. No doubt, people still talked about their village and customary laws but preferred formal law to settle disputes. Values associated with individualism came to the forefront.

Relationships between disputants also changed in the new environment of freedom of action. They behaved more like strangers to each other. Each one became an island in a fragmented society that was protected by law. Clarity of community justice was replaced by the clarity of law in the process of adjudication. The social ramifications of legal decisions were lost sight of. Communal security and bonds were replaced by freedom and protection under law. Community ended when law began.

17

THE NEPALIS IN ASSAM
A Question of Identity

LOPITA NATH

The Nepali presence in Assam is an established fact. Historically, there is evidence that Nepali had strong links with Assam, matrimonial, or otherwise as early as the eighteenth century, when the ancient kingdom of Kamrupa, extended to eastern Nepal. Thereafter in the second decade of the sixteenth century, the Koch King Biswa Singha married Ratna Kanti Devi of Kathmandu, followed by Nildhwaj and Nar Narayan, the two kings of Kamrup who also married in Nepal. As a consequence of these matrimonial alliances, a number of Nepali Brahmin priests, Chetri warriors, farmers, herdsmen and artisans were brought from Nepal to Assam (Sinha, 1990 : 222). These immigrations, however, did not have much impact on the social, economic or demographic balance of the region.

It was only in the colonial context, 1817 to be precise, that migrations of the Nepalis to Assam with serious socio-political ramifications took place. They first came in the wake of the Treaty of Sagauli (1815-16), with the deployment of the Gorkhas in the Sylhet operations as a part of the Cuttack legion, later known as the Assam Light Infantry (Sinha, 1990 : 226-27, Shakespeare, 1977 : 6). These soldiers after their retirement from service were encouraged to settle in the foothills, forest fringes, as well as in other strategic points on the frontier, thus creating certain compact pockets of Nepali settlements in Arunachal Pradesh, Assam, etc. (Sinha 1990 : 229). They soon emerged as loyal citizens and faithful allies of the British Government (Sinha, 1990 : 229). This view is however contradicted in reports of the contemporary British officials (Government Files : 1929) where the Nepalis were severely criticized for "their dirty sanitary habits, and learning bad habits from the local people". Lieut. Col. T. Keyes in his *Treatise on*

Nepal has written that the Nepali migration to the North-East was "not entirely undesirable", and since this migration cannot be stopped, it should be allowed to continue.

Thus, in the colonial period the migrations of the Nepalis to the region increased as a consequence of British colonial expansion. Besides grant of waste lands on favourable terms, the Nepalis were reported to have been given pecuniary assistance for their onward journey to Upper Assam. They came mostly under the lure of economic opportunities. There were strong push factors like : increasing fragmentation of land- holding; indebtedness; ecological crisis through deforestation; rising population without further land to cultivate and chronic deficit of food production in the hill areas of Nepal, which constantly pressurised Nepali migration. This migration to Assam and the North-East was propelled by certain pull factors, which included, besides colonial patronage, abundance of land, both in the plains and hills of Assam; thinness of local population and their refusal to work in the hard fields opened up after colonization; similarity of natural environment; scope for employment. This was found in the colonial army and police, in the offices as chaukidars, darwans, chaprasis, peons, as well as avenues in agricultural sector, dairy, transport and construction works. Thus, the Nepali herdsmen and marginal farmers trickled down to Assam at least from the first quarter of the present century (M. Hussain, 1993 : 256-57). These migrations were not without some implications. This chapter is an attempt to focus on the Nepali migration to Assam and its implication. We propose to examine briefly the losses and gains of Nepali migration and the levels of their assimilation in the post-colonial period. The analysis is of an exploratory nature, and will attempt to draw conclusions on the issue of Nepali identity and ethnic conflict in the region in the light of the above issues.

Nepali Migration to Assam

In the post-colonial period, the immigrant population in the region had to adjust to the change in rulers and participate in the democratic system. The Nepali migration to the North-East continued unabated and there was tremendous increase in the Nepali population.

Table 17.1 demonstrates the growth of Nepali population in Assam both numerically and percentage-wise in the colonial as well as the post-colonial period. Although in the colonial period, they showed signs of the growth, to serve the colonial interests, it was very high in the post-colonial period, specifically during the years from 1951-1971. Within a span of twenty years, their population rose from 1,01,338 to 3,49,116 indicating a growth of 3.5 times. This was a very significant period for the Nepalis in Assam, as they actively participated in the electoral process to ensure the success of the ruling government during those years, attributing their success to their numerical strength. Table 17.1 also gives the population figures for 1991, which although increased to 4,32,519, numerically, decreased percentage-wise to 1.93 per cent from 2.38 per cent in the total population. This may be due to the Assam movement, when the Nepalis labelled as foreigners, were at the receiving end of a backlash. Many left their homes and moved out settling in the border areas of Kakaribhita, Biratnagar, Dholabari, Dhannagar, Suryanagar etc. Most of the Nepalis settled in these areas hail from Tezpur, Sonitpur etc. (as told by Lil Bahadur Chetri, Interview No. 2).

Table 17.1 : Growth of Nepali Population in Assam

Year	No. of Nepali Population in Assam	Percentage
1901	21,347	0.35
1911	47,654	0.67
1921	70,344	0.94
1931	88,306	1.02
1951	1,01,338	1.26
1961	2,15,213	1.98
1971	3,49,116	2.38
1991	4,32,519	1.93

Source : Census of India Reports, 1901-71; M. Hussain, 1993 : 258

In the post-colonial period, the Nepalis became a significant immigrant group. Although encouraged by the push factors, and supported by the Indo-Nepal Friendship Treaty of 1950, and the border roads construction following the Chinese aggression of 1962, Assam became a home for many Nepali labourers. They sought employment as marginal farmers-*cum*-small-dairymen, while others continued to engage in construction works, as labourers, wood-cutters as well as chowkidars, drivers, peons, securitymen etc. Even in the present times for a Nepali, dairy farming or marginal farming are common avenues, although they seemed to have graduated from being engaged only as labourers, chowkidars or peons to white collar jobs. These are the Nepalis, who have moved to the urban centres and being educated they have begun to fill in the role of the professionals. But since the number of these in competition is not so great, they do not pose a threat to the local people.

Assimilation among the Nepalis

As important feature of Nepali presence in Assam is the assimilation of the immigrant Nepalis into the land of their migration. They speak the language (Assamese) fluently, are educated in the Assamese language, scholars are writing in the Assamese language and have more or less merged into the host society. A survey of the Nepalis in and around Guwahati city testifies to this fact. Mr. Lil Bahadur Chetri, Retd. Professor in Economics, Arya Vidyapith College and Sahitya Academy Award winner for Nepali in 1987 for his novel *Brahmaputrar Ahe Pahe*, has remarked :

> "There is too much assimilation in the Assamese way of life. The Nepalis in Assam has studied in the Assamese medium and celebrate Assamese festivals like *Bihu*. The feelings are reciprocated for in the Nepali celebration of *Bhanu Jayanti*, there is full Assamese co-operation and participation" (Interview No. 2).

A visit to the interior Nepali villages in Rowta, in Darrang district also supports the point stated. The residents of the villages spoke the Assamese language, and even communicated with each other in Assamese. Mr Indra Sharma, Subject teacher, Dikrai Higher Secondary School and resident of Rowta, commented that :

> "We speak Assamese, educated our children in Assamese schools, we have adjusted. Even the fact is that we preferred to speak more

in Assamese than in Nepali, even among our Nepali friends" (Interview No. 4).

However, it cannot be denied that assimilation was not complete; and they have retained their own distinctive cultural traits. They converse in Nepali, and celebrate their own festivals, the Dasain with gaiety. A look at Nepali house in a village, with the haystack and cowshed in front and the double storeyed Tungsi house are evidences that they have retained their own identity even in a land for away from their homeland. Perhaps assimilation was a necessity from the point of view of economic and political integration.

The Losses and Gains of Migration

Edward Shils has written that immigration results in some loss of what is objectively valuable to the immigrants and their descendants. The immigrants gradually lose the memory of place and of landscape, this in turn furthers the loss of language, a sense of historical continuity with their ancestors, as well as of beliefs and images. The Nepalis in Assam, who have been here for two or three generations have lost all contact with their Nepali homeland. Most of them have never been to Nepal and any visits are to that of a foreign country. In this context Mr. Chandralal Gautam, teacher and resident of Rowta had said :

"I have been to Nepal in 1975 and again in 1993 but there is not much contact; although we have our relatives, we do not know where they are". (Interview No. 7)

The Nepalis in Assam speak in language which is very different from the one spoken in Nepal. Much of their culture has been diluted by the loss of contact. For example, as a beginning to the festival of *Dasain*, there is the symbolical ceremony of *Raja Tika*, whereby the tika is first applied to the head of state, which in Nepal is the monarch or Raja, on the main door. But the Nepalis in Assam (those in the Rowta village) have given up the habit and instead symbolically apply it to the picture of the head of state or the country.

Perhaps the greatest loss of the Nepalis in Assam has been that of an identity. In spite of their assimilation and greater Assamisation, they have been labelled as foreigners and are at the receiving end of a backlash.

As told by Indra Sharma :

> "In reality, although we are living in Assam and are Assamese, we have to identify ourselves as Nepalis". (Interview No. 4)

Nonetheless, with all this unreplaced waste, there is also a very great gain. The gain lies in the widened scope of reference, awareness and appreciation in the hybrid culture to which the immigants contribute. To the Nepalis in Assam, who have assimilated in the multi-cultural society of Assam, the sense of gain is much more compared to the loss. They have acquired much of the culture of the land to which they migrated.

Mr. Rebati Upadhyay, politician and teacher, had remarked :

> "We have gained by coming here, learnt a new culture, in addition to our own culture, we are gainers, we have not lost anything" (Interview No. 9).

They speak Assamese as well as Nepali fluently, have been Assamised to a great extent and are a part and parcel of the Assamese society. This point has been reiterated by Mr. Chandra Sharma, 64 years, Interview No. 10, who was born in Nepal and came to Assam during the British times, when he remarked that :

> "There is no difference between Assamese and Nepali, the only difference lies in language" (Interview No. 14).

Conclusion

Yet, the Nepalis in Assam have remained on the periphery of the Assamese mainstream in particular and Indian in general. Those born and brought up in Assam and the later immigrants from Nepal are accorded the same status as a peripheral community. During the Assam movement, the question of identity of the Nepalis in Assam transformed the existing relations between the Nepalis and the Assamese in Assam. That, they came to be labelled as unwanted foreigners in a land where they were born and brought up, also generated an awareness of their own ethnic identity. In their hearts every Nepali in Assam believes himself to be an Assamese and an Indian, but when they are sidelined as foreigners, the Nepali identity started becoming very strong. This awareness is more pronounced among the new category of white collar Nepalis in Assam. Born, brought up and educated in the region, speaking the local languages fluently and aware of the contributions and sacrifices of their forefathers to the consolidation and development of the region, they know of Assam as their home. But as they compete for their jobs with the local people, they are made aware of their peripheral position. They have become politically aware and culturally conscious of their status in the state and citizenship rights. They are made more conscious of their position when they are called for hearings to prove their identity in the 'voters list' in Assam after the movement. Residents of seventy-eighty years are summoned as they have been marked with a 'D' or doubtful voter in the lists.

Mr. Chandralal Gautam remarked :

> "There are hearings; names have been struck off the voters lists and there are enquiries. The person called, have to go with all their documents, as many as 13 times. There is a lot of harassment. Even on the day of festivals, we have to attend hearings". (Interview No. 7)

These Nepalis, some even without any papers, have nothing to prove their long presence except they themselves. This has generated a feeling of hurt and lack of hope for the future. They are thus left with no alternative but to fall back upon the Gurkha past and identify themselves with the pan-Nepali solidarity movement. The white collar professionals try to provide the leadership for airing the genuine Nepali grievances. But even in this, the Nepalis in Assam feel that their interests have not been properly focused.

Thus, the actual status of the Nepalis in Assam have to be determined. In spite of their long presence in Assam and a large degree of assimilation, they are still labelled as unwanted foreigners. Although there is hope for the future and a change in the situation, the delay has generated a feeling of frustration. The reasons for the unfulfilment of their hopes and aspirations is the lack of a strong ethnic solidarity among themselves. Even the leadership among the Nepalis has not been able to provide the necessary support, mental and physical. However, the Nepalis in Assam are still participating in the social and political processes of the region, hoping, if not anything else, a peaceful co-existence.

REFERENCES

Danda, A.K. *et al.*, (1997) *The Nepalis in North-East India : Politics, Aspirations and Ethnicity in North-East India,* Calcutta.

Census of India, Reports, 1901-1991.

Government File No. 26 of 1929, "Treatise on Nepal by Lieut. Col. T. Keyes. Confidential B, March, 1929 Nos. 269-271, Serial No. 287 (Assam Secretariat).

Hussain, Monirul, (1993). The Assam Movement – Class Ideology and Identity, Delhi.

Interview No. : 2, Date : 22.12.2000.

Interview No. : 4, Date : 24.03.2001.

Interview No. : 7, Date : 24.03.2001.

Interview No. : 9, Date : 24.03.2001.

Interview No. : 10, Date : 25.03.2001.

Sinha, A.C. (1982). 'The Nepalese in North-East India : Ethnicity and Resource Appropriation' in *Social Tension in North-East India*, J.B. Bhattacharjee (ed.), Shillong.

Sinha, A.C., (1990). 'The Indian North-East Frontier and the Nepalese Immigrants', in *Himalayan Environment and Culture*, Shimla, Indian Institute of Advanced Study.

18

IMPLICIT COMMUNALISM
The Case of Contemporary Assam

SAMIR KUMAR DAS

Even an elementary definition of communalism views it as the use of religion for purposes other than the religious ones. Since political entrepreneurs use religion as an instrument in order to promote and further their narrow economic and political interests, it has no relationship whatsoever with religion *per se*. A believer is very unlikely to be a communal person for the simple reason that he/she will not use or even allow his/her religion to be used for non-religious purposes. The distinction between a believer and a communal person in other words coincides with that between religion and religiosity. While religion may even make one sacrifice one's self-interest, religiosity is meant to demonstrate before others how religious one is and to cash in on it. Jinnah for example, was not particularly known as a staunch believer of Islam. Yet he was the one who fathered the Pakistan demand. Although communalism refers to use of religion for non-religious purposes, the nature and role of its use are not the same in all parts of India or for that matter, the world, *Hindutva* as some of the leading researchers inform us, does not seem to play the same role in the North-East as it plays for example, in northern India. In the North-East, the issue of infiltration especially of the Muslims from across the borders has acquired tremendous significance and played a key role in the articulation of the ideology of *Hindutva*. On the other hand, the issue of constructing 'the Ram Janambhoomi' in Ayodhya has its appeal in the northern part of the country, but seldom does it hold out the same appeal to the people of this region for reasons not unknown to us. For one thing, a significant portion of the population in the North-East happens to be of 'tribal'[1] origin for whom the ideology of

Hindutva does not have as much appeal as it has to the Hindus of northern India. For another, even the Hindus living in the region for historical reasons, have been and of course, are by and large free from many of its orthodox ingredients. The spread of Vaishnavism particularly in the valley areas contributed enormously to the softening – and in many cases, obliteration of many inegalitarian social practices, rituals, orthodoxies and dogmas prototypical of Hindu caste system.[2] Contemporary empirical researches have also been carried out to show that unlike its counterpart in the northern India, caste system in Assam is not characterized by any kind of steeply vertical asymmetry.[3] In simple terms, not all societies are equally vulnerable to the instrumental uses of religion and other cultural practices by the political entrepreneurs that dominate them. Assam was and to some extent, is by and large free from the communal abuses of casteism and religion. Thus to cite an example, Assam was surprisingly spared of the kind of communal violence that otherwise rocked nearly all parts of India in the wake of partition.

This chapter is not meant to be a paean in praise of Assam's enviably 'secular' track record. In fact, the cultural historians – almost without any exception, writing on the region have been very generous in showering their words of praise on Assam. This chapter in fact turns our attention to a kind of communalism that still remains implicitly in the society and politics of Assam. Indeed, it is so implicit that we often lose sight of it and that is what precisely makes it doubly dangerous. Dangerous because it is communalism that has the menacing potential of eating into the secular-democratic foundations of our body politic and secondly, because it remains unseen and sometimes, unseeable. Since it remains unseen and at times, unseeable, whatever harm it does, it does very imperceptibly, that is to say, without letting us know of the greater danger that is lurking behind our apparently tranquil body politic. Implicit communalism in other words, refers to the greater danger that lurks behind this apparent veneer of tranquillity and civic order. It is the civility of the danger (or 'the orderliness of disorder' as Romain Rolland once called it) that makes it all the more dreadful—much more dreadful than what one notices in northern India. Unlike some run-of-the-mill researches on this subject that are churned out in this part of the country—albeit with alarming regularity, this chapter proposes to focus on the rhetoric of civility that is seen to accompany the phenomenon of communalism in north-eastern India. Since I have dwelt at length on why communalism bodes ill for our body politic[4], I have chosen to turn my focus away from this otherwise beaten track. Instead, we tend to concentrate on how communalism works in Assam not simply by keeping the civil order intact but precisely through it.

The 'Civility' of Communalism

The 'uncivil' nature of communalism has attracted the attention of most of the analysts and commentators for its very apparent nature.[5] When one is threatened, maimed, incapacitated or killed in the name of religion, one loses one's right to life and liberty guaranteed by the Constitution of India. The civil order, in other words, exists through a regime of rights. Similarly, right to elect the governors of the country is believed to be indispensable to the persistence of a civil order. Any disruption in elections by creating communal troubles or by mobilizing religious communities *en bloc* is officially construed as an attempt at wresting away from the people their inalienable rights. Some recently enacted laws prohibit the politicians of India from mobilizing people for elections along communal lines. Civil order *per se* is not valuable; it is valuable because it guarantees the enjoyment of rights enshrined in the Constitution. Secondly, civil order also exists through a balance of political forces – whether political parties or pressure groups or both. In theoretical circle, balance is always regarded as the pivot of civility. Civility is destroyed as soon as the balance is disturbed. If the political parties are of highly uneven size and strength, they are unlikely to be able to balance each other. The larger and stronger amongst them can and do of course, tilt the political balance in their favour and literally rock the political system. The operation of the civil order requires that no political party is big and strong enough to devour another. Similarly, if the nature and composition of the political alliance change too frequently the political balance gets disturbed. If in any society mobilization along communal lines turns out to be only modality of mobilizing people politically, then the political parties and groups that are otherwise known for their firm commitment to secular values may feel compelled to join the bandwagon. Such political theorists as

William Riker and his associates have demonstrated that balance is an integral part of the civil order.[6] The civil order exists through state's 'legitimate monopolization of the instruments of violence' in the society. The monopoly not only sanitizes the larger social sphere and 'internally pacify' it but enables the state to come down heavily on the detractors of the civil order. Should violence take place in the society, it is theoretically the duty of the state to counter it and restore the civil order. The state in short, is the repository of civil order. The theoreticians of the civil order have usually been ardent statists.[7]

Explicit communalism directly comes into conflict with the civil order brought into existence and defended by the state. It is ultimately the state that as the repository of the civil order is called upon to handle the communal menace. A state that promises to act as the repository of civil society is described as secular. If civility in a multi-communal society implies the establishment of a regime of rights and a balance of forces irrespective of the communal differences, then of course the state cannot be theocratic, that is to say, cannot identify itself with any particular community and act as its spokesman. A secular state is one that positions itself above the warring communities and vows to act as a neutral body. While civility is associated with the presence of the state, uncivility is necessarily associated with a lack of it. The reason why the third-world societies could not successfully free themselves from the bane of uncivility is precisely that they are at very rudimentary levels of 'stateness'.[8]

Implicit communalism is not anathema to the persisting civil order. On the contrary, it is a phenomenon that works through it. In so far as it works through it, the civil/uncivil dichotomy no longer seems to coincide with the state/non-state dichotomy. We have reasons to believe that in the given context of Assam, communalism is implicit in the sense that it is located within the civil. When communalism works from within the civil, the state as the repository of the civil cannot free itself from the vice. It debilitates the state's competence in handling and dealing with communalism. The state as it were is embroiled in it. In this chapter, we make a brief attempt at reviewing how communalism is seen to be working through the regime of rights and balance of political forces and supplementing the functions that any modern state promises to undertake and discharge in pursuance of its claim to uphold and defend the civil order.

The Regime of Rights

The Constitution of India holds that under all normal circumstances the Fundamental Rights pertain to the individuals rather than the Indian citizens, irrespective of their communal differences. In other words, communal differences will not be allowed to play any role in the enjoyment of these rights. In simple terms, the regime of rights is established beyond the realm of social and communal differences. The civility of the regime lies in the fact that it establishes itself beyond this realm. The civil and the communal thus appear as two completely separate and separable realms. Their mutual separability is crucial to the coming into being of the civil order. Similarly, an adult's right to vote is an integral part of the regime of rights. The civility of the right lies in the fact that the individual (voter) is required to vote in his or her individual capacity – as an abstract individual. His or her communal affiliations are not expected to influence him or her in a manner that is at variance with if not, detrimental to his or her self-interest. The civil is compromised as soon as the communal overtakes the individual and prevails over his or her self-interest. Since the argument is somewhat complex, let us elaborate the point with the help of a commonplace example. A kind of ultra-rightist argument that is currently gaining ground in our political discourse has more to do with *Hindutva* than to democracy. In fact as we will try to show, there is always the danger of being seduced by its pseudo-democratic trappings. The argument albeit is in conformity with the formal rules of syllogism. For example :

(A) Democracy everywhere is the rule of the majority.
(B) The Hindus are the majority in India. Therefore,
(C) Democracy is the rule of the Hindus in India.

The problem with this argument is that democracy seldom looks upon the majority as being constituted as the Hindus. Their being the Hindus is only incidental. If they exercise any influence on the outcome of what they choose by casting their votes, democracy is jeopardized. The outcome of choice according to the Democratic Theory cannot be influenced – let alone determined by their social background. Liberal Democratic Theory may have been criticized for having taken the individuals as absolutely abstract and 'disembodied' beings; but that is what the theory is. More than the majoritarian rule, democracy presupposes civility. But when communal compulsions set forth the parameters of electoral politics, the so-called democratic elections get tainted and the rule of civility is blatantly violated. The point may be illustrated with reference to the recently held Assembly elections in Assam – one in 1996 and another in 2001.

In both the above-mentioned elections, the oscillation of the Asom Ganga Parishad (AGP) is quite interesting. The defeat of 1991 led the party to realize at great cost that they would not be successful in coming back to power without wooing the minorities including the immigrant Muslims (not necessarily 'foreigners'). Even at its heyday in 1985, AGP could poll exactly the same percentage of votes that the Indian National Congress (INC) and the United Minorities Front (UMF) could do together. In a sense, the division between the INC and the UMF aided AGP's so-called 'thumping victory' of 1985. In 1996, the party soft-pedalled on the issue of 'foreigners'/immigrants almost to the point of forgetting it. It dropped the demand for repealing the Illegal Migrants' (Detection by Tribunals) Act of 1983 and joined hands with such parties as UMF and Communist Party of India (Marxist) that in Assam, are for whatever reasons identified as the party of the Bengalis. The more it alienated the *Varna*-Hindu, Assamese sections of the voters. In fact, the signs of discontent within the party amongst its rank and file were visible and began to take their toll.[9] It enraged such eminent leaders as Atul Bora, Pulakesh Baruah and Bhrigu Kumar Phukon and led them to leave the party. But it paid rich electoral dividends so much so that AGP came back to power in 1996. The run-up to the Assembly elections of 2001 is interesting. This time AGP's decision of forming an electoral alliance with Bhartiya Janta Party (BJP) and *vice versa* signified a reversal of this trend. The decision enraged many leaders and supporters of both these parties alike resulting in large-scale desertions. But what is important to note in this connection is the fact that the more it moved closer to the BJP, the more it alienated its former allies. The UMF, CPI and CPI(M) were first to go. High-profile Mr. Abdul Muhib Mazumdar was one to resign from the Mahanta ministry in April 2001. The party as we know, fared miserably in the elections. It could not muster the minority votes for obvious reasons. Since the alliance left many fissures and cracks, it could not consolidate even the *Varna*-Hindu, Assamese votes. As a result, there was a split in these votes benefiting Indian National Congress.

Why do we refer to the complex election scenario of Assam? Perhaps the most important reason is that Assam has become a fractured society—much more fractured than what she was in the pre-1985 period. Alarmingly, the faultiness are very deep and sharp—indeed unbridgeably so. The electoral compulsion today is that either you woo the Assamese-speaking *Varna*-Hindu mainstream or you woo the minorities including the immigrant Muslims. The middle-of-the-road policy does not pay. It is a politics that gradually marginalizes the centrists and the fence sitters. The choice has become exclusive. This has certainly polarized the electorate on communal lines in a hitherto unprecedented manner and most importantly, in blatant violation of the norm of civility. AGP today is faced with the strange obligation of making a clear and exclusive choice. Besides it is the Hobson's choice that has pushed the party literally at the end of its tether. This is a classic illustration of how communal divisions in the society compel the parties to be tied to them and force them to gradually turn away from the realm of civility. When the communal enters the electoral, the civil takes a backseat. But, it does not necessarily obliterate the civil. Never before in the history of Assam have the foundations of the civil been so fragile and superficial.

When the electorate is scarred by the communal faultiness of this nature, the balance of forces naturally gets jeopardized. Political alignments are made and unmade in keeping with the communal requirements. If AGP found in UMF, CPI and CPI (M) its 'natural' allies in 1996, it faces the imperative necessity of discarding all of them in 2001. What was so 'natural' in 1996 turned out to be so unnatural that the party took pains to discard them altogether. Political alignments revolve around communal axis and there is no way by which AGP can make both ends meet. The AGP dilemma sharply illustrates the crisis of the civil. Either AGP has to play the same game by facing the crisis of making exclusive choices or it has to turn the tables around and re-establish the secular and civil rules of the game. At this state of the party, the important question is : Can the party take such a bold step? Who is going to initiate it? Which of the parties is going to set the ball rolling? This chapter has no easy answer to all these questions.

The Balance of Forces

But how has communalism cut into the state's otherwise legitimate monopoly over the instruments of violence? We may refer to the recent rise of Islamic fundamentalism in Assam. It is true that fundamentalism has never been absolutely alien to the political practice of the immigrant Muslims. Yet, its present-day version is remarkably different from its earlier versions. One, there is reason to think that the newly ascendant Islamic fundamentalism has acquired an organized and militant character. Security agencies in India reportedly have the information that as many as 15 different militant Islamic organizations are operating in the state of which three (viz. Muslim Liberation Tigers of Assam or MULTA, Muslim Liberation Army or MLA — formerly known as the Muslim United Liberation Front of Assam or MULFA and Islamic Liberation Army of Assam or ILAA) are quite strong. Many of them are acting at the behest of such foreign espionage agencies as Inter-Services Intelligence (ISI) and ultra-fundamentalist bodies as Islamic Chhatra Shibir and Jamiat-I-Islami of Bangladesh. Formerly their activities were restricted to the multi-ethnic areas of the Brahmaputra valley (like, Nagaon and Mariani) where Muslims have always been in sizeable numbers. But now their activities have spread out to the vast areas of Barpeta, Goalpara and Dhubri and even to such far off areas as Cachar of the Barak Valley.[10] While their activities are engulfing the ever-newer areas, they are also undergoing a certain militarization. The roots of fundamentalist militancy among the immigrant Muslims may be traced back to the days of the large scale anti-Muslim pogroms in the Brahmaputra valley organized during the tumultuous days of 1983. A Muslim Volunteers' Force was raised in Assam as a vanguard for protecting the Muslims against the attacks from the Hindus. It stated objectives are :

> .... to impart training in the Muslims for self-defence, to form 'death squads' to enrol people and training them for protecting the people belonging to the Muslim community in buses, trains and in public places, to take suitable measures against those who by virtue of their power and high ranks are condemning the Muslims, torturing and killing them, to take counter-measures then and there, to take steps for restoring Muslim interests wherever they are in jeopardy,

> to extend help to Muslims who are in dire straits, to convert Assam into the Waterloo of RSS (Rashtriya Swayamsevak Sangh) and to take a constant vigil on government employees and to inform the authorities about their misdeeds.[11]

Even Saiyad Azad Madani, widely appreciated for his moderate views, called upon the Muslims to get united against the Asom Gana Parishad, a proclaimed successor to the forces loyal to the erstwhile Assam movement and to take up arms whenever necessary.

The religion has not prevented Muslims from fighting the enemies. If someone comes to attack you, then try to make him understand with sympathy; but if someone does not understand, then be engaged in a formal battle against him.[12]

He also in the same public meeting held at Doboka exhorted upon them to train themselves in karate and kung fu in self-defence and to spend 3 to 4 hours at the minimum in a day for arms training. The Muslims, he added, should remember that AGP had killed 'thousands of their brothers' in earlier years. Muslim fundamentalism has so far made it a point to see the Indian state as the ultimate saviour and the protector of their interests. But now it seems that the fundamentalists no longer show the patience of keeping faith in the state. Their faith has to late been severely eroded with the effect that they either fall prey to foreign forces or feel the necessity of standing on their own and resolving their problems without resorting to the Indian state or both. That immigrant Muslim faith has considerably eroded in recent years is evident from the fact that *Kalam* that by its own admission is the spokesman of the Muslims, accused Hiteswar Saikia, the then Chief Minister of Assam, of falling a 'victim to the Hindutvawadi game-plan."[13] The more this feeling gets entrenched, the less they are likely to approach the state for the ventilation of their grievances. Thirdly, the fundamentalists are seen to insist on political mobilization along religious lines and ask all Muslims – irrespective of their subdivisions, to form a unity against their stronger adversaries. In the process, it seeks to wean away a portion of Muslims – known as 'Assamese Muslims' whose identity as the Assamese was not only too-taken-for-granted by them to require any further proof, but was never questioned by the members of the Assamese community. They are ones whose ancestors came to and settled in Assam long back and have been effectively assimilated into the so-called Assamese mainstream. The argument is simple: Since the immigrant Muslims are endangered, it is a sacred duty of all Muslims – native or otherwise to come to their rescue and lend a helping hand to them. Implicit in it, there is the call for de-culturation – of doing away with the 'Assamese' identity of the 'Assamese Muslims' and join the ranks of their Muslim brethren. It is true that the 'Assamese Muslims' have more or less remained indifferent to these calls. But if fundamentalist forces become strident the Assamese community might lose one of the otherwise reliable partners and have to pay a heavy price for its own chauvinistic excesses.

Communalism is usually viewed as a threat not just to our otherwise fledgling multi-religious body politic but also to the very religion that is under use. By subjecting religion to political and economic uses, it degraded religion. This chapter argues that we usually ignore the eaıly warnings until it erupts into riots and engulfs a wider area. Notwithstanding the not-too-negligible riots of 1992 that rocked some of the immigrant-inhabited pockets of Brahmaputra Valley. Assam does not fall in line with the overall pattern of the country as a whole. But there is reason to believe that the politics of Assam of late seems to be taking on a communal overtone. This is expressed in many ways like, people's electoral choices, political alignments of different parties and interest groups, the growing militancy of some fundamentalist groups alleged acting in connivance with the foreign espionage agencies etc. This chapter concludes that communalism as it exists in Assam is of more implicit nature and if early warnings are ignored, it will not take much time to become explicit. The distinction between explicit and implicit communalism is too crucial to be ignored.

NOTES

1. The term 'tribe is used here not in any pejorative sense, but in the sense in which social scientists particularly anthropologists use it. The vernacular equivalents of the term (like, the *hao* in Meitei) are often used to connote the cultural inferiority of these communities. For us on the other hand, 'tribes' are communities that are situated outside the framework of Hindu society necessarily ridden by castes. For a theoretical discussion see, Samir Kumar Das, 'Tribes in Contemporary India' in Rakhahari Chatterji (ed.), *Politics India : State-Society Interface*, New Delhi : South Asian, 2001.

2. For a brilliant analysis of the contributions of the Vaishnavite saints of Assam (like, Srimanta Sankaradeva and Madhavadeva) see, Hiren Gohain, *Asomiyeea Jatiyeeya Jiwanat Mahapurushiyeeya Parampara* (in Assamese) (Guwahati : Lawyer's Book Stall, 1990). I have not come across any study of comparable standard on the spread of Vaishnavism by Santa Das Gossain of Sylhet in the Imphal Valley.
3. For an excellent review of the system in Assam see, Audrey Cantile, *The Assamese – Religion, Caste and Sect in an Indian Village*, London Studies on South Asia, No. 3, London : Curzon Press, 1984.
4. See, Das, Samir Kumar. 'Sampradaiyakatar Dawai Naki Munider Matibhram' (in Bengali), (The Panacea of Communal Riots or the Errors of the Eminent?) in *Subhashree*, Calcutta, Vol. 37, 1988, pp. 20-41.
5. If we define communalism in a somewhat broader way to include conflicts between ethnic communities, then of course, the term 'uncivil' has actually been in use in the official cricles. See, Ved Marwah, *Uncivil Wars : Pathology of Terrorism in India,* New Delhi: Harper-Collins, 1998.
6. Riker, William. *The Theory of Political Coalitions*, New Delhi: Oxford & IBH, 1964, Chapter One.
7. Following Bakunin, a section of anarchists however believe that a civil order can exist independently of the state's mediation if a society attains a particular qualitative state.
8. Thus the law-enforcing agencies' lack of neutrality in handling communal riots points to the limitations of the state. See, Vibhuti Narain Rai, 'Communal Riots' in *Seminar*, 483, November, 1999.
9. For a detailed analysis of this see, Samir Kumar Das, *Regionalism in Power: The Case of Asom Gana Parishad,* New Delhi: Omsons, 1988, Epilogue: 'Community Goes to Polls: A Study of Assam Elections of 1996'.
10. Chandan, Dileep. 'Assam: Closing Ranks' in *Sunday*, 11-7 May, 1997, pp. 59-60.
11. *Saptahik Neelachal* (in Assamese), 20 July, 1983.
12. *Agradoot* (in Assamese), 25 February, 1990, trans. mine.
13. Imran, A.H. 'Anuprabesh: Sharanyantrer Neel Naksha' (in Bengali) in *Kalam*, Calcutta, August, 1992.

19

IDEOLOGICAL ASPECTS OF BODO SEPARATISM IN ASSAM

DHRUBA PRATIM SHARMA

Amongst the plains tribals in the state of Assam, the Bodos are the largest group, their population being concentrated mostly on the north bank of the Brahmaputra river, with some of them staying on the south bank as well. In the late 1980s, the Bodos started a massive agitation demanding establishment of a separate Bodo state north of the Brahmaputra river, comprising nearly half the area of Assam, the creation of Autonomous District Council for the Bodos living on the south bank, and the addition of the Bodo-Kacharis living in the hill district of Karbi Anglong to the list of Scheduled Tribes in the Indian Constitution, entitling them to certain privileges and safeguards. They also demanded increased job reservation for Bodos and the inclusion of their language in the Eighth Schedule of the Constitution of India. Like similar movements elsewhere, the Bodo movement showed both integrationist and secessionist tendencies and had almost parallel strands of non-violent protests and violent activities. Due to the tactics adopted by the movement leaders, the violence it generated, and the strategic location of the Bodo-inhabited areas, the movement attracted nationwide attention. The agitation formally ended in 1993 with the signing of an accord, and the setting up of an Autonomous Council. This chapter shall attempt to examine the ideology and direction of the Bodo Movement (1987-93).

The separatist ideology that the leadership of the Bodoland Movement articulated with a powerful impact among the Bodos is rooted in a deep sense of alienation in relation to the Assamese society of which they had been considered to be a peripheral part. Their hostility towards the politically powerful and educationally advanced sections of the Assamese, especially the caste-Hindus, was aroused by the latter's continued neglect and indifference in regard to the cultural richness and socio-economic problems of the tribals. Imbued with the mentality of caste-stratification, dominant Assamese opinion tended to view tribal cultures as inferior, though at times adopting a patronising attitude towards them, and encouraged them to merge with the Assamese way of life and adopt the Assamese language. The radical ideology of the Bodoland Movement is the reaction to this condescending and contemptuous attitude of the local elite towards the tribals, their culture and their problems.

The ideology of the Bodo Movement is based on the assumption that Bodos constitute a nationality distinct from the Assamese nationality. An ABSU memorandum says, "The problems of the Bodos and other plain tribes are nothing but a nationality issue. The Bodos have a genuine aspiration to establish a distinct Bodo nationality and to get recognized in the world as being civilized and advanced. Without a separate state this is not possible"[1]. The pamphlet claims that the original natives of Assam, the Bodos have become the oppressed of the land due to the domination of the Assamese who came in as immigrants during the Ahom rule. "The outsider Assamese has unjustifiably overthrown the original masters, the Kacharis"[2].

The propaganda circulated by the ABSU seeks to delegitimise the concept of a composite Assamese identity encompassing or submerging the identities of smaller tribal groups. About the Assamese nationality the ABSU holds, "There is no clear-cut definition of Assamese. In practice one whose mother-tongue is originally Assamese and is not converted from non-Assamese speaking community is known as Assamese. As such, Bodos are not Assamese, Tribals are not Assamese, Rajbanshis are not Assamese. Similarly all Mongolians are not Assamese"[3]. Thus the ABSU sets up a racial criterion for defining the Assamese identity. The ABSU alleges, "the Assamese language and community are nothing but only artificially defined. Language and community ... but surprisingly and cleverly this artificial Assamese community has captured Assam and its administration and now dominating the once master-ruler of Assam—the Kacharis—the Bodos"[4]. The ABSU condemns the 'conspiracy of assimilation' carried on by the Assamese (contemptuously referred to as the 'caste Hindu Assamese clique') aiming at inclusion of all the people of Assam within the 'greater' Assamese nationality.

The ABSU's tirade against the Assamese culture and community, significantly questions the historical and linguistic validity of the Assamese language terming it as a mixture of other languages like Bengali and Oriya, which developed among the immigrant caste-Hindus only after the thirteenth and fourteenth centuries.[5] Such a view, while being scientifically untenable, serves to glorify the Bodo culture which had 'held sway in the region from time immemorial', as against the caste-Hindu Assamese culture which is not rooted in the soil and which developed relatively very late. Hence the Bodos are exhorted to reject Assamese culture and to resist all forms of assimilation into it. It finds a parallel in the ideology of the DMK which extols the virtues of Dravidian culture as against Aryan culture.[6]

Further, the Bodoland agitation leadership, in a curious imitation of the despised assimilationist mind-set of the Assamese caste-Hindus, views the other plains tribal communities of the Brahmaputra valley as part of the 'larger Bodo nationality'. This led to fear of Bodo dominance among the smaller plains tribes like the Rabhas and Mishings who, therefore, did not actively associate with the Bodoland Movement.[7] The changing of the nomenclature of the proposed homeland from 'Udayachal' to 'Mishing Bodoland', and finally to 'Bodoland' indicated an assertion by the leadership of the agitation that the Bodo people, being the largest tribal group in the state as well as in the North-Eastern region, felt no need to be apologetic about asserting their hegemonic status.[8]

The literature of the movement stresses the separate ethnic character of the Bodos, and highlights the economic exploitation of the tribals by the ruling elite. Hence the ideological under-pinning of the movement is a mixture of ethnicity and class-conflict between the privileged and the deprived. The memorandum of the ABSU on the basis of which the Movement was started, contains 92 demands of which 89 related to socio-economic issues like supply of drinking water in the interior areas, electrification of villages, higher recognition and protection of Bodo language and culture, and protection of tribal lands. Later on, the movement leaders dropped these 89 demands and retained only 3 political ones relating to granting of a separate state and autonomous councils, saying that socio-economic grievances could not be fulfilled in the absence of political will on the part of the state.[9] The achievement of a separate state is seen as the panacea to resolve all socio-economic problems.

The growing class-division within the Bodos is never mentioned in the literature of the movement, nor is any clear blue-print provided of their economic programmes once a homeland is achieved. The slogan of 'ethnic identity in danger' provided a powerful mobilising instrument in the hands of the emerging middle class. The influence of leftist ideology on the Bodo movement appears to be limited to the mention in some of their literature that they desire a socialistic pattern of society and that they support the concept of smaller states with more powers as advocated by the late Jaiprakash Narayan.[10]

The ideology of the Bodoland Movement carries strong elements of nativism and revivalism. But this nativistic ideology has been presented as one of liberation. Basic economic factors lying at the roots of social movements are often obscured by the manner in which the ideology of movements is presented, and only the more apparent realities are highlighted. Hence the Bodo leadership propagates the idea that assumption of political autonomy by the Bodos will remove their deprivations.

At least in outward appearance and in the official stand of the Movement leaders, the Movement was strictly Gandhian – peaceful and democratic – and the leaders disowned all acts of violence that occurred. The ABSU uncompromisingly stuck to its demand for a separate state till the time of the Bodo Accord when it reneged on this demand, but never did it threaten to secede from India. This gave a type of legitimacy to the ABSU which an openly violent and secessionist organisation like the Bodo Security Force (BASF) could never aspire to.

Although the demands of the Movement were manifestly political ones, the ABSU itself was a 'non-political' body and the ABSU leaders repeatedly asserted this saying they were not like the selfish politicians who manipulated people for their own political gains.[11] The ABSU constitution authorises the organisation to take up political issues when the 'political diplomacy of the so-called politicians threatens the national existence of the Bodos'.[12] Thus the ABSU leaders appeared to the Bodos in the image of saviours and not in the shape of politicians seeking narrow electoral gains. This mobilisation of the ABSU served to thoroughly discredit the established political elite among the Bodos, especially the PTCA leaders who were received as being hand-in-glove with AGP Government.

Conclusion

The Bodoland Movement was an example of mass mobilisation carried out along ethnic lines leading to a sharpening of pre-existing ethnic cleavages and a heightened sense of group awareness amongst the people bounded within these cleavages. The contextual background helps to understand the spontaneous and intense response of the Bodos to ABSU's call for a mass movement, as also to understand the response of the state and the non-Bodo people towards the Movement. The Movement occurred at a crucial movement in Assam's history when political aspirations of different ethnic groups in the state were rising rapidly after the conclusion of the six-year long Assam Movement and the settlement of the foreigners issue with the signing of the Assam Accord. The coming to power in the state of the newly-formed AGP party in the 1985 elections strengthened this tendency. The cyclonic Assam Movement which was perceived as having achieved spectacular success for the Assamese-speaking community lit the path of agitation to the people especially the youth of various communities in Assam's remarkably plural society as a means of highlighting their grievances, asserting their ethnic identities and pursuing their aspirations to political power.

The Assam Movement, led by students along supposedly Gandhian lines, disowning all incidents of violence and affirming their faith in the Indian Constitution but refraining from participation in elections, became the model for other ethnic movements that cropped up throughout Assam in the post-1985 period. Of these the most significant and enduring was the Bodoland Movement, which indeed finds many parallels with the Assam Movement in its strategies of collective mobilisation and political bargaining.

As to the level of structural change that the Movement aimed at bringing about, we may note that the Bodo Movement was neither a reform movement nor a revolution but rather in between these two, i.e., a transformative movement aiming at bringing about middle level structural changes in this distribution of power and in the system of differential allocation of resources. The element of conflict in this movement acquires a sharper focus than in the reform movements, of which the Brahma Movement among the Bodos is a good example. Again the Bodoland Movement is not a revolutionary one as the conflict is not based on the ideology of class struggle but is more between ethnic groups with some elements of class struggle being built into its ideology.

NOTES

1. "Why Separate State?" Memorandum submitted to the President of India, the Prime Minister of India, and the Home Minister of India, ABSU, Kokrajhar, 10 November, 1987, p. 59.
2. *Ibid.*, pp. 9-10.
3. "Divide Assam Fifty-Fifty" Pamphlet, ABSU, Kokrajhar, 23 August 1987, p. 17.
4. "Why Separate State?" pp. 9-10.
5. *Ibid.*
6. Rao, M.S.A. (ed.), *Social Movements in India*, New Delhi, 1985, p. 17.
7. Misra, Udayon. "Bodo Stir: Complex Issues, Unattainable Demands", *Economic and Political Weekly*, May 27, 1989, p. 1147.
8. Kamaroopi, "Assam: Back to Bad Old Days." *Economic and Political Weekly*, June 27, 1992, p. 1307.
9. "Why Separate State?"
10. *Ibid.*
11. Dasgupta, Barun. "Bodo Agitation: Background, Prospects", *Mainstream*, June 24, 1989, p. 16.
12. "Constitution of the All Bodo Student's Union", March 2, 1969.

20

MOVEMENT OF LESSER KNOWN ETHNIC GROUPS OF ASSAM

VASHYATI BHUYAN

With the treaty of Yandaboo in 1826, Assam came under the British rule. Despite a series of geographical and administrative reorganizations the self-determination and aspirations of the ethnic groups remained unfulfilled. These unresolved ethnic desires in Assam are constitutional and partly extra-constitutional, depending on the respective nature of declaration.

For most of the people in general ethnic movements in North-East meant, for a long time, the Naga-Mizo type insurgencies of the ethnic groups of Assam. That various other ethnic groups of Assam have been agitating for long is not known to most of the people.

This chapter is just an attempt to bring forth the various movements of lesser known ethnic groups of Assam.

Introduction

Even before the days of Indian Statutory Commission (Simon Commission) in 1930, different ethnic groups in Assam were fighting for identity. This identity consciousness among different ethnic groups in Assam is nothing new. It is a well known fact that hill men always reported higher degree of consciousness than their counterparts in the plains, but that does not mean that the plainsmen of Mongoloid origin lacked identity consciousness. What was the cause of this identity consciousness? It was with the emergence of a 'middle class' through expansion of modern education and entry to jobs under colonial administration that the seed of identity consciousness were sown. And this very class of people, later on named 'tribes' played a pioneering role in spreading identity consciousness among the members of their own society. However, many in the early stage of consolidation, identified themselves with the larger Assamese society, even distancing themselves from their respective ethnic roots. But as their volume increased they found themselves exposed to unknown competitions as advancement in various economic spheres were not expanding at an identical pace. Again social discriminations, superiority complex of the caste Hindu Assamese society and the caste based social equation gradually started pushing them away from the larger Assamese society. Gradually this started getting a political direction. The atmosphere of neglect and indifference was potential enough to provide motivation for them to start thinking in terms of their own political boundary. In fact they were never taken into confidence and the growing caste Hindu Assamese elite never seriously thought of sharing power with them. Hence it was not a very difficult task for them to arouse this existing but not developed identity consciousness among their own people and direct it towards self-determination aspiration.

The Ahom Movement for Recognition

The Ahom who first established their region in Assam, ruled during 1228-1826 AD, a remarkable period of dynastic rule in the Indian subcontinent. But the Britishers had deprived this ruling race of everything, after the annexation of Assam. They were almost reduced to the level of poor cultivators. The alien government did not recruit Ahoms in responsible positions in the bureaucracy because of the latter's initial hostility towards the British rule. Even in the subsequent years in matters relating to employment the government systematically followed a policy of discrimination against the Ahoms and deprived them of benefits of new economic orders. Larger number of people from outside were brought to Assam to run the government machinery. Similarly the entire labour force employed in the tea industry was brought from outside the province. All these had far reaching effects on the social conditions of Assam. Thus the Ahoms as a community were driven into the lowest rank of the social order of the British administration. To voice against the plight of the Ahoms some of the community leaders pioneered the Ahom movement and ultimately formed an organisation known as the All Assam Ahom Association in 1893. After uniting themselves they later proposed before the Simon Commission for a quota of legislative seats in the province be allotted to the Ahoms, but it was rejected because Simon Commission has treated the Ahoms as high caste Hindus. And as a result, the Ahoms lost the special privileges enjoyed by them since 1909. Even the Government of India Act, 1935 excluded the Ahoms from the list of the minority communities. But soon, a split occurred in the Association apparently over the issue of minority rights. The militant fraction of the organisation wanted a new political framework for the Ahoms as a minority community in Independent India, while the other fraction thought that Ahom Association should be linked up with the Congress which was going to be the ruling party in Independent India. While efforts were being made for political integration of the various ethnic groups of Assam, along with constitutional safeguards devised for protection of their peculiar culture and traditional values, but the Ahoms who still maintained distinct ethnicity did not receive due attention of the makers of the Constitution. Growing economic imbalances in the region, negligence of the state and Union government in the maintenance of the Ahom monuments and large scale destruction of the historical ramparts, government's failure to make necessary arrangements for proper research into the Tai Buranjis and other literatures as well as their proper preservation and the educational backwardness of the Ahoms, all these once again made them conscious of their glorious past and asserted their separate identity from the rest of the Assamese society. The proposal for further reorganisation of Assam and creation of Nagaland gave fillip to the Ahom organisations and was activated with a new name, the All Assam Tai Sabha. Immediately, two other organisations of Ahom Tai and Mongoloid people had emerged with similar demands. They were all Assam Ahom Association and Mongoloid National Front. After demanding separate state individually, the three organisations having similar objectives decided to amalgamate themselves as *Ahom Tai Mongolia Rajya Parishad.* Then in 1970, the *Ahom Tai Mongolia Rajya Parishad*, without changing its ideology and objectives decided to contest the said election under the *Ujani Asom Rajya Parishad* (UARP). UARP was primarily a revivalist organisation of the Ahom community with an identical socio-cultural pattern and also a territorial identity since its activities were confined to the geographical limits of upper Assam. The UARP demanded the creation of a new state in upper Assam. Although the Central Government fulfilled the demand of the Naga Nationalist Organisation, Mizo National Front, and All Party Hill Leaders' Conference by creating Nagaland, Mizoram, *Meghalaya* and *Arunachal Pradesh*, but it did not concede the demand of UARP.

Various factors have been responsible for this:

(a) Unlike other ethnic organisations of undivided Assam, a programme of mass movement and direct action did not back UARP's demand.
(b) The demographic structures of upper Assam are such that it could not mobilise all sections of the region's population.
(c) Even sizeable section of the Ahom community who had long association with the Congress had not openly supported the demand, the demand for a separate state of upper Assam.

All these had weakened the UARP, and when subsequently the Parishad merged with the Janta Party during 1978 to contest the Assembly election on the banner and symbol of Janata Party, it lost its separate identity and its community appeals became ineffective and illogical.

Karbi-Dimasa Autonomy Movement

We can trace back the root of Karbi-Dimasa autonomy demand during 1946 when a demand for a separate district with functional autonomy was articulated by the leaders. But it is not more than thirty years back that a planned collective stand and mobilisation took place. Many students of ethnic movements opines that the root of Karbi-Dimasa autonomy demand may safely be traced back to the events of 1960, when All Party Hills Leaders Conference was formed, where both the leaders of N.C. Hills and Karbi-Anglong were also members. Then in 1969, when the proposals for reorganisation of Assam and granting of autonomous statehood to Khasi-Jaintia and Garo Hills was in the process of finalisation, the M.L.As. of N.C. Hills and Mikir Hills opposed the idea of joining the Hill state on the grounds of religion, culture, customs and language. By now the leadership of the Mikir and Dimasa were convinced that without a separate state, no meaningful solution to their problems could be achieved. Analysing the issues raised through different memoranda etc., till 1882 by the Karbi-Dimasa leadership the following become apparent: (a) They opposed the idea of establishing Assamese language both in official matters as well as medium of instruction; (b) Yet they were against joining Meghalaya on several grounds including numerical ground; (c) According to them the then Assam administration was least bothered about other communities and ethnic groups, so it was impossible to develop either economically or culturally under the Assam administration; and (d) They were convinced that they had no future even if there is a change in the Government as the leaders of Assam Movement were already taking anti-tribal stand publicly.

However the year 1985 brought a turning point to the three-decade old movement with the emergence of a youth-led and youth-based mass movement organisation called People's Democratic Front (PDF), under whom in May 1986 the Autonomous State Demand Committee (ASDC) was born. The birth of ASDC can definitely be said to be the turning point because for the first time a mass-based movement was attempted to be organised in Karbi-Anglong, which was not an elite oriented. The earlier committees never thought to educate the masses. For the students of ethnic movements the evolution of ASDC opens up an altogether new horizon. It has been observed that all the ethnic movements of North-East aspired to attain emancipation for themselves in isolation and have never thought of linking themselves with the movements of larger Indian masses. But ASDC happens to be the first organisation to link up with the movements of larger Indian masses. They are also well aware of the fact of emerging inter-differentiation within the society. Further, ASDC is the only ethnic organisation in North-East to take up very much democratic stand on the question of future status of smaller ethnic groups of non-Karbi-Dimasa origin in their proposed autonomous state. No other organisation has dared to raise these issues. Under the present political economic circumstances, ASDC may not reach its target, but it will be of great interest to the students of ethnic movements in the tension prone North-East, to observe ASDC's future course in fixing the above target.

The Movement of Koch Rajbongshi for Scheduled Status

Gait has remarked in the Census of India, 1891 that "whatever may have been the racial affinities of the original Koch tribe, there can be no doubt that the present Koch of Assam belong to the Mongolian rather than to the Dravidian stock". Although most of the people of North-East having Mongoloid connection were included in the first list of scheduled tribe in free India but the Koch-Rejbongshis of undivided Assam could not find any place in that. However, because of their inclusion in the scheduled castes list, the Koch-Rajbongshis in North Bengal district secured some special protection. It remained a sociological mystery as to how and why there was differential treatment to the same ethnic category distributed between two political units. Then in 1953, the Backward Class Commission, headed by Kaka Saheb Kalelkar, declared them as OBC, which aggravated the dilemma of the Koch-Rajbongshis. Again the Koch-Rajbongshis of undivided Assam were divided into two segments, Koch-Rajbongshis of undivided Goalpara district were categorised as MOBC while the rest of them in other districts of Assam remained OBC. Thus the same ethnic group now achieved three statuses – scheduled caste in North Bengal, MOBC in Goalpara and OBC in other districts of undivided Assam. It was only in 1968 for the first time, Koch-Rajbongshi Sanmilani, which was established in 1959-60 for the socio-economic upliftment of the group of people, demanded for scheduled status although there was no clear stand whether they wanted scheduled tribe or scheduled caste status. Then in 1969, this problem of scheduled status was resolved and a categorical demand for scheduled caste status emerged. In 1970 they opposed the inclusion of Koch of Meghalaya in scheduled tribe list and they repeated their demand for inclusion in scheduled caste list. But in 1980 the demand for the scheduled caste status was revised and instead a demand for scheduled tribe status was put forward. It is apparent that the Koch-Rajbongshis of Assam has been suffering from identity crisis. If we see academically then this process of tribalisation may appear to be a retrograde step. But if we look at the character of unequal and unethical distribution of wealth and privilege of the Indian states, then even this reverting step appears to be natural and just one. Unlike the "Udayachal" or "Karbi-Dimasa movements the Koch-

Rajbongshis do not have a specific control zone of their own and are scattered all over the state, but it would be perilous to ignore their demand for a tribal status. Although in comparison to other ethnic movements of this part the Koch-Rajbongshis of Assam appear to be much docile, but if their demand is kept pending for long the movement may not be so docile in the near future.

The Minority Movement – The United Minority Front

The United Nations has described 'Minority' as those non-dominant groups in a population which possess and wish to preserve stable ethnic, religious or linguistic traditions or characteristics which are different from those of the rest of the population. If we accept this suggestion, as far as population pattern is concerned, Assam is a state made up of group of minorities. No single group of people, no community – ethnic, religious or linguistic – can claim absolute majority. According to the United Minority Front, all groups in Assam are minorities at one level or another. The emergence of the United Minority Front in the political scene of Assam during 1985 election is not an isolated event. It emerged out of a collective movement for safeguarding the constitutional right of all the minority groups against those who have been trying to shun them out. The organisations, who were instrumental in bringing the United Minority Front into being, were the Citizen Rights Preservation Committee, Jamiat Ulema Hind, and the All Assam Minority Students Union. These organisations were active right from the beginning of the Assam agitation to build up public awareness against the snatching of political rights from the people belonging to the minority communities. It was rather at first felt by Fazal Golam Osmani, who was a minister in the Janata Party minister of Golap Borbora (1978), the urgency to build a common platform of different minority communities, particularly the Bengali Hindus and the immigrant Muslims as a defensive measure. Just like all other movements of North-East the United Minority Front suffers from an inherent insularity in the sense that they never thought of linking the micro and macro situations. It is a known fact that all the issues of different movements are basically democratic demands, relating to rights. But knowingly or unknowingly the United Minority Front has been showing total indifference to this aspect. They have rather preferred to remain isolated from the democratic movements. If they can shun this attitude, their original motive of safeguarding themselves will definitely bear fruits.

Conclusion

Identity consciousness and identity assertion that has emerged in the 'tribal' societies of Assam and the human rights issues of the religious and linguistic minorities is of paramount importance to all the members of our societies, as it has far reaching consequences. These assertions and demands hardly depends on our liking or disliking them. It seems these movements were destined to occur. Therefore, there is a serious need for a keen attempt to solve these problems, which should be independent of any politics. Indeed it is a great responsibility of all the right minded members of our society to find solution to the question as to why the friends and neighbours for centuries are accusing and asking for social and political separation. Without solution to the issues raised by these movements any permanent solution to the ethnic tangle in Assam will remain a far cry. Development in all spheres of life is the only solution to this problem.

REFERENCES

Borah, B., (1993). 'Ethnic movements and the problems of development in N.E. India', (paper presented in Regional Seminar in *Processes of Development & Planning in the N.E. India*, (March 26-27).

Dutta, K.N., (1969). *Landmarks of the Freedom Struggle in Assam*, Guwahati Lawyer's Book Stall.

Dutta, P.S. *Ethnic Movements in Poly-cultural Assam.*

Hunter, W.W, (1975). *A Statistical Account of Assam*, Delhi, BR Publishing Corporation, (1975 reprint).

Sen, S. *Tribes and Castes of Assam.*

21

TRIBAL POPULATION AND ETHNIC PROBLEM IN ASSAM

M.M. DAS

The total tribal population of Assam was 28,74,441 according to 1991 Census showing an increase of 12,67,793 from that of 16,06,648 in 1971, registering a growth rate of 78.9 per cent during 1971-91 compared to the growth rate of 53.25 per cent for the total population as a whole during the same period. Such an abnormal growth rate of tribal population is confusing in view of the fact that the birth rate during the period has been remaining the same and also there is no evidence of tribal immigration into Assam. Therefore, there is every possibility that a large chunk of Hinduised tribals have turned back to be tribals. Thus the process of detribalization has been changed to the process of retribalization as a result of ethnic movement during the recent decades. However, in six districts – Goalpara, Kamrup, Morigaon, Nagaon, Karbi Anglong and N.C. Hills, there has been slight decrease in percentages of the tribal people, perhaps because of the fact that the increase in immigrant people in all these districts has reduced the percentages of the tribal people.

Though tribal people are found in all the 23 districts of Assam, there is a wide variation in their spatial distribution. It is interesting to find that except Karbi Anglong and North Cachar Hills, there is not a single district where the percentage of tribal population is more than 50 per cent of the total population in 1971 as well as in 1991. In 1971 only Dhemaji district had a percentage between 30-50, but in 1991, Kokrajhar and Dhemaji were included in this category. All other districts had percentages below 30 in both the years. In as many as 12 districts had percentages below 10 in 1971 and 9 in 1991.

There are as many as 60 tribal groups of people in Assam constituting a total population of 28 lakhs (1991) which is 12.50 per cent of the total population of Assam. The major tribal groups, each of whom has more than one lakh population are Bodo, Mishing, Karbi, Santali, Garo and Rabha in order of their size of population, whereas the Dimasa, another major group of tribe with their concentration in North Cachar Hills has a population of 84,654. All these major tribal groups constitute 84.35 per cent of the total tribal population of the state, while the remaining 15.65 per cent is constituted by the other 53 minor groups. It is interesting to find that as many as 16 minor groups are only in the name as each of them having a population of less than 100 and 18 of the minor groups also have a population between 100 and 1000 only. Among these major tribal groups, Bodo, Mishing, Karbi, Rabha and Dimasa have started movement for the protection of their ethnic identities and in order to fulfil their ethnic aspirations, they have demanded separate political unit of different forms for their own. Among the minor groups, only the Tiwa (Lalung) having only a total population of 32,633 constituting a mere 1.16 per cent of the total tribal population has demanded a separate Tiwa Land for the protection of their ethnic identity.

The total and percentages of population of major tribal groups are shown in Table 21.1.

Table 21.1 : Population of major tribal groups, 1991

	Tribes	Total Population	Percentage of total tribal population	Percentage of total population
1.	Bodo	11,84,569	42.17	5.28
2.	Mishing	3,81,562	13.59	1.70
3.	Karbi	3,55,032	12.64	1.58
4.	Santali	1,35,905	4.84	0.61
5.	Garo	1,14,779	4.09	0.51
6.	Rabha	1,12,424	4.00	0.50
7.	Dimasa	84,654	3.01	0.38
	Total	23,68,925	84.35	10.57
	Others	4,39,492	15.65	1.96

It is seen from Table 21.1 that each of only six tribal group has a population more than one lakh, the Bodo being the biggest group followed by Mishing and Karbi, each with more than 3 lakh population. Dimasa is the smallest group having only 84,654 population.

The main concentration of the Bodo tribe is found in the Kokrajhar district. But there are secondary concentrations in Udalguri, Paneri, Barama, Tamulpur, Kakilabari, Sorbhog, Dudhnoi, Boko and Mariani. Thus it is seen that the Bodos do not actually have a distinct geographical territory for a separate political unit or a state.

The settlement of the Mishing is concentrated on the banks of the Subansiri river, Majuli, Jonai and Dhemaji areas. They also do not occupy a distinct geographical territory for their own.

Though the Karbi Anglong district is the homeland of the Karbis, they account for more than 50 per cent of the total population only in the Hamren sub-division, whereas their percentage is below 50 per cent in the Diphu sub-division. Yet the Karbis have a distinct geographical territory to justify their claim for a separate political unit for which constitutional safeguard has been given under Sixth Schedule to the Constitution creating an Autonomous District Council. Similarly, the North Cachar Hills district is the homeland of the Dimasa and so they are also brought under an Autonomous District Council.

Dudhnoi and Bodo are the main settlement areas of the Rabhas. Besides, they are scattered in Chaygaon, Paneri, Kalaigaon and Mangaldai areas. Without having a distinct territory of their own, a separate administrative set-up known as 'Rabha Hasong' (Rabha Land Council) has been carved out in Dudhnoi and Bodo regions to provide them ethnic protection.

The Tiwa tribe, which is numerically a small tribal group with only 32,633 persons, has their settlement confined to Morigaon, Mikirbheta and Raha thanas of Marigaon and Nagaon districts. This tribe is very much conscious about the preservation of its ethnic identity and agitation has been started for their separate administrative set-up. Like the Bodos, the Rabhas and, the Mishings, this tribe is also brought under Autonomous Tiwa Council (Das, 1989).

Among all the tribal groups, the ethnic movement takes a most virulent form in the case of the Bodos. The Bodo activists are divided into many groups on the basis of their different kinds of demand. Some groups demand a separate Bodoland state and some others who are hardcore extremists adopting terrorism and violence of different forms are found to be restless till they achieve a Sovereign Bodoland seceding from India.

The plains tribes people of the Brahmaputra Valley after

Independence organised themselves under the banner of "Plains Tribals Council of Assam" (PTCA) to fight for equitable social order free from exploitation and injustice. They started the 'Udayachal Movement' in 1967. This movement was not a revolutionary movement as it was never aimed at bringing about structural changes. It was rather aimed at achieving an autonomous region within the existing political set-up through the redistribution of power and the system of differential allocation of resources, rights and privileges.

In 1974, the PTCA had shed a lot of blood and achieved the recognition of Bodo language as a medium of instruction in the schools in tribal 'Belts and Blocks'. They developed an ideology based on relative deprivation in various fields and involved themselves in conflicting relations with the upper caste Hindu privileged ruling groups to bring about change in the traditional distribution of power. So the conflict is based more on ethnic track-tribal and non-tribal groups, not on class struggle in terms of 'privileged' and 'deprived' classes, the exploiters and the exploited. The aim of the 'Udayachal Movement' was to achieve a separate Union Territory for the plains tribals stretching in the northern part of the Brahmaputra from the border with West Bengal to the Jonai area on the east (Paul, 1989).

The movement has passed through certain stages in its career. In 1974, they shed blood and agitated for the recognition of Bodo language to establish their separate ethnic identity. But they are not satisfied with the mere recognition of their language. Being conscious of the glaring socio-economic injustice and deprivation, some of the Bodo youths have organized militant groups for a separate state called 'Bodoland' in the geographical territory they claim to predominate from the border with West Bengal to Panchnoi in the east. During the six-year long Assam agitation against foreign immigrants, a student organization called 'ABSU' was formed. This organization becomes very active in organizing the Bodo people for a separate 'Bodoland' within the Constitution of India. The Bodo Sahitya Sabha was also formed to raise voice for the realization of a Bodoland to be carved out of Assam. In the mean time, the PTCA as the recognized political party has been weakened among the Bodo people and a breakaway group led by B.K. Basumatary called the United Tribal Nationalist Liberation Front (UTNLF) becomes stronger as it adopted an extreme method of agitation and started mobilizing the tribal youths for the creation of a Bodoland state. ABSU and Bodo Sahitya Sabha have resorted to peaceful, democratic movement for the creation of a separate Bodoland.

Several militant and extremist group like NDFB, BLT, BEF, ABWWF, BSS among which NDFB and BLT have started vigorous violence and terrorism in varied forms demanding a sovereign Bodoland seceding from India. They have started 'ethnic cleansing' within the area of Bodoland Council which is created by the Central and the State governments in 1991 according to the recommendations of the Bhupinder Singh Committee as an expected solution of the Bodo problem. By ethnic cleansing, larger number of non-Bodo people have been already killed and driven away from their hearths and homes within the area of the Bodoland Council with the objective of raising the percentage of Bodo people so that their claim for separate Bodoland can be justified.

Recently there has been a ceasefire between the BLT and the Indian Government and dialogue has been going on for the solution of the Bodo problem. Unlike NDFB, the BLT has now dropped their demand for a sovereign Bodoland, but they are negotiating for more autonomy to the extent of a state and more areas including villages and towns mostly inhabited by non-tribal and non-Bodo tribals, tea gardens and even the Manas Game Sanctuary and the Bongaigaon Oil Refinery and Petro-Chemical Industries. They also raise demands for a Central University, a Medical College and an Engineering College. On the whole, the ABSU, the Bodo Sahitya Sabha and the BLT are not satisfied with the creation of Bodoland Council. But the activation of the Bodo movement will largely depend on what the exploited and oppressed Bodo want, the extent of their mobilization, the strength of organization and leadership, on the one hand and the stand and measures adopted by the ruling class both in the Centre and the State of Assam, on the other. What is urgently needed is the radical transformation of our socio-economic system which at present promotes inequality, injustice and exploitation in one form or the other (Paul, 1989).

REFERENCES

Das, M.M. (1989). 'Tribal Problem of Assam : Movement and Solution', *Ninad*, an Assamese Journal published from Gauhati University Campus.

Paul, M.C. (1989). *Dimensions of Tribal Movements in India : A Study of Udayachal in Assam Valley*. Inter-India Publication, New Delhi.

22

ISSUES AND PROBLEMS OF ETHNICITY IN ASSAM

P.C. DUTTA AND B.C. PRADHAN

Introduction

The most debatable topic of the present day Assam in North-East India is increasing tension and turmoil arising out of the ethnic crisis among the people of the state. The geographical situation of Assam has given the state its special position and importance situated in the North-East (N.E.R.) corner of India and surrounded by four foreign countries like China, Burma, Bhutan and Bangladesh. Assam stands like a sentinel of the country in a most sensitive region. It is a meeting ground of the people with different cultures. It is unique in the sense that the migration to the state was mainly from the east whereas migration in the rest of India were from west to east. Immigration or influx of foreign nationals into Assam is not a recent phenomenon but has a strong historical past. A very significant fact about Assam is the assimilation of Indo-Aryan and Mongolian cultures. However, the present-day ethnic composition is something from Assam of the past.

The whole population of Assam can be divided into two broad and distinct racial types like (i) the Caucasoid and (ii) the Mongoloid. Caucasoid type is represented by the Caste Hindus, the Muslims and some professionals. The two broad categories of castes are the Brahmins and the Koch, the latter represents a heterogeneous type. Many people believe that after Hinduisation of different tribes, they were included in the caste-fold of Assamese society. But the Rajbanshis claimed that they have separate entity since long past. The Assamese Muslims are medium statured having leptorrhine nose and mesocephalic head. With the recognition of the immigrant Muslims as the Na-Asamiya, four groups of Muslims are found like the Syeds, the Marias, the Sheikhs and the Na-Asamiyas.

The Indo-Mongoloids can be identified by yellow brown colour of the skin, stretched or flat wave and coarse hair of the head. The broad face has scanty hair growth, the body hairs are also scanty. From the study of the formation of Assamese nationality it would appear that the bulk of the population of Assam is of Mongoloid origin. However, most of these communities through assimilation have lost their tribal characteristics. According to the Constitutional Amendment Act of 1976, 14 tribes like Chakma, Dimasa, Cachari, Garo, Hajong, Hmar, Kuki tribes, Khasi-Jaintia etc. Lakher, Man, Mizo, Mikir, Naga, Pawi, Syntheng were scheduled in the autonomous hill districts of Karbi-Anglong and North-Cachar. The 9 tribes scheduled in the plains of Assam are like Burmans in Cachar, Bodo and Bodo-Cachari, Deori, Hojai, Cachari and Sonowal, Lalung, Mech, Miri and Rabha. The Ahoms now occupy special position in respect of distribution in upper-Assam districts. Originally Thai or Shan speaking Ahoms soon became Hinduised and accepted the Indo-Aryan language Assamese.

In the border areas of Nagaland and Mizoram, there are Naga and Mizo people speaking their respective Naga and Kuki-chin languages. Broadly speaking, the population of the plains of Brahmaputra and Barak Valley speak Assamese and Bengali of the Indo-Aryan family. Thus, Assam presents a unique picture of multi-ethnic state of India. But since the advent of the twentieth century and till now there is a crisis of ethnic identity in the state of Assam. Sometimes it posed a serious threat to the unity and integrity of the state by changing the geography of Assam. Due to ethnic conflicts, the geographical boundary of the state has been reduced to such an extent that present Assam cannot be identified by the students of other provinces, who have gone through the past history.

In this chapter, an attempt has been made not only to identify various ethnic groups of Assam but also to examine the causes for the growth of resentment and dissatisfaction among the different ethnic groups. Finally, attempt has also been made to explain the consequences of such ethnic conflicts in the state of Assam resulting in the further decadence of the state.

Religion and Ethnicity

At the time of country's independence in 1947, Assam attracted attention of the entire nation for foreign national issue. However, this issue is not a trend developed on the eve of independence, it is as old as British occupation of Assam. The products of the New English Education in Bengal by the end of the nineteenth century overflew into Assam for livelihood. During this time, the dominance of middle class Bengalees in employment by virtue of their educational superiority started in Assam.

During the years of Muslim League ministry under Sir Mohammed Sadullah and before there was a heavy flow of people from East Bengal. It is possible that the Muslim League ministry encouraged the land-hungry peasants from East Bengal to settle in the fertile plains of Assam out of purely communal considerations though in the name of agricultural development of the state. Before independence, there had always been a latent fear in the Assamese mind of being swamped by the Bengali-speaking people and such suspicions were strengthened when Assam was included in the group "C" category by the Cabinet Mission.

Taking language as an issue, the then leaders of Assam headed by Gopinath Bordoloi committed a serious blunder in Assam's history as a result of which there was every possibility of Muslim dominance in Assam. The separation of Bengali-speaking district of Sylhet from Assam in 1947 through a referendum greatly helped to calm Assamese fears of being outnumbered by Bengali-speaking population but the path for future ethnic conflicts were cleared from that day onwards in Assam.

In 1951 Census, the rise in the population of Assamese-speaking people was substantial as the migrated Muslim population adopted Assamese as their language leaving their mother-tongue Bengali. Meanwhile, the refugees from East Pakistan poured into the state in thousands leading to an abnormally high rate of population growth in the state. During that time the Bengali-speaking population in Barak Valley districts was in majority. To change the political situation of Assam, they started "Purbanchal" movement which was suppressed when the plan for "Purbanchal" was rejected by the State Re-organisation Commission of 1954.

Before independence Sir Sadullah bore the responsibility for settling the Muslim infiltrators in Assam and after independence the task was carried on by others. Newspapers alleged that Moinul Hoque Choudhury was encouraging Muslim communalism in Barak Valley districts as a Pro-Pakistani and supporter of "Azad Cachar Party", for which he was drained by the D.C. of Cachar under Preventive Detention Act for providing shelter to the Muslim infiltrators from Pakistan[1]. During that time the linguistic nationalism of the Bengalees in Barak Valley was at its peak against the Official Language Bill passed in Assam legislative Assembly. Besides, the leaders of the Indian National Congress encouraged Muslim infiltrators into Assam for their vote-bank which was clearly manifested in one of the election meetings in which a leading Congressman of Assam expressed "So long as Alis and coolies are with the Congress, we have nothing to fear." Later on A.G.P. Government of Assam continued to appease the Muslims by making them as their vote bank too. To reduce the Hindu Bengalees into minority in Assam, the Government of Assam is still trying and the process of Assamization has not stopped.

Language and Ethnic Conflicts

(A) Prior to the partition of the country, the province of Assam was divided mainly into two regions – Surma valley and Brahmaputra valley. In Surma valley, according to 1931 census report, the Bengali speaking people were 28,48,454 and Assamese speaking people were 3,692. In Brahmaputra valley including N.E.F.A. and Hill Districts, the Assamese speaking people were 19,78,823, the Bengali speaking population were 11,05,581. Thus, 70 years ago, Bengali speaking people in Assam numbered 39,60,712 and Assamese speaking people were 19,92,848. This figure in census report was a great headache to the Assamese leaders headed by Gopinath Bordoloi and others of Indian National Congress. For the domination of Assamese in the politics of Assam they wanted to separate Sylhet from Assam. They persuaded the Central leadership of Indian National Congress as a result of which "Sylhet Referendum" took place. Only three and half Police Stations of Karimganj sub-divisions remained in India along with the then Cachar district.

Just after independence, disappointment and resentment overtook the Bengali speaking people of Cachar and considering the linguistic, racial and cultural affinities they wanted to integrate Cachar district with Tripura under the New Scheme of "Purbanchal". When the "States Re-Organisation Committee" was set up, the Bengali speaking leaders of Cachar submitted the memorandum again with full of facts and figures in support of it. However, the Commission rejected the proposal for which the Bengali speaking people expressed their resentment. Assam is a multi-lingual state but on 24th October, 1960, the Government of Assam declared Assamese as the sole official language of the state. The people of Cachar launched a movement of protest against the language policy and to put it down, the Assam Government opened fire on non-violent Satyagrahees on 19th May, 1961. As a result of police excess, 1 girl and 10 boys were killed. Cachar Zila Sangram Parishad and Bhasa Andolan Samiti launched a non-violent movement demanding Bengali as the second official language of the state. Three language formula called as "Shastri Formula" was evolved by Lal Bahadur Shastri by which "Assam Official Language Act" was amended so as to make Bengali as the official language in Barak Valley. In 1972, on 12th June, Academic Council of Gauhati University passed a resolution making Assamese as the sole medium of instruction in the educational institutions of Assam. Tension mounted again in the Barak Valley of Assam. On 18th June, 1972, Cachar Zila Sangram Parishad lodged a protest against the decision of the Gauhati University. On 28th July, 1972 'Cachar Bandh' was observed and in continuation of the movement. Satyagraha movement took place in November 1972 and continued till January 1973 in a phased manner, organized jointly by 'Chatra Yuva Sangram Parishad' and 'Cachar Sangram Parishad'. Due to step-motherly attitude of Assam towards the Bengalees of Barak Valley, the "Union Territory Demand Committee" (UTDC) was formed under the leadership of Paritosh Paul Choudhury. The UTDC organised agitation to get Barak Valley enrolled as one of the members of North Eastern Council (NEC) for preserving the language and other interests of the people of the valley. Barak Upatyaka Banga Sahitya O Sanskriti Sammelon (BUBSOSS) started different types of movements after its formation through its first conference held at Silchar in January 1977 and protested against the strategy followed by the State Government towards Barak Valley. In the year 1980, another student organisation named All Cachar Students' Association (ACSA) was formed and started movement demanding one Central University in Barak Valley. Afterwards its name was changed first as All Cachar Karimganj Students Association (ACKSA) and then as All Cachar Karimganj and Hailakandi Students Association (ACKHSA). In the year 1985, a movement again started under the banner of "Cachar Siksha Sangrakshan Samiti" formed in 1973, to protest against the 6th Article of historic Assam Accord and for the demand of a Central University in the valley. Fresh tension mounted in the valley created by the SEBA Circular (No. SEBA/AB/Syllabus/11/85-86-1 dated 28.2.86) imposing Assamese language in the valley. On 21st July, 1986 there was a police firing on students at Karimganj, as a result of which 2 students were killed.[2] Very recently, on 4th April, 2001, a memorandum submitted to the D.C.s of three Barak valley districts by the BUBSOSS demanded total implementation of Official Language Act for using Bengali in all official works. The very attitude of State Government towards the valley in different forms has not stopped till date. Though the demand for Union Territory is suppressed, it may crop up again and may take violent turn if the harmonious relationship between the people of the valley and their counterparts in the Government of Assam are not properly maintained.

(B) Another language movement in Barak Valley attracted the attention of the politicians, administrators and others in the state is the conflict between Meitei and Bishnupriya groups. In 1962, the Nikhil Bishnupriya Manipuri Bhasha Parishad (NBMBP) was formed and placed its demands for the recognition of Bishnupriya as Manipuri. Then the movement was spearheaded by the "Bishnupriya Manipuri Andolan Parishad" through peaceful and democratic means. In 1975, the Information and Broadcasting Ministry declared that broadcasting facilities through All India Radio would be extended to Manipuri language both Metei and Bishnupriya. In this respect memorandum was submitted on 5th August, 1983 to the then Chief Minister by jointly Nikhil Bishnupriya Manipuri Mahasabha, Nikhil Bishnupriya Manipuri Sahitya Parishad and Bishnupriya Manipuri Samaj Sanstha headed by Monoranjan Sinha. However, the said language has been implemented as a medium of instruction at the primary stage education in the Barak Valley *vide* Government notification No. EMI. 169/74/

Pt-III/310 dated Dispur, the 14th November, 1983 and (ii) No. EDG. 459/86/217 dated Dispur, the 21st July, 1989. One of the main demands is the correction of 1961, 1971 and 1981 figures of this linguistic minority, and to record correctly this linguistic minority as Bishnupriya Manipuri. A memorandum was submitted by the NBMSP to the then President of India in this regard. Tension mounted in Barak Valley when the Government of India gave recognition to the language of Metei group as one of the languages in the Eighth Schedule to the Constitution of India. Since then and till now the Bishnupriya group have lost all faith on the government both Central and State and their agitational programmes are going on.

Tribal Issues and Ethnicity

In the post-independence era, some remarkable ethnic conflicts took place which changed the current of Assam's political history. To safeguard the language, culture, customs etc. the different hill tribes through their organisations and leaders have separated themselves from the mainstream of Assam and got the status of statehood. At present, separate states like Nagaland, Mizoram, Meghalaya and Arunachal Pradesh have been emerged as separate political entities in this region but the problem of ethnicity is yet to be sorted out.

(A) The demand for a separate State of 'Kamata' or 'Koch Land' in North Bengal as well as some parts of Assam has taken a violent turn during the last few years, organised by 'Kamatapur Liberation Organisation (KLO), Koch Rajbanshi Liberation Organisation (KRLO), Koch Rajbanshi Liberation Tiger Force (KRLTF) and Koch Rajbanshi Security Force (KRSF). This movement has received help and assistance from extremist groups of Assam like the outlawed United Liberation Front of Assam (ULFA), Bodo Ultra groups etc. The movement originated with a view to protecting their rights and interest in social, political, cultural and economic spheres. The chief aim of these organisations is to win the right of self-determination of Koch Rajbanshi people in North Bengal as well as the western parts of Assam. As a result of their movement, the areas of Assam worst affected are Dhubri, Bongaigaon, Goalpara and Kokrajhar. According to security sources, the KLO, the KRLO, the KRITF, the KRSF, have been training militant groups of Assam in the dense forests and hilly areas of Assam, Bhutan and Bengal trijunction. The Koch Rajbanshis fear that they would lose their ethnic identity because of the steady influx through the porous Indo-Bangladesh International Border of Lower Assam and North Bengal. They swear to restore and regain their lost identity by carving out a separate state. In this respect they have sent eleven-point charter of demands to the Government of India and their movement is going on.[3]

(B) The plain tribals of Assam can broadly be divided into two groups like (i) the Bodo groups and (ii) the Miri and the Michings. The Bodo and the Miri groups belong to Mongolian origin and they are ethnologically different from rest of the Assamese people. They are the earliest known inhabitants of Assam. From time immemorial they had been maintaining their sovereignty till their last king Tula Ram Senapati died in 1854 A.D. The language spoken by the Bodo group of the plain tribals belongs to the Tibeto-Burman group and it widely differs from the Assamese language. Among the hill tribes of Assam, the Dimasa and the Garos belong to this Bodo stock. The All Bodo Students Union (ABSU), a student organisation of Bodos has been demanding that Assam must be divided on fifty-fifty basis between the tribal and the non-tribals. The present area of Assam is 78,523 sq. km. and half of it becomes 39,261.5 sq. km. Tribals are demanding 25,478.1 sq. km. as Union Territory along with 15,222 sq. km. for Karbi Anglong and N.C. Hills autonomous state totalling 40,700.1 sq. km. which is slightly more than 50 per cent. The areas of Union Territory included the whole of Kokrajhar and Lakhimpur districts, Majuli and Sodia Sub-division, northern parts of Dhubri, Goalpara, Barpeta, Nalbari, Kamrup, Darrang and Sonitpur districts. They claimed that they had been the masters and rulers of Assam at one time and the present Assamese society was formed by the influx from Kanauj, Mithila, Magadha etc. of the Central India in the thirteenth and fourteenth century only whereas the Bodos and other tribals are the aboriginal people of Assam. The Assamese people and the government are having a deep conspiracy to swallow and assimilate the tribals with Assamese people and the Assam will finish them gradually. The tribals of Assam claim their distinct linguistic and cultural heritage and hence Assam should be separated on the basis of language and culture. The tribals want to enjoy the right to political self-determination and a separate state would fulfil their desires[4].

(C) The Hmars are the inhabitants of Mizoram Barak Valley and North Cachar Hills. The Scheduled Castes and Scheduled Tribes Order (amended) Act of 1976 includes not only the Lusais and other 37 tribes or subtribes but also Lakher, Pawi and Hmar apart from the Chakma settlers from Tripura. The Mizos or Lusais in general opposed this classification as well as granting of autonomous status to the Lakhers, Pawi and Chakmas. To their great dissatisfaction and under the banner of Hmar People's Convention (HPC), Hmars have been carrying on agitations since 1954 for autonomy to safeguard their interests in Hmar dominated areas. In a memorandum to the Prime Minister of India on 21st January, 1987, HPC raised the demand for a separate state called, Hmar Ram. They wanted the reorganisation of North-Eastern states to satisfy their political aspirations. The demand made by the Hmars was unacceptable to the Mizos. They staged agitational programmes and were capable of cutting off the lines of communication to the people of Mizoram as they had their control over a part of the Silchar-Aizawl Road. In 1989, the state government of Mizoram decided to grant autonomy to the Singlung Hill Development Council (SHDC) for social, economic and cultural development of the people under its jurisdiction.

An accord was duly signed on 27th July, 1994 and this was followed by an agreement on 8th August, concerning the settlement of SHDC's jurisdiction. A three-member Commission verified the SHDC area but the state government delayed its implementation. HPC president Hmingchunghenung complained that Mizoram government had shown total disregard to the findings of the Commission set up to ascertain whether the Hmars are in a majority in the HPC demanded area or not. Despite surrender of a number of cadres of the HPC to the Mizoram government in 1994, some of the dissidents who remained underground had been able to reactivate the organisation and a nexus between the NSCN and the HPC has been established. The militants had enabled the Hmars to set up camps in dense forests along Assam-Mizoram border and their active support extended operations to the Barak valley and North Cachar hill region of Assam.

(D) Karbi-Anglong and North Cachar Hills are the only two autonomous Hill districts remaining in Assam after independence as the Naga Hills district got a fullfledged statehood status in 1962 and Khasi and Jaintia Hill and Garo Hills districts formed the State of

Meghalaya. Later on, the Mizo Hills district got the status of Union Territory and finally become a state under Indian Union. The Karbi-Anglong and North Cachar Hill of Assam is bounded by the plain districts of Nowgong and Sibsagar on the north and Meghalaya on the west, Nagaland and Manipur on the east and the district of Cachar on the South. During the days of British Rule North Cachar Hill was a sub-division under the plain district of Cachar and the Mikir Hill was part of the Nowgong and Sibsagar districts. These two districts were administered as "Excluded and partially excluded Area." The Constituent Assembly of India appointed a Sub-committee for these areas known as Bordoloi Sub-committee to enquire into the aspirations of the tribal people. The tribal people of this area represented for autonomy to safeguard their language, culture, customs and ways of life. The Bordoloi Sub-committee report was that Autonomous District Council for all the hill districts of Assam will be created under the provision of Sixth Schedule to the Constitution. In 1951, the Mikir Hills, came into being out of the portions of Sibsagar and Nowgong districts of Assam and a new civil district with North Cachar Hill sub-division was formed. In 1970, the North Cachar Hill sub-division was raised into the status of a district. The Karbis and Dimasa Kachari are the main tribes living in the Mikir hills district. While North Cachar hill district is inhabited by the Dimasa Kachari, Hmar, Kuki, Karbi and other tribes. They have their own languages, cultures and traditions but one thing they have in common is their backwardness, educational, economic and political. At the time of State Reorganisation of 1969, the Mikir Hills and the North Cachar Hills District Councils were given option to join the proposed Meghalaya sub-state but the people of those hills did not see the solution of their problems in joining Meghalaya. On the other hand, they received certain significant assurances from the highest authority of the government of Assam and the APCC (Assam Pradesh Congress Committee). They wanted to develop in all spheres by preserving their own separate entities as tribes.

The main discontent mounted in these hill districts when Assamese was imposed as medium in the University and secondary schools of education. The customs, traditions and manners of these two districts differ greatly from the contiguous tribal area. Considering all these the Mikir hills and the N.C. Hill leaders' conference submitted memorandum for a separate state to the Prime Minister of India in June 1973. The Central Committee of Karbi Anglong and North Cachar Hill State Demand Committee again submitted memorandum to the Prime Minister of India on 18th January, 1982 for creation of a separate full-fledged state. They expressed their desire due to the economic, political and cultural backwardness of their people along with the issue of medium of instruction. Their agitation took violent turn when the Autonomous State Demand Committee (ASDC) and the Karbi Students Association (KSA) jointly submitted a memorandum to the Prime Minister of India on 18th May, 1987. They proposed English as the official language of the Autonomous State having a separate legislature to be located at Diphu, besides other proposals. Till now, the issue is pending before the Central and State governments. Due to their strikes, demonstrations and road blockade, normal life has been paralysed and delay in government's decision into the matter is taking the dangerous turn in these areas[5].

(E) The most important burning issue of the present day Assam is the extension of Naga Ceasefire to other states of North-Eastern Region. The Government's representative and negotiator, Mr. Padmanabhaiah has opened a new pandora's box of problems in a highly volatile region, known for insurgency, agitation and bloodletting. On 14th June, 2001, an agreement was signed between Padmanabhaiah and the National Socialist Council of Nagaland (NSCN) General Secretary, Muivah at Bangkok. While the earlier Accords were operating within the Nagaland territory, the fresh ceasefire has been extended to the geographical territories of Assam, Manipur and Arunachal Pradesh where there are Naga inhabitants. It not only affects nine districts of Manipur but also applies to Tirap and Changlang districts of Arunachal Pradesh and Sibsagar, Jorhat, Golaghat, Karbi Anglong, North Cachar districts and some portion of Barak Valley district of Assam which contain a sizeable Naga population. In these areas i.e. so called greater Nagaland, the NSCN is recruiting fresh cadres, establishing larger militant networks and camps and collecting taxes when the ceasefire is in operation since August 1997. As a reaction to it various political parties and leaders of Assam and Manipur lodged protest against the Centre's decision. The Chief Minister of Assam was not consulted by the Central government but only informed about the decision of the ceasefire. The Assam government is not in a mood to give an inch of Assam's land to the NSCN leaders for their aspiration of greater Nagaland. Whether the Naga ceasefire will bring peace in the region or not, one thing is certain that the region will face the same consequences as happened during the days of partition on the eve of independence. It will change not only the geography of North-Eastern region but also the history of the region. In its wake it may bring bloodshed and several new terrorist organisations as it is a great lesson to all other militant groups of the region that the extremist activities are the only means to achieve the political aspirations.

Conclusion and Suggestion

Going back to the past history of Assam, it may be proved that the process of separation and demand for autonomy started from the year 1947 when Sylhet was separated from Assam for the causes well known to the leaders of Assam. However, the process of separation is still going to the discriminatory attitude of the state government towards other ethnic groups of the state.

Sub-nationalism movements in Assam have resulted in the formation of different states and ongoing movements of the Bodos, Bengalees, tribes of North Cachar hills, Karbi-Anglong, Koch Rajbanshis etc. are very much in the air and a day will come when they will secede from the Assamese mainstream. It is noteworthy to mention that the recently held ceasefire agreement with the NSCN Chief by the representative of the Central Government will pose a serious threat to the Government of Assam. Hence, it may be revealed that due to the lack of foresightedness of both the Central and State governments, the unity and integrity of the state is jeopardised. In the pre-independence era, the tribals demanded for simply autonomy but the leaders of Assam were adamant in their attitude as a result of which they got themselves separated from the mainstream.

In conclusion, it may be said that the ethnic conflicts in Assam were due to the repressive attitude of the Government of Assam from time to time. Had the leaders of Assam been liberal to all the ethnic groups and sympathetic to safeguard their language, customs and culture ethnic movement in different parts of Assam would not have taken place.

NOTES

1. "Ruinous Tendency to Side Track the Main Issue in Assam", *Hindustan Standard*, July 2, 1961.
2. (b) "Pradhan Mantri ki Balitechen-Kitchu na kintu Tadanta Report ki chilo-Bangalee Hindu Uchchedane Sarbansh Jote-Ekti Aprakashito Dalil." July 2, 1961, *Ananda Bazar Patrika*.
3. "Certain Aspects of Social Movements in Barak Valley" P.C. Dutta & B.C. Pradhan in *Social Movements in North East India*, (Ed.), M.N. Karna. Indus Publishing Company, New Delhi, 1998.
4. "Separate Kamatapur Demand of Koach Rajbanshi" by S.S. Chatterjee, *The Assam Tribune*, June 3, 2001.
5. "Autonomy Movements in Assam : Documents", A memorandum to Rajiv Gandhi submitted by ABSU, ed. by P.S. Dutta, Omson's Publications, New Delhi, 1993.

REFERENCES

Extension of Naga Ceasefire, article by : Shibnath Sharma, *Assam Tribune*, July 13, 2001.

Jogen Das (ed.). *Reflections on Assam (1944-1983)*, Harendranath Barua Memorial Society, Guwahati, 1992.

Naga Ceasefire – An Impetus to Separatism? article by : M.K. Dhar, *Assam Tribune*, July 4, 2002.

Naga Ceasefire – Dangers and Opportunities, article by : Sanjay Hazarika, *Assam Tribune*, June 28, 2001.

Naga Ceasefire and Manipur, article by : Sino Angom, *Assam Tribune*, June 6, 2001.

Pankaj Thakur (ed.). *India's North-East : A Multifaceted View*, Prakash Publishing House.

The Crisis of Ethnic Identity in Assam article by : Arijit Bhattacharjee, *Assam Tribune*, May 29, 2001.

The Naga Ceasefire Imbroglio, article by : Satish Ch. Kakati, *Assam Tribune*, July 6, 2001.

Udayan Misra. *North-East India : Quest for Identity*, Omsons Publications, New Delhi.

23

ETHNICITY, SECULARISM AND RELIGIOUS TOLERANCE
The Role of Ahoms in Assam Society

LIPI GHOSH

Introduction

Ethnicity and religion are two important aspects, which are put to use by people to identify themselves in a society. North-East India may be termed as a unique region in its historical setting, which in spite of many ethnic diversities has a tradition of religious harmony. Of this region Assam valley again presents a distinct picture which absorbed migration of the Tais – one of the remarkable Mongoloid races of people. The neo-Brahmanical influence, with its Vaishnavite morals of secularism in Assam valley has a related history of its own with the Ahoms – the migrant Tai-Shan community people in the valley. This chapter makes a micro level study of the religion of the Tai-Ahoms of Assam in its historical setting. It, with reference to the works of two different schools, attempts to show the religious interaction of the migrant community people in the historical set-up. It attempts to review the question if the Ahom monarchs followed a policy of religious tolerance and thus were secular in their attitude.

Defining 'Secularism'

The term 'secular' with its corresponding Latin word *secularis* literally means worldly rather than spiritual, not relating to religion or bound by monastic restrictions. It means the spheres of secularism and religion are distinct, independent, exclusive and separate without penumbral zones. It also means that secularism derives its *raison d'etre* from state unfettered by theology whereas religion derives its validity and justification from God or some divine authority.

In Encyclopaedia Britannica, 'secularism' has been defined as "any movement in society directed away from other worldliness to life on earth." In the European Middle Ages there was a strong tendency for religious persons to despise human affairs and to meditate on God and the afterlife. As a reaction to this medieval tendency, secularism, at the time of the Renaissance, exhibited itself in the development of humanism, when people began to show more interest in human cultural achievements and the possibilities of their fulfilment in this world. The movement towards secularism has been in progress during the entire course of modern history.

In short, secularism, is a religion of humanity; it embraces the affairs of this world; it is interested in everything that touches the welfare of sentient being. It is a protest against theological oppression and tyranny. Secularism means the cultivation of friendship and intellectual hospitality. It means the living for ourselves and each other. It proposes to give serenity and content to the human soul.

Secularism in Indian Context

That being the definition of secularism by modern social sciences and while it is clear that Middle ages upheld the antipathetic attitude towards secularism in European history, it follows our task is to see the situation in context of Indian history. India in just present day context is multi-religious, multilingual, multiethnic and secular democracy. About 85 per cent of Indians are Hindus which also include Sikhs, Buddhists, and Jains; 11 per cent Muslims; 2.5 per cent Christians and the rest include Zorastrians and others. India is not a theocratic Hindu state and religious pluralism and secularism is the core of state policy where freedom of religion enshrined as a fundamental right of man with equal respect and status to all religions. Although in India, prior to 1947, the term 'secular' was not in much vogue, instead the word 'nationalist' was in common use to differentiate from communal or religious elements.

That being the characteristic feature of modern age, much prior to this period was the period of India's medieval history, when state used to play a direct role in the religion of the country and religious practices of the countrymen. The state connected itself with religious establishments and concerned itself direct with affairs of the world, both spiritual or sacred.

Assam, Ahoms and Secularism

Assam over the period of history from early thirteenth to early nineteenth century was under the control of the Ahom rulers. The Ahoms were an important offshoot of the Tai race of people. The Tai-Ahoms entered the Brahmaputra valley from the east in the early part of the thirteenth century and carved out a small kingdom in its easternmost corner after having conquered the Morans and Borahis, the two small indigenous tribes. By the first half of the sixteenth century, this Ahom kingdom grew in size and population after the conquest of the Chutiya kingdom on the north-east, that of Kacharis in the south-west and the Bhuyan chiefs in the west and the north-west. During the seventeenth century, the kingdom was further enlarged by the annexation of Kamrupa. By 1682, the repeated Mughal invasions were wiped out for good and since then the western limit of the Tai-Ahom kingdom had been the river Manaha on the north and the Nagarbera hills on the south of the Brahmaputra which remained in tact till the British annexation of the kingdom. Scholars now generally agree to the fact that the Tais lived in the south of the Yaun-tse-Kiang river and that Southern China was their early homeland wherefore they might have spread out to different parts of South-East and South-West Asia, in time and space continuum. There is now positive evidence that the Tai people of North-East India, particularly the Tai-Ahoms, the earliest migrants, had their original homeland at Moung Mao in Dehong prefecture, in Yunnan province of Southern China.

But so far the element of Tai religious tradition of these Ahom rulers are concerned, we find there was the notion of nature worship mixed with spirit beliefs and other old Tai religious rituals. Thus in most Tai societies the most significant aspect apparent is the notion of *Phii* (spirit) and *Khwan* (life essence). Spirit and life essence, representing the fundamental concept of power, relate to a wide range of cultural practices in ritual, mythology and literature and to various aspect of social and political relations. The period of first millennium A.D. is generally considered as the period of ancient Tai culture. It is well known and largely accepted phenomenon that before the great exodus of the Tai-Ahoms in Assam in the thirteenth century, almost all the

Tais lived together in Southern China and northern Vietnam complexes and some others in northern extremity of Burma and Thailand. It is not unlikely the period all held the same religious beliefs, customs and practices in common. As early as 1905, G.C. Barua noted that "the Ahoms migrated to Assam and before that the Tais were converted to Buddhism" Haliram Dhekial Phukan, noted that ancient religion of the Tais was sort of animism. To many historians like Phya Anuman Rajadhon, it is not known what religion was in their homeland before their exodus to outer places. However, many hold that it is almost certain that animism formed the part of the early belief and they may perhaps have been some traces of Buddhism through Tibet and China. According to historian like H.G. Quaritch Wales the early Tais must have been animists and probably they received Mahayanism at a fairly early period. Luang Suryabongsa argues that religion of the Tais when they lived in Yunnan was animism and ancestor worship. Erik Seidenfaden also says that original religion of the Tais was probably animism, coupled with ancient worship. He however thinks that prior to the arrival at the Shan land of present day Myanmar, the Tai-Yais of Yunnan were animists and perhaps few of them have imbibed the tenets of Taoism and the Mahayana doctrines. About ancient Tai religion B.J. Terwiel is of opinion that ancient Tai religion system is to be understood in context of Ahom practices and thus he makes a movement in a reverse direction from Ahom to the Tai and not from Tai to the Ahoms. However, he holds that notions of *nat* and spirit worship, sacrificial rituals etc. among the Ahoms is to be understood in context of surrounding culture of China and other neighbouring countries and thus he upholds the notion of existence of a culture prior to their culture in Assam.

Before we look into the subject it is an academic necessity to look into the existing literature and research work on the subject under review. About Ahom religious belief system, spirit worship, vitality of soul and related divination practices many scholars from different parts of the world tried to arrive to a specific conclusion.

We can broadly classify two schools of scholars who worked on the subject – they may be identified as the Supra-Tai and the Proto-Tai schools. The first group or the Supra-Tai school of scholars may be identified as those who believe in non-identity or lack or original Tai identity among the Ahoms. Among this Supra-Tai scholars, to take chronologically, the first and foremost generalized work with reference to Ahom history, society and culture is the work of Edward Gait's *A History of Assam* (1905). It goes to Gait's credit to use Ahom Buranji chronicle in the Tai language along with Assamese chronicles and Persian documents from Mughal dynasty and English documents of the East India Company. Gait's primary object was to write a history of Assam and not of the Ahoms and he started the book by recounting the influence of Brahmanism and Aryan culture in the land of Assam before the advent of the Ahoms. He then went on to narrate the history of interaction of various ethnic groups after the arrival of the Ahoms, the domination of Hindu culture and the Sanskrit based Assamese language from the sixteenth century onwards. Like Gait, G.E. Harvey in *History of Burma* (1925), E.R. Leach in his *Political System of Highland Burma* (1954) and German Scholar Erik Seidenfaden in his work *The Thai Peoples, Book I : Origin and Habitats of the Thai People with Sketch of their Material and Spiritual Culture* (1958) comment that the Ahoms are completely Hinduized. Seidenfaden in his work gave the statement that "they (the Ahoms) had been taken to Hinduism as regards religion, customs and manners as well as language." According to him Ahoms are no more Tai and hence Ahoms cannot be considered as a separate group. Among the Assamese scholars the most important historian of Assam history is Surya Kumar Bhuyan. He has many works in English and Assamese. Bhuyan believed that Assam had been an inseparable organic part of India since antiquity and Assam was a case study of Hinduization – the process whereby the cultures of indigenous people as well as of the Ahoms gradually yielded place to Hindu culture. In his opinion Assam at the time of Ahom rule was already under the domination of Hindu culture. The next important work is by Maheswar Neog. His most important contribution relating to our present subject of research is the *Early History of the Vaisnava Faith and Movement in Assam* (1965). In his opinion Assam was not an original settlement of any particular tribe. Assamese culture was a blend of culture of many tribes, including the Ahoms. To him the Ahoms could rule their kingdom for 600 years because they had given up their language and way of life. They freely and voluntarily accepted the language and religion which all other tribes in the area could accept. Along with Maheswar Neog we can cite the work of Satyendranath Sharma – *The Socio-Economic and Cultural History of Medieval Assam, 1200-1800 A.D.* (1989). He like Neog describes the revival of Hindu Vaishnavism by Sankardeva in Assam in the fifteenth century. This school of Hinduism could reach the villagers through literature, dance, drama, music and painting, which were used as media of propagating this doctrine. Neo-Vaishnavism was the means of Assamese culture and religion to spread to every corner of Ahom kingdom. Next to Sharma, one Dutch historian B.J. Terwiel took interest in Ahom culture. He wrote a two-volume work on *The Tai of Assam* (*1972, 1981*). Terwiel read the Ahom language and he studied the Ahoms within a perspective of other Tai groups. He made a thorough study of Ahom religion, rituals and different divination practices. Terwiel says that the original religion of the Tais probably was animism and he rejects any propositions to Buddhist elements in old Tai religion and to quote him – "Ancient Tai seem to have share with many folk religions surrounding them. Sacrificial religion is almost ubiquitous and essential in the methods adopted here". As a whole Terwiel too like Assamese scholars believes that the language, religion, rituals and cultures of the Ahoms are dead. The latest scholar belonging to this school is S. Yasmin Saikia. Her Ph.D. thesis entitled – *A Name Without a People : Searching to be Tai-Ahom in Modern India* is a work from Wisconsin Madison University, USA in 1999. To Yasmin Saikia the images of Tai-Ahom identity are elusive, unhistorical, fuzzy and ambivalent (Saikia, p. 326). She calls Ahom as a dead subject. The pity is that Ms. Saikia's work placed emphasis on political movements and political identity of these groups of people and did not care to look into their socio-cultural traits. With limited research on Tai cultural aspects, she insisted that the leaders of the Tai-Ahom movement are re-reading their past according to their own terms (p. 85). To her arts, architecture, coins and inscriptions of Assam are viewed by the Tai-Ahoms as a source of their history but these actually do not tell us much about a people and the customs of a group called Ahom. By analyzing four categories of Buranjis, Saikia tried to show influence of Hindu mythical ideas on these. Her research shows that there is no reference of the term 'Ahom' in local language (p. 154). Following colonial mind she applies the epithet *Ahom : A Dead Subject* (p. 190). The most impressive conclusion of the thesis is – "The study of Tai-Ahom identity remains perennially open for more research and analysis".

Thus from Gait to Saikia according to all researchers' interpretation Tai culture and Tai language are not considered central to the history of Assam. To them central pole of the history of Assam is the Aryan, Hindu culture and the Sanskrit language. These works on cultural and religious history conspicuously emphasize the influence of the Hindu religion in Assam. So the readers are made to believe that the Ahom, the Tai culture, language and religion have all been totally absorbed. There are no rituals or beliefs or divination practices except Hinduism.

The second school of historians belongs to the Proto-Tai school, who have studied Ahom history with an approach opposite to the Western and the Assamese school. They studied Ahom history separate from the history of Assam and the history of India. They see Tai culture and language as distinct from the Hindu culture and Assamese language. They believe that western and Assamese researchers have nothing but superficial outlook. To them if someone looks Ahoms with a keen eye he would be able to understand the real picture of Ahom and then would be able to realize how much Tai cultures are living along with the Ahoms.

Padmeswar Gogoi wrote *Tai-Ahom Religion and Customs* (1976). His work shows that the Ahom had their own religion and their rituals. He identified their objects of worship and ritualistic forms of worship and concluded those as the Tai cultural traits in India. His another work entitled *The Tai and Tai Kingdoms : With a Fuller Treatment of the Tai-Ahom Kingdom in the Brahmaputra Valley* (1968) is an important work to examine Ahom history as a part of the history of Tai nation and its various kingdoms. In the realm of religion and ritual the most important intellectual of Ahom revival movement is Nagen Hazarika. He wrote on *The Ahom Philosophy of God* (not dated) arguing that the Ahoms have their own god and their own religious text. Unlike the Western and Assamese school, he claimed that Assamese culture was Ahom culture. Another significant work is by Swarna Lata Barua – *A Comprehensive History of Assam* (1985). Her work speaks about Ahom identity. She wrote comprehensively with a Marxist approach. Romesh Buragohain's edited work *The Lost Trails* (1994) also proposes a theory of Ahom state formation and his book speaks about Tai-Ahom's own religion and divination practices. Girin Phukan in his book expressed his opinion that at present majority of Ahoms came to realize that their adherence to Hinduism was a fundamental cause of their downfall. Through their acceptance of Hinduism, Phukan concluded the Ahom common people allowed themselves to be positioned at the lowest level of caste hierarchy – as outcaste – lower even than the Sudra caste. Finally, he spoke about present day Ahom consciousness. The work of Pushpadhar Gogoi, i.e. *Tai of North-East India* (1996) is an important addition to Tai school of literature. To Gogoi, the priestly clan of the Ahoms represents their traditional culture and Ahom religion and divination practices have not lost its original flavour. Thai scholars have also taken interest in the subject and all of them absolutely belong to this second school of thought. Scholar like Pharya Anuman Rajadhon (1888-1969) wrote in *The Story of Thai Nation* (1940). Rajadhon thinks it is almost certain that animism formed the art of the early belief. Luang Suryabongsa also argues that the past religion of the Thais was probably animism and ancestor worship. The best of Thai works on Ahom is by Sarnath, i.e. *Visiting Tai Ahom : Our Blood Relatives* (1954). Sarnath's work makes us feel that the Ahoms were the relatives of the Thais in Thailand. Wilaiwan Kanittanan has utilized this approach of comparative cultural history. She wrote an article, "A Linguistic Approach to Khwan : An Ancient Tai Belief" (1981) with an important conclusion that the calling of the life's Essence is a genuine ancient Tai ritual. Chatthip Nartsupha, Ranoo Wichasin, Ranee Lertleumsai – all Thai scholars tried to study along the line of comparative cultural history. Chinese scholar Cheah Yangcheong writes "Thai-Tai family had a common ancient culture prior to their acceptance to Theravada Buddhism" and in this context he refers to the ancestor worship and offering sacrifices of Tai culture in other parts of Asia. Amalendu Guha, a famous non-Assamese historian of Assam history also is of similar view when he compares the spirits of the Tai-Ahom religious cult as a form of animism tinged with elements of ancestor worship with that of degenerated *Tantrik* Buddhist and tribal fertility rites.

It is pertinent further at this juncture to look into the view of the social scientists who specifically speak on homogeneous *vs.* heterogeneous character of Assam society. According to N.N. Basu, the North-Eastern region may be looked upon "as a federation hall, where the most ancient and the most modern, the most antiquated and the most up-to-date, are found to meet together upon terms of perfect cordiality. The followers of all the schools of philosophy – the Vedic, The Puranic and the *Tantrik* – have thrived here equally well, and people of all races, Aryans and non-Aryans, Hindus and non-Hindus, have equally contributed to the building up of the social fabric." The view of B.K. Barua is that, the North-East is racially and linguistically homogeneous, that is to say, its inhabitants form a distinct entity among the people of India, united by a common tongue, an Aryan dialect of great antiquity. This view is contested by P.C. Choudhury who holds that though the process of Hinduisation or Sanskritisation of the non-Aryan tribes went on from early times, the region remained a land of heterogeneous racial strains with linguistic divergences, notwithstanding the fact that modern Assamese language is of Aryan origin. To what extent the pan-Indian dominant culture, otherwise known as Sanskrit or Sanskritic culture, which made the composite system later known as Hinduism the vehicle of its expression, was able to influence the North-Eastern zone inhabited by peoples belonging to various Mongoloid racial stocks and the Mon-Khmer and Tibeto-Burman speech families is the principal subject of our enquiry.

In perspective of this debate of the researchers, it may be observed that the history of Assam points out that in Assam before the entrance of the Ahoms at the beginning of thirteenth century, Aryan culture was already established, especially the Sakta doctrine which taught that power in this universe came from women particularly the goddess Kali or Parvati. Five hundred years before the in-migration of the Ahom, there was a kingdom named Kamarupa, which was centre of Sanskritic culture.

The characteristic evolutionary pattern of Sanskritic culture in Indian soil has attracted attention of social scientists. N.N. Bhattacharya, the noted historian is of opinion that Sanskrit in its origin is an Aryan or Indo-European language, but during its evolution on the soil of India, the non-Aryan peoples had a share in its development. It was thus a joint product of both Aryan and non-Aryan, so that it could become by 500 B.C. the most natural vehicle of a composite pan-Indian culture. The subsequent history of civilization in India is the expression and elaboration of this Sanskrit culture and its slow but inevitable acceptance by the peoples of India, directly or indirectly. And this went on hand in hand with the spread of Sanskrit culture, which became synonymous of Indianism. This progressive Sanskritisation of the various pre-Aryan and non-Aryan peoples in their culture, outlook, world-view and way of life characterised the history of India through the ages. And in the course of this Sanskritisation, the peoples who were influenced by it, also brought their own spiritual and material milieu to bear upon the Sanskrit or Sanskritic culture, which they were adopting, and thus helped to modify and to enrich it in their own circles. A study in Sanskrit literature shows that Sanskritisation was never a one-way traffic; Sanskrit culture had flexibility and adaptability of a unique kind; and nowhere did it enforce a single structure or pattern. It could always be tailored according to situation, convenience and local condition. While dealing with the question of Sanskritisation in the North-Eastern region, one has to take note of the methods adopted by its protagonists, the range of their success, outstanding features of their emphasis, areas in which they were to compromise or lose and so forth.

It is difficult to ascertain precisely the period when Sanskritisation began to take place in the Brahmaputra valley. But there is hardly any doubt that it began at a fairly early period, even before the beginning of the Christian era. The language of the ancient inscriptions of Assam is Sanskrit, the earliest of which belongs to the fifth century A.D. The Assamese language developed out of the Sanskrit language as early as the seventh century A.D. Its direct ancestor is, however, Magadhi Apabhramsa. According to Grierson, "Magadhi was the principal dialect which corresponded to Prakrit. East to Magadha was spoken Pracya Apabhramsa. It spread to the south and south-east and here became the parent of modern Bengali. Pracya Apabhramsa also spread to the East keeping north of the Ganges and reached the valley of Assam where it is represented by the Assamese. Each of the three descendants of Magadhi Apabhramsa, Oriya, modern Bengali and Assamese, is equally directly connected with the common immediate parent." The ancient inscriptions of Assam, though written in Sanskrit, show that as early as the seventh century A.D. some of the Assamese formations are there. In the seventh century A.D. Hiuen Tsang wrote that the

Kamarupi dialect differed only a little from that of mid-India. Thus the seventh century A.D. may be regarded as the *terminus ad quem* because by this time the rulers of Assam, whatever their original ethnic and linguistic features might have been, had adopted Sanskrit as the language of their official proclamations and religious expressions in the same way as many centuries later the Ahom rulers adopted Assamese. In the popular level also the people of the Brahmaputra valley followed a kind of Prakrit which had very little difference with the languages of Northern India. But to determine the *terminus a quo* is a matter of greater difficulty. The Sanskrit inscriptions are written in North Indian Brahmi structurally connected with the Kutila variation of the Gupta script of Eastern India. So direct evidence goes as far back as the fifth century, and for a earlier stages we are to depend on indirect evidence. One should not fail to recall in this connection that the Brahmaputra valley always lay on the highway for all Indian emigrants to the Far East and this kept the region with the perpetual contacts with the rest of India, and as such the linguistic and cultural contacts must have started from a remote period.

According to the traditional accounts, Sanskritisation in the North-East was due to Naraka, the first mythical king of this region. The Nidhanpur grant states that Naraka was the son of Vishnu who, assuming the form of a boar, lifted up the earth. Bhagadatta was the son of Naraka who challenged Indra in a battle and became famous as a conqueror. Naraka and Bhagadatta are also mentioned in the Doobi, Tezpur, Nowgong, Bargaon, Gauhati and other grants.

Apart from the mythical elements of Naraka's being the son of Vishnu (this might have also been in figurative sense meant for glorification of the royal office), the account is realistic, which refers to Brahmanical settlements in the Brahmaputra valley in a remote period of history. These Brahmanas were the torch-bearer of Sanskritisation through the ages, and subsequent kings also followed the tradition introduced by Naraka of bringing and settling learned Brahmanas from Northern India. Facts are lacking regarding the achievements of the kings intervening between Naraka-Bhagadatta and Pusyavarman, the founder of the Varman line. But the Nidhanpur copper plate grant records the king Bhutivarman of the sixth century A.D. granted special *agrahara* (religious gift of land to the Brahmanas) settlements to more than two hundred Brahmanas of various *gotras* and *vedasakhas* (pertaining to various branches of the Vedas) for promotion of Vedic religion and scholarship. The Brahmans not only established their own settlements, but absorbed the earlier inhabitants in their fold by initiating them to the Brahmanical religion, ritual and language. The process of Hinduization was there in north-east India since the days of Kamarupa rulers when a large number of Brahmins were patronised and there was process of Sanskritization which led to the development of the Assamese language. With these Brahamana settlers Sanskrit culture and its various manifestations began to influence the political, public and religious life of the people in the Brahmaputra valley. The theory of the divine origin of kinship which was propounded by Manu was adopted by the rulers who liked to compare themselves with the gods of the Hindu pantheon.

This Brahmanical influence, various aspects of which have been canonised in Sanskrit scriptural and secular texts, paved the way of Hinduisation not only in the Brahmaputra valley, but in the greater North-Eastern region as well. The sporadic Brahmanical settlements were places in which aspects of Sanskritic culture were conserved and from which spread far and wide. The royal patronage helped in the spread of Brahmanism, more appropriately the *Arya Dharma, or* in popular term Hinduism. Among the settlers and preachers, who were granted lands, there were Brahmanas also from Madhyadesa or Aryavarta, as we come across in the Khonamukhi grant.

According to Nirmal Kumar Basu, the social structure of Hinduism was a federated organisation in which there was a spirit of harmony which wielded together the discordant elements. As a result, we find a tendency towards forming a social whole out of diverse and conflicting elements. A derivative social organisation was thus developed in ancient India which sought to put an end to the other alternative of ethnic wars and the extermination of the conquered. Such an organisation came into existence with hierarchical grades for diverse communities and with social duties and means of livelihood allotted to each of them. Under this character of Hinduism assurance was given to the tribes and detribalised castes. Every group was allowed to follow their original tribal and traditional social practices, cults and rituals, laws and customs. This accounts for the Hinduisation or near-Hinduisation of many a tribe of North-Eastern India, and the

Brahmana settlers tried only to make the process smooth. They did not impose any system. It was a natural flow which the Brahmans tried to channelise under certain given circumstances. S. Barkataki seems to be right when he says, "There never was on the part of the Hindus any overt effort anytime to convert others to their faith. There is little doubt that but for the advent of the British, and in their wake that of Christian missionaries, all the tribes would have been assimilated into the Assamese Hindu fold like numerous other tribes before them, who came and settled in Assam, the Kacharis and the Ahoms being the most notable examples." The Rabhas, Kacharis, Mechs, Kochs and kindred tribes to follow to a considerable extent the mode of social behaviour as prescribed in the Hindu legal texts. Moreover, Hindu caste laws are not the same everywhere. The emphasis given on *svadharma* (the typical socio-religious and cultural characteristics of a given people) and *lokacara* (the existing popular customs) by the law-givers made the caste-system of the North-East liberal and flexible. As a result, the Brahmanas of the North-East did not look down upon men belonging to the lower ranks of the social hierarchy and were not also strict in the observance of the rules relating to food and profession.

It may be guessed that such characteristic feature of Hinduism provided a favourable environment to the Ahoms to intrude in North-East India. Moreover, the area in present day upper Assam where the Ahoms developed their settlements was outside the jurisdiction of the Kamarupa kingdom. It was under Kachari influence and the Kacharis were animistic too like the Ahoms and so there was no immediate absorption of Ahom culture within the fold of Sanskritic culture.

For the first two hundred years there was no appreciable departure in the religion of the Ahoms. They continued to follow their traditional religion. Then there came a change. However, leaning towards Hinduism at the beginning did not mean any mass scale conversion. To Romesh Buragohain gradual leaning towards Hinduism was more due to some historical accidents than that of religious zeal. He refers to some accidental occurrences for which Ahom kings leaned towards Hinduism. For instance Ahom king Siu-Sheng-Pha *alias* Pratap Singh was under the grip of an evil spirit which he got rid of by performing some Brahmanical rites and, therefore, because of gratitude he patronised the Brahmins. Although such occurrences are likely to be figments of imagination, those were good causes influencing the monarchs.

As we already noted the process of Hinduisation was there in North-East India since the days of Kamrupa rulers when large number of Brahmins were patronised. The disappearance of the Kamrupa kingdom in course of history and in the absence of a strong centralized polity, the process received a setback. However in the Bhuyan chiefdoms and in the Chutiya kingdom, the process continued to hand on the Aryanization or Sanskritization did not lose its ground. Nevertheless the process was slow in Upper Assam and when the Ahoms landed there, an Ahomisation process was emerging. But with the annexation of the Chutiya state and Bhuyan chiefdoms, the Ahomisation process had gradually given way to the Hinduization process.

The initial process of giving way to Hinduism shows that the early Hindu kings of Assam were for the most part exclusive devotees of Siva. Siva seems to have been the guardian deity of the kingdom and this would almost justify the claim in the *Kalikapurana* that the land was reserved by Sambhu for his own domain. When HiuenTsang visited the country during the reign of Bhaskaravarman, he found that "the Deva temples were some hundreds in number and that the various systems had some myriads of professional adherents". Many of these temples were probably consecrated to Siva, and Saivism was possibly the dominating religion of the time. After Hinduization the Ahom monarchs erected more temples to God Siva than to any other deity and also reconstructed several older shrines of Mahadeva. Pratapasimha (1603-41) constructed the present Siva temples at Biswanath-ghat and Negritting (Dergaon). It is said that a highway covering some 48 miles in length was constructed for the purpose of carrying *nirmalaya* on horse-back every morning from the Negritting temple to the Ahom capital, and that the monarchs would not take their midday meal without first taking such *nirmalaya*. Under the auspices of Gadadharasimha (1681-96), a patron of Sakta Hinduism, the standing temple of Umananda opposite Gauhati town was built. Rudrasimha (1697-1714) built several temples on the banks of the Jayasagara tank near the town of Sibsagar and one of those temples enshrined Siva. The queens of Sivasimha (1714-44) built temples on the Gaurisagara and

Sivasagara tank both near the capital, the main temple in each place being dedicated to Siva (Sadasiva Muktinatha). Pramattasimha (1744-51) built the Rudresvara Siva temple at Gauhati. Rajesvarasimha (1751-69) had the temples of Vasisthasrama, Manikarnesvara and Citracala built about the town of Gauhati under the supervision of his viceroy, Dasaratha Tarun Duwara Barphukan. The Rudrasagara tank was excavated in the capital under the orders of King Laksmisimha (1769-80). In their coins also the Ahom kings betray their Saiva-Sakta proclivities and it is interesting to note from the coins of different monarchs how they came more and more into the grip of Sakta priests.

The Neo-Vaisnavite movement initiated by the Saint-poet Sankradeva in the last decade of the fifteenth century proved to be an epoch-making phenomenon in the religious and social history of medieval Assam. The Neo-Vaisnavite movement launched by Sankradeva and his worthy disciple Madhavadeva found a great mass base and in the course of time it got itself crystallized into four *samphatis* or sects, namely, the Brahama Samhiti of which the greatest exponent was scholar-saint Deva Damodara; the Purusa Samhiti, named after its founder Purusottama Thakur, the Nika Samhiti or 'pure sect' so called because of its strictly conforming to the rules and regulations prescribed by Madhavadeva; and Kala Samhiti which owed its origin to Gopaladeva, popularly called Gopal Ata of Bhawanipur. Twelve *satras* (Vaisnavite monasteries) were established by Gopaladeva, six of which were presided over by Sundra *mahantas* and six by the Brahmanas. Among these the Mayamara *satra* played a very significant role in the history of the North-East. It was founded by Aniruddhadeva who was born in 1553. His earlier name was Harakanthagiri. He was initiated by Gopaladeva who advised him to preach the doctrine of *bhakti* among the backwards. He first made his centre at Visnu Balikunchi. But because of frequent Dalfa (Nishi) raids he shifted the location of his centre to Nahar-Ali on the bank of the Maranj river in the present North Lakhimpur sub-division. He, however, stayed for a short period in Majuli on the bank of a lake called Moamari and converted many people of the neighbouring area into the new creed. He used to send his apostles, or visit himself the tribal areas and spread the messages of the *bhakti* cult. Amongst the tribes, the Morans were the first to be converted. They were followed by the Kacharis,

Chutiyas, Barahis, Ahoms and Brittials. Here we have a very important clue to the understanding of the process through which the tribes of the North-East came under the influence of liberal Vaisnavism.

The neo-Vaisnava reformer, Sankaradeva (1449-1568 AD), inculcated the monotheistic doctrine of *ekasarana namadharma*, based mainly on the *Bhagavad Gita* and the *Bhagavatapurana*, in the very early years of sixteenth century. The worship of all gods other than Hari (Krisna) was interdicted in this system of religion. In fact conversion to Hinduism, finally gathered momentum when there started the revival of Hindu Vaisnavism by Sankardeva in Assam in the mid-fifteenth century. Maheswar Neog in *Early History of Vaisnava Faith and Movement in Assam* (1965) and Satyendranath Sharma in *A Socio-Economic and Cultural History of Medieval Assam* (1989) describe the revival of Hindu Vaisnavism by Sankaradeva. The neo-Vaisnava reformer, Sankaradeva (1449-1568 AD), inculcated the monotheistic doctrine of *ekasarana namadharma*, based mainly on the *Bhagavad Gita* and the *Bhagavatpurana*, in the very early years of sixteenth century. The worship of all gods other than Hari (Krisna) was interdicted in this system of religion.

Neo-Vaisnavism was a religion of the masses and this school of Hinduism was able to reach easily down to the grassroot level. Neo-Vaisnavism reached every corner of Ahom kingdom and many Ahoms being attracted by its new philosophy trend to this sect of Hinduism. This was the gradual conquer of Ahoms by the Vaisnavite philosophy.

The three Assamese states of Eastern India, namely Assam, Kamarupa and Kooch Behar, were covered by the end of the seventeenth century and the beginning of the eighteenth century with a network of these Vaisnava establishments, and almost the whole Hindu population was now divided among them. Some of the adherents of the Vaisnava order have made serious departures from the original tenets of the faith, or have relapsed into heterogeneous doctrines discarded by the *gurus*. Others again have carried the puritanic zeal of the new faith far indeed. The followers of Gopaladeva formed into a school, characterized by catholicity and a democratic outlook and freedom from the tyranny of creeds. It particularly thrived and acquired large following in the north-eastern parts of Assam with their predominantly Tibeto-Burman population, and reclaimed large numbers of people from animistic practices. The followers of the

Mayamara *mahanta* within Gopaladeva's order rose in revolt as one man against royal oppression (1769), and succeeded in subverting Ahom power for a time. The history of Assam Vaisnavism is one of many conflicts and persecutions. The course of political history of this eastern part of India also has been changing considerably from time to time. But the renaissance, which had its beginnings in the activities of Sankaradeva has wrought itself into fulfilment in many ways, and marked out a definite place of Assam in the cultural map of India.

Laksminath Bezbaroa says that it was not the intention of Sankaradeva's sect to do away with the traditional Vedic rites for the initiate. Madhavadeva held an ideal in this respect to all people by performing the *sraddha* ceremony of his mother. But this was during the transitional stage of his life, when he was passing from an *avirakta* to a *virakta*. After this, however, Madhavadeva never performed the ceremony; and this rite was also never performed in his monastery manned by celibate monks only. When a monk died, Brahmanical rituals, attendant upon cremation, were not observed.

The great Sankradeva movement thus brought about a new and comprehensive outlook on life and a distinctly healthy tone to social behaviour. It accelerated the pace of a renaisssance of literature and fine arts like music and painting. The dignity of the individual endeavour of man as a distinct religious being and not as 'the thrall of theological despotism' was declared. Assam discovered herself as an integral part of the holy land of Bharatavarsa, and gloried in that discovery. The holy books in Sanskrit, the literal humanoids of India, could no longer be sealed to the common man's view by a rigid oligarchy. The use of local language in expositions of theology and philosophy was in itself a challenge to the erstwhile guardians of secret doctrines, who understood the significance of the challenge and 'protested very much'. The humanism eyed askance at the numerous blood sacrifices, including the immolation of man, and the sacred that was the order of day in Hindus but an island in a Tibeto-Burman ocean, as the medium for the propagation of the neo-Vaisnava faith led to its emergence as the language of all the people. The ancient kingdom of Kamarupa was now undergoing a huge change, and it was having almost a regeneration, political and social, which time well with the cultural resurgence initiated by Sankaradeva; and the first possibilities of a unified and modern Assam were now in evidence.

Conclusion : How and to What Extent the Ahoms were Secular?

It is substantial question as to how and why the Ahoms gave up their anecdotal religion and took to the process of Hinduization. There arises a related question – were the Ahoms secular and to what extent? There is no doubt that their approach in an indirect way helped to develop a zeal of secularism in Assam society. To the Ahoms goes the credit of embracing the policy of assimilation. Being ruling class they neither tried to stick to their own religion nor tried to impose it on their subjects. Rather they displayed the ardency for assimilation. All the Ahom rulers followed a policy of toleration and assimilation with heterogeneous races and tribes around them. The Ahoms, increased their community by conferring upon new entrants the status and privileges of the members of ruling race. In other words, they needed collaboration of the surrounding multi-tribal people and won them up with their attitude of assimilation.

The records of these affiliations were carefully maintained. There was an exhaustive scrutiny during the reign of Swargodeo Pratap Singh. From these records, many leading Ahom families appear to have been founded by patriarchs belonging to many non-Ahom races like Varahi, Chutiya, Garo, Koch, Kachari, Moran, Miri and others. The cultural fusion very often associated with admixture of blood between the tribal and non-tribal elements and it promoted a cultural synthesis. Thus the Ahoms had an indirect role behind this formation of one nation with many fragments.

The Ahoms also followed a policy of peaceful co-existence. They kept peace and friendly relationship with neighbouring hill tribes. The hill people living exclusively in the hills were living in comparative isolation from the other non-tribal communities in the plains. But there existed some sort of relationship from the beginning of the Ahom rule. The Ahom ruler's catholic attitude towards caste and creed, policy of intermarriage, recruitment of hillmen in the army and civil offices, grant of estates to the hill chiefs and other commercial concessions to tribal chiefs in the plains further strengthened the bond of friendship. At times there might have been clashes or misunderstandings but as soon as they were resolved amity and concord prevailed between the hills and plains and trade and social intercourse resumed. It was under Ahom patronage that Sankaradeva could exert Vaisnavite influence which resulted in greater cultural assimilation between people of different categories and cults. A good number of Daflas, Miris, Singhpos, Nagas, Kacharis, Manipuris, Goras etc. were admitted into the Ahom society resulting in emergence of a greater Assamese society.

Thus the Ahoms were free from theological oppression and tyranny rather they were highly accommodative. Secularism was the dominant undercurrent of Ahom royal policy which meant the cultivation of friendship and extending intellectual hospitality instead of imposing their own religion on the subjects.

REFERENCES

Barua, Golap Chandra, (1930). *Ahom Buranji,* Calcutta.

Barua, (1978). Indira. *Social Relations in an Ahom Village*, New Delhi.

Baruah, S.L., (1985) *A Comprehensive History of Assam*, New Delhi.

Bhattacharyya, N.N., (1995) *Religious Culture of North-Eastern India.* New Delhi.

Buragohain, Romesh, (1994) *The Lost Trails,* Dhemaji.

Dhayani, S.N., (1996). *Secularism, Socio-legal Issues,* New Delhi.

Erik Seidenfaden, (1958). *The Thai Peoples, Book 1 : Origin and Habitats of the Thai People with Sketch of their Material and Spiritual Culture*, Bangkok.

Gait, Edward., (1905). *A History of Assam.*

Gore, M.S., (1991). Ed. *Secularism in India,* Allahabad.

Gogoi, Padmeswer, (1976) *Tai-Ahom Religion and Customs*, Guwahati.

Gogoi, Pushpa. (1996) *The Tai of Northeast India,* Dhemaji.

Hazarika, Chao Nagen, (1996) *We Revive We Survive*, Guwahati.

Kanittanan, Wilaiwan, (1999) "Khon Thai Nai Prathet India : Phasa lae Wathanatham, [Thais in India—Language and Culture] (In Thai), *International Conference on "The Tai People before the Coming of Civilisation",* Prince Mahachakri Sirindhon Anthropology Centre, Bangkok, 27-28 May.

Lambert, Eric T.D., (1952) "A Short Account of the Ahom People", *Journal of Siam Society,* Bangkok, Vol. 40, Part 1.

Miri, Sujata, (1993). *Communalism in Assam : A Civilisational Approach,* New Delhi.

Neog, Maheswar., (1965). *Early History of the Vaisnava Faith and Movement in Assam*, Guwahati.

Neog, Maheswar, (1984). *Religions of the North-East,* New Delhi.

Phukan, Haliram Dhekial, (1929). *Assam Buranji,* Calcutta.

Rajadhon, Phya Anuman. *A Brief Survey of Cultural Thailand,* Bangkok, B.E. 2496.

Suryabongsa, Luang (1954). *Buddhism in Thailand,* Bangkok.

Saikia, S. Yasmin, (1999). *A Name without a People : Searching to be Tai-Ahom in Modern India*, unpublished Ph.D. Thesis, Wisconsin Madison University, USA.

Terwiel, B.J., (1981). *The Tai of Assam and Ancient Tai Ritual, Centre for Southeast Asian Studies*, Vol. II : Sacrifices and Time Reckoning, Gaya.

Wales, H.G., (1931). Quaritch. *Siamese State Ceremonies,* London.

24

SECULARISM, ETHNICITY AND MONGOLIAN CULTURE IN NORTH-EAST INDIA

GIRIN PHUKAN

Secularism is an ideology which seeks to determine the place of religion in public life. Unlike the western doctrine of secularism, the Indian version grants to religion, a place of honour in public life. This has however degenerated into the aberration of politicisation of religious sentiments and communal identities. Thus secularism in India has acquired a connotation different from what it carries in the west. In the west secularism signifies a policy of exclusion of religious consideration from the sphere of public policy while in India it implies accommodation of religious sensibilities in state policy and symbolizes a preference for preserving cultural pluralism. In fact, secularism obliges the state to express equal regards for all religions. However, in practice, it has resulted in several unintended consequences such as the politicisation of religious identities and incompatibility between the rights of the individual and collectivity besides the problem of minorityism and majorityism. In its basic thrust on religious tolerance. Secularism in Indian Constitution expresses itself in terms of three basic provisions—right to freedom of religion, non-discrimination on the basis of religion and preservation of religious, ethnic and cultural diversities (*vide* Articles 15 and 25-28). But the policy of secularism as equal respect for all religions has turned religious diversities into religious animosities. By and large, inter-religious hostility is a very significant feature of Indian polity. This hostility sometimes assumes militant forms leading to bloodshed, arson, rape and brutalities. The communal elite have organised militant movement to preserve the separate identity of their respective communities.

Thus the virus of politicisation of religious sensibilities and securing civil liberties from the galloping command of religion have been the challenges before secularism in India. It may, however, be noted that politicisation of religious identity is not similar to political participation. Politicisation, in fact, refers to a process of appropriation of religio-cultural sensibilities of the people by certain vested interests for their parochial, political and economic purposes. The main actors in the act of politicisation are the elite of emerging middle class particularly the business and power entrepreneurs who unscrupulously use religious identities, sentiments, and symbols for material and power pursuits. The class which is expected to be a pace setter of a civil society, has itself turned into its subverter. They play the game of the power sockers impelled by their religio-cultural sensibilities and their economic vulnerabilities. In view of all these, it would be an interesting point to examine how far this state of affairs of secularism in India as noted above has been a general phenomenon throughout the country? Does religious sensibility act as a powerful instrument of political mobilisation in all the regions of the country? In this exercise an endeavour has been made to examine these questions in the context of North-East India with special reference to the Mongoloid people.

II

The demographic composition of North-East India is unique. A great majority of indigenous people of this region fall within the fold of Mongoloid culture. The Mongols who derived their culture from the rural agro-based culture of the Austrics started to immigrate into the North-East and spread all over the hills and the plains of Assam and tried to mould their culture within the framework of the new geographical environment. In course of time the geographical situation compelled the Mongoloid population to spilt into smaller tribes, sub-tribes and communities. In this way, a process has been completed resulting in swarming the vast tract of land.

From linguistic point of view, the main branch of the Tibeto-Burmese people now live in the northern part of Assam and Arunachal Pradesh like the Miris (Misings), Mishmis, Akas, Daffalas (Nishis), and Adis fall under one variegated and colourful Mongolian culture. Another linguistic branch of the Tibeto-Burmese group of people are the Bodos of Assam. The Bodo language and its different branches, namely Mech, Rabha, Cachari, Hajong, Tripuri and Lalung fall within this fold. The various dialects of the Nagas are akin to the Bodo language. The Ao, Angami, Lotha, Sema, Tangkhul, Kanyak, Mao, Rengma and many other tribes fall under Mongoloid culture group. The Wangchoo, Tangchang and Nokte tribes now living in Arunachal Pradesh also belong to this group. Even the Austro-linguistic Khasis and Jayantias belong to the great Mongoloid race. Over and above, the Tibeto-Burmese tribes like Deuris, Chutias, Morans, Borahis, Koches whose distinct language and dialects are either extinct or are partially alive also belong to the same Mongoloid race. Another branch now living in Assam is the Sino-Siamese linguistic group which includes the Ahoms, Khamtis, Khamyangs, Pakhial, Aitons, Turungs. In fact, all the indigenous people living in Assam except the Brahmins, Kayasthas and Kalitas originated from the same Mongoloid race. Most of them still maintain their distinct linguistic and cultural traits.

The consciousness of social distinction based on caste and creed which is a predominant trait of the people of Aryan origin is completely absent among the Mongolians. They do not believe in untouchability and distinction based on caste and social status. In fact, they are free from religious inhibition and caste prejudices. They are not orthodox and are prepared to receive new ideas. More importantly, the Mongolians have tremendous qualities of adaptability. Thus they are practical, unprejudiced and tolerant of others. These Austro-Mongoloid cultural traits have greatly influenced the culture of the North-East. Therefore, unlike other parts of India, the caste-war and communal conflicts are considerably absent in the region.

III

The Mongolian people of North-East India may broadly be divided into two categories – Mongolian of the hills and the plains. All the indigenous hill people of the North-East are Mongoloid and a great majority of the aboriginal groups of the plains are of also Mongoloid origin. While the Mongolians of the hills still maintain their original culture, though most of them have accepted Christianity, the Mongolians of the plains such as the Ahoms, Chutias, Cacharis, Koches have adopted Aryan language, religion and culture. More importantly, they became the ardent and liberal patrons of Aryan language and religion and greatly contributed to the growth of composite Assamese society and culture. But this is, however, not to imply that they completely abandoned their traditional basic cultural traits. A larger section of Mongoloid groups like the Bodos, Misings, Rabhas, Tiwas, Tais still continue to profess their own traditional Mongoloid culture and rituals. It is worthwhile to note that all sections of Mongoloid race possess similar cultural values.

Unlike upper-caste Aryans, traditionally the Mongoloid people are basically agriculturalist. It is the main source of living of the large majority of Mongolians. Therefore, their traditional cultural foundation is agriculture. In fact, rice has been an important cereal, responsible for creating a cultural identity and determining the social values and way of life of the Mongoloid people.

As is well-known, food habits are an important variable of culture. Rice is the staple food and home-made rice-beer is the traditional drink of the Mongolians. They take naturally grown plants as vegetables which possess medicinal properties and the stickily rice cooked in an unmatured bamboo pipes is liked by them. Besides, pork, chicken, duck, frog, many kinds of fish, dry preserved fish, cocoon seeds of endi and muga worms and eggs of red ant are their typical dishes. Even some kind of insects are also relished by the Mongolians. Like other Mongolians of the world, they prefer to take boiled food having no spices and directly burn fish, meat and vegetables like brinjal, tomato etc. Most of the Mongolians also take beef. Thus it appears that food habits of Mongoloid people is secular in nature which has an international character.

Another very important ingredient of culture is the clothes worn by the people. In fact, dress is a reflection of many aspects of their lives depending on the wearers's society and the place of the wearer within a particular social setting. Dress is often used and perceived as a marker of identity and as such traditional textiles are commonly identified with group identity. By and large, clothing serves as an indicator of identity in terms of culture. Most of the Mongoloid people in the North-East still maintain their traditional dress to a considerable extent. The excellence and special character of textile such as the woven dresses made from cotton, muga silk bear the imprint of Mongoloid textile culture among them. Weaving being a way of life with the Mongoloid society, every rural girl is adept in weaving silk, cotton and endi cloth. Most of the Mongoloids are adept in making thread from muga and endi-worms. This practice of rearing endi-worms is quite similar to the traditional Mongoloid society from the rest of the world. However, the village handicraft seems to be diminished if not died out as now-a-days most of them purchase cloth and tools instead of making them themselves. In any case, like the food habits, the types of dresses are considered as important symbol of identity unlike religious sensibility in the case of Aryan communities.

Further, it is remarkable that in Mongoloid society, the status of women is higher as they are considered as a system of creativity. Women are not only giver of offspring, they are also associated with various agricultural activities. Some of them, particularly in the hills are even associates in the commercial field too. The absence of dowry system in the North-East can be ascribed to the Mongolian influence. It may also be noted that Mongoloid women, who are not completely influenced by Hinduism, do not use veil and keep their head bare and do not use vermilion which is considered as a symbol of slavery. Inter-caste marriage is not a burning problem among them.

Besides, another outstanding feature of the Mongolians is the collective manner of working. The Mongolian villagers stand untidily at the time of merry making. Co-villagers are invited at the time of house-building and perform the job of harvesting collectively. Similar collective approach is noticed even at the time of fishing and hunting.

Thus it appears that the consciousness of social distinction based on caste, creed, social status and even profession which is a pre-dominant trait of the people of Aryan origin, is completely absent among the Mongoloids. As such they have no social taboos and they are free from caste prejudices and untouchability. By and large, Mongoloid culture is itself secular in nature and as such Mongolians are born secular. Therefore, religious sensibility, a vehicle of communalization of politics in the country does not act as a powerful instrument of political mobilization in North-East India.

Notes:

1. This writeup is based on personal investigation and observation.
2. Secularism in Indian Constitution expresses itself in terms of three basic provisions—right to freedom of religion, non-discrimination on the basis of religion and preservation of religious, ethnic and cultural diversities (*vide* Articles 15 and 25-28).

25

ETHNIC ISSUES AND CONFLICT RESOLUTION
A Case Study of the Karbis in Assam

R.P. ATHPARIA

I

Louis (2000:4087) states that "Tribal societies in India have a very ancient and alive history and heritage of their own. They have their own culture, religious, social, economic and political structures handed down generations for centuries. The indigenous people's myths, stories, tales and songs reflect their social, political and cultural organisation. Nature, environment and ecology play the most important role in their lives while studying the Jharkhand movement". Louis (2000:4087) has formulated several issues, namely, common platform for political awakening and the sense of being original settlers; Christianity contributed to tribal identity formation by providing education. It also gave them a history, a myth about the 'golden age', it accentuated the notion of private rights in hand; it also emphasised the sense of separateness from the rest (K.S. Singh, 1987) and lastly, the ethnic sense of 'we' tribals and 'they' the outsiders united the entire tribal population for a protracted struggle.

In North-East India, the tribal societies have also a long history and heritage of their own. They have their own cultural, social, economic and political structures keeping in view Louis' hypothesis. In this chapter an attempt has been made to see how the Karbis, a hill tribe of Assam, have resolved their ethnic issues when they had settled in the Jaintia territory, and in the Ahom territory. It is also an attempt to see how they have resolved their issues in the colonial period and after India's Independence.

The Karbis long known as Mikirs, constitute a major hill tribe of Assam. They are mainly concentrated in Karbi Anglong District of Assam formerly known as Mikir hills. They constitute 1.14 per cent of the tribal population of Assam. The tribal population of Assam as a whole constitutes 12.82 per cent of the total population of Assam. As there is no detailed historical work on the Karbis, it is difficult to present a picture of the Karbis' social, political and economic aspects of the past. Ethnic issues and conflict arise when the folk feel or visualise the situation where its existing socio-cultural, socio-economic and socio-political systems are in danger or in a state of being overwhelmed due to some external force or contact with a stronger culture. Such situations have occurred among the Karbis in the past.

The Karbis came in contact with the Jaintias after their migration to the Rongkhang area for settlement as the first instance of external influence. They lived in the Jaintia territory for many centuries. During that, the traditional Karbi identity had undergone changes to a considerable degree in respect of language, culture, economic activities etc. As a result, traits of Mon-Khmer culture (borne by the Jaintias) particularly in respect of language, religious faith and activities, religious songs and dances etc. had gradually entered into the Karbi social life. For example, a good number of Khasi-Jaintia words are used by the Karbis and the popular *chomankan* dance of the Karbis is believed to have originated from the Khasis. Upto certain extent the Karbis did not consider the entrance of the Mon-Khmer culture as a problem to their culture and identity. But when they found that their mythological hero and great warrior Nokbe was killed by the Jaintias and thereafter when they could smell that the Jaintias were going to impose their matrilineal norms on the Karbis they felt very much insecure as their patrilineal identity was going to be destroyed. The Karbis were not prepared to forsake their traditional patrilineal system at any cost. As a result, many Karbi families came down from the Rongkhang hills to the Ahom territory in the Nagaon plains across the Kopili river. The Ahom king not only rehabilitated the Karbis but also provided them protection, and reinstated their king at Rongkhang under the Ahom king thereby helping the Karbis to fully practise their traditional norms and culture and their ethnic identity in their own way.

During the colonial period, the Karbis had two main conflicts with the British, namely, (1) spread of Christianity and (2) land and revenue settlement. In the latter part of the nineteenth century, a few Karbi families at Tika of Baithalangso were converted to Christianity by the Baptist Christian Missionaries. Their new religion brought them a new faith as well as modern education. The Christian families and their children thus got the opportunities to know about the western and the most developed societies of the world. This also brought to them a new perception and a tremendous change in their outlook towards the age old religious faith and practice, and to a considerable extent in their day-to-day life. There was also the change brought by the land and revenue settlement introduced by the British Government. In the hilly areas, however, this arrangement did not affect them at all; but the lower portions such as the villages of the Kapili and the Langpi of Nagaon (now within Karbi Anglong District) practically come under the cadastral areas. By this new administrative system the individual Karbi families became land owners – earlier land was owned by the entire village under the headmanship of the village headman, Sarthe (or *gambura*). As a result of this the community system of cultivation locally known as *Jirkedam* began to erode, and gradually it spread to the hilly areas where non-cadastral lands were (still today are) freely cultivated under the method of shifting cultivation (locally known as *rit*) by the individual families.

The creation of separate administrative unit that is the autonomous district in post-independence period is a landmark in the history of the Karbis. The very purpose of the autonomous district is to give them the opportunity of self-administration for development and progress according to their own genius under the norms of the Sixth Schedule of the Indian Constitution. In this context, it is worth mentioning that their traditional political system has not been discarded which is still well in existence although it has nothing to do with the pace of development in the modern context. The modern administration apart from giving them the taste of true democracy, has given them modern education, agriculture, transport and communication and infrastructure of development.

In the early days of creation of the district, the district and the state authorities took up some means regarding the utilization of land and forest resources in the district by passing acts and undertaking schemes to stop *Jhumming* and shifting of villages. The notable acts and regulations and Mikir Hills District (*Jhumming*) Regulation, 1954, scheme of model villages 1964 and coffee and rubber plantation scheme in 1975 etc. As a result of the development process under the modern administration, urbanization at some point is the eventuality. This has opened up opportunities for outsiders to come over here for permanent settlement in due course. In due course of time some urban centres have become the growth points/centres causing a great impact on the socio-economic and socio-cultural life.

Opening of mining and hydroelectric power generation industries at few places of Karbi Anglong such as Amtreng (hydro-electric project) and Bokajan (cement factory) have also attracted employment and job seekers from within and outside the district. Following them businessmen and traders also come there, and thus significantly contributed to the rapid growth of non-agricultural population.

Availability of vast open cultivable lands in foothills that are contiguous to the plains and even some interior places of Karbi Anglong have attracted agricultural and landless people of the plains districts of Assam and elsewhere mostly non-Karbi. These people do not get the land settlement but in a couple of years economically dominate the cultivable lands of the Karbis under *Paika, Sukti* or *Bandhak* (mortgage) system. Under such situation, the actual land owners become poorer and lose everything except the ownership of land by name.

During the sixties, the hill tribal leaders of the united Khasi and Jaintia hills and the Garo hills district of Assam launched a movement for the creation of a separate political unit for the hill tribals basically with the intention to provide safeguard to tribal culture and identity. When the autonomous state of Meghalaya comprising the two hill districts was formed, the united Mikir and North Cachar Hills (now Karbi Anglong and North Cachar Hills) was given a choice whether or not to join the new born political unit under Article 244 (A) of the Constitution of India. The article has also provided for a right to its people to form a separate political unit who never desired. The Karbi leaders opted for remaining with Assam. It may be mentioned that Meghalaya is a tribal Christian state while the united Mikir and North Cachar Hills is a Hindu Tribal area. This fundamental difference in religious faith and sentiment was perhaps the root cause of this district not joining the Christian state of Meghalaya. Here, we find another instance of Karbi people's crucial decision on the question of religion and socio-cultural identity.

Basing on the provision given by Article 244 (A), the Karbis, mostly the youth, with the help of the Dimasas and other tribals launched a movement during the eighties and the nineties. They demanded the implementation of the article with the intention to form a separate political unit for the Karbis and the Dimasas. The youth organisation like ASDC (Autonomous State Demand Committee), KAASDCOM (Karbi Anglong Autonomous State Demand Committee), KSA (Karbi Students' Association), ADSU (All Dimasa Students' Union), KANCHASDCOM (Karbi Anglong and North Cachar Hills Autonomous State Demand Committee) engineered the entire movement. This movement was virtually inspired by the historic Assam movement on foreign nationals' issue, and the former took its birth soon after the latter died down following the signing of Assam Accord in 1985. The Karbi movement has given a tremendous impetus to the Karbi youth on issues like social modernization, modern identity and of course the creation of an autonomous state for better self-administration and so on. Later, however, the idea of implementing the Article 244 (A) vanished after signing the MOU (Memorandum of Understanding on 1st April, 1995).

By looking at the present trend in respect of socio-political and socio-economic development in the Karbi Anglong district, the Karbi tradition and identity can be said to have reached a transitional state – the question of Karbi identity on the traditional foundation and the question of progress of the people both seem to have equal importance. It is observed that during the colonial rule, when the whole of North-East became a part of British India, material conditions facilitating change in N.E. opened up development of railways and roadways, introduction of modern education, emergence of private property in land and common subjection to a highly centralised political authority. It was during this period that immigrants, some representing more advanced nationalities and ethnic groups settled in Karbi Anglong. Earlier, migrations at times did generate religious and racial conflicts, but as far as livelihood was concerned nature had enough to give to everyone. Since people were living at subsistence level, there was no need for any ethnic issues like insecurity. But migrations that began during the British period, apart from creating the ground for cultural and linguistic conflicts, generated competition among different ethnic groups for new economic and political opportunities thrown open to the public by the colonial rulers. The Karbis did not feel threatened by the neighbouring ethnic groups like Dimasas, Jaintias etc. who were living peacefully in the same environment. But the Karbis became apprehensive of the educated Hindu, Bengalis and the Assamese middle class, the hardworking Muslim Bengali peasants and the enterprising Marwaris, who entered the bureaucracy, agriculture and business respectively. The Karbis who did not compete with the new immigrants, began to worry about domination by these new immigrants in all spheres. Their sense of insecurity and feeling of alienation made them conscious to their own identity. As a result, internal differences and conflicts between the Karbis and the non-Karbis remained unresolved.

REFERENCES

Louis, Prakash, 2000. Jharkand : Marginalisation of Tribals. In *Economic and Political Weekly,* November 18-24. Vol XXXV, No. 47, pp. 4087-4091.

Singh, K.S., 1987. *Tribal Societies in India*. New Delhi, Manohar Publications. p. 197.

Srikanth, H., 2000. Military and Identity Politics in Assam. In *Economic and Political Weekly,* November 18-24, Vol. XXXV, No. 47, pp. 4117-4124.

26

BODO ISSUES

S.K. MUKHERJEE

The Bodo Kacharis, one of the earliest settlers of Assam are numerically the largest tribal groups in North-East India. They are Indo-Mongoloid people and speak Bodo, a branch of Tibeto Burman language. The Bodo-Kacharis inhabit primarily along the northern bank of Brahmaputra, but their concentration is highest in the Kokrajhar district of Assam. The Bodo-Kacharis have retained their cultural traditions to a large extent and are inspired by the legends of their past history. They have been practising wet cultivation for a long period, and are well-known for their traditional skill in cultivating paddy by irrigation and also for sericulture of Endi and Muga of Assam. They have also contributed to a large extent in the cultural and ethnic configuration of Assam valley (Chatterjee, 1951).

In a composite state of Assam, the Assamese were politically the most powerful group, consisting of a mass cultivating families led by a number of educated and landed families who had branched out into government service, the professions of tea and small trade. They had begun a struggle with the Bengali middle class for political and cultural supremacy already in the late nineteenth century and by fifties were powerfully entrenched both in the state administration and in the Congress organisation. Their dream was now to turn Assam into a homogeneous society with the Assamese way of life and the Assamese language. This cultural campaign also paid political dividends as it legitimised the Assamese way to grab the largest share of the cake and acquire a vertical monopoly of power in the state administration. Eventually, the hill tribes got their own states like Meghalaya, Nagaland and Mizoram.

Before independence, the leaders of the Assam provincial Congress

Committee had entered into an alliance with tribal leaders guaranteeing limited self-government in aid of certain safeguards in the plains. But most of the hill tribes are not happy with such limited self-government. The plains tribes too have been more or less restive for a long time because the Bodo peasants or large proportion of them had been squeezed out of their land. Secondly,Bodo inhabited areas had been badly neglected during the successive Congress government. Thirdly, the Bodos and other tribals resented the campaign of Assamisation and felt they had no chance of preserving their own cultural heritage in that atmosphere.

Initially, a socio-religious movement began under the guidance of Srimat Kalicharan Brahma in the early part of nineteenth century. The religious reform movement called Brahma Movement was instrumental in the cultural and political consciousness among the Boros. Guru Kalicharan represented to the Simon Commission for reservation of seats in the State Legislature and government services for the tribals. He also supported the formation of the tribal League to focus the attention on their social, political and economic problems. In the late sixties the movement assumed a new phase and developed into a socio-political one for a separate state within the Indian Union. The leadership of the movement was vested in the Plains Tribals Council of Assam (PTCA) constituted in 1967. The Bodo Sahitya Sabha established in 1952 and Bodo Students' Union also played important role in the organisation of the movement. Historically, the plains tribals movement emerged out of the demand for linguistic rights of the Bodo Kachari. It has been aptly stated that language is the most favourite political issue in Assam (Chaube, 1973). In fact, most of the similar movements of this region developed from language issues especially after the enactment of the Official Language Act of Assam in 1960.

They have been easy targets for many glaring injustices for decades due to their illiteracy and simplicity. The problem of land alienation assumed a very alarming proportion. From the beginning of this century immigrants from East Bengal (now Bangladesh) and the Adivasis from Chotanagpur area infiltrated into their area swallowing up many of their old villages and most fertile areas. The age-long activities of the non-tribal traders and money lenders and adverse socio-economic effects of recent urbanisation and industrialization without careful arrangements for their economic protection and rehabilitation have engendered a feeling of deprivation, discrimination and injustice among the Bodos. Further, the imposition of ceilings on agricultural land holdings had seriously affected the illiterate and ignorant Bodos. They complained that the plains tribals had been uprooted in a systematic and planned way from their own soil and step-motherly treatment of the administration dominated by the Assamese speaking people only reduced them to the status of second class citizens of the state. The PTCA demand for an Autonomous Region in 1967 was upgraded to a demand for Udayachal, a Union Territory in 1973. But in 1977 the top layer of their leadership announced withdrawal of the demand for Union Territory in favour of the demand for Autonomous Region. This announcement (by the PTCA leaders who were by then with the Janata Dal after the lifting of national emergency) shocked the diehards and within a short span of time they organised themselves under Plains Tribal Council of Assam (Progressive) shortly known as PTCA (P). The demand of PTCA (P) was for a Union Territory called Mishing-Bodoland and they submitted a number of memoranda to the Prime Minister between 1980 and 1983.

At the instance of All Bodo Students Union (ABSU) which has been active all along since 1967, attempts were made to unite the PTCA and the PTCA (P). But the unity efforts failed. In 1984, PTCA (P) was dissolved and a new organisation was floated with the name of United Tribal Nationalist Liberation Front (UTNLF) which too, in support of its demand for a Union Territory, named Tribal Land, submitted a number of memoranda between 1984 and 1990. The ABSU too, between 1972 and 1988, submitted a number of memoranda to the Prime Minister, in support of their demand for a Union Territory. However, the Twentieth Annual Conference of the ABSU held at Bastibari in Dhuleri district during December 1988 ushered in a very militant phase in the movement when they decided to suspend all other demands except three political demands. This conference also upgraded their demand for a Union Territory to full-fledged statehood for more autonomy and political power and gave the nomenclature Bodoland to the proposed state. 'However, Bodoland was not meant only for the Bodos but was merely a nomenclature of a tribal state including the plains tribals of Assam. The non-tribals were also to be guaranteed with all the constitutional rights in the proposed Bodoland'. This was asserted by the ABSU communique in December 1988 that was signed by none other than late Upendra Brahma. Since then almost everyday, by masterly utilisation of pressure tactics, ABSU-BPAC continued to remain in the headlines and ultimately the Government of India had to initiate rounds of tripartite talks and then the much publicised three-member panel on Bodoland was constituted. The three-member committee submitted their report on 31st March, 1992 but the Bodo leaders rejected it. On 21st February, 1993 the seven-year old Bodo agitation came to a dramatic end with the Assam Government and the Bodo leadership signing a memorandum of settlement that gave the plains tribals an autonomous Council. The accord was signed in presence of the Union Minister of Home, Rajesh Pilot and the state Chief Minister Hiteshwar Saikia. The Bodoland issue was sought to be solved without further reorganisation of Assam. According to the recommendations of the expert committee the Bodo demand was for the establishment of a Central University in Kokrajhar. The State Government was required to take effective steps to uplift the Bodo language and its literature in the State of Assam.

The Centre resumed talks with the Bodo Liberation Tigers (BLT) on July 13, 2001 in its bid to work out the modalities for the formation of proposed Bodoland Territory Council. The talks started well ahead of July 31 the deadline set by the All Bodo Students Union. The ABSU had threatened to launch a vigorous mass movement for a separate state for the Bodos from August 2001. The talks, however, remained inconclusive as a concrete decision on the shape of the proposed BTC could not be taken which would replace the existing Bodoland Autonomous Council (BAC) structure formed on the basis of the vexed 1993 Bodo Accord. The BLT was represented by senior outfit leaders like Chandan Basumatory, Kamal Mushahary and Mainao Diamary. The Central team was headed by P.D. Shenoy, Additional Secretary, Home Affairs. The Bodo leaders however alleged that the newly elected Congress Government in the state had not done its homework before participating in the talks. Dispur adopted delaying tactics and only prove counterproductive. Although the talks had reached an advanced stage it was temporarily suspended because of the Assembly elections. It is understood that Centre and BLT leadership had reached an amicable understanding about the redrawing of the boundary of the BAC to be reconstituted as the Bodoland Territorial Council (BTC). The BLT had acceded to the Centre's request of leaving out 105 of the 353 villages not originally included within the Council areas after the hastily signed 1993 Bodo Accord as they were not Bodo dominated. A central intelligence agency report apprehended "further controversies and trouble causing serious ethnic/communal violence and breakdown in the law and order situation in the state." The exclusion and inclusion of villages in the renotified BAC could spark off "communal and ethnic turmoil in the districts of Darrang Nalbari, Kamrup, Bongaigaon, Dhubri and Kokrajhar." Based on the ground situation since 1993 Accord, the report anticipated trouble in various BAC districts. According to the report, 158 immigrant Muslims and nine Bodos had been killed in communal clashes in Barpeta and Kokrajhar districts while clashes between the Bodos and the Adivasis claimed 308 Adivasis and 80 Bodos.

REFERENCES

Chatterjee S.K., (1951). *'Kirata-Jana-Kriti.* Royal Asiatic Society of Bengal, Calcutta.

Chaube, S.K., (1973). Plains Tribals in Assam Politics, *North Eastern Affairs.*

Kalita, J, (1996). Tribal Problems, A Reorganisational Matter of Assam, *Reorganisation of North-East India since 1947*(ed.), B. Datta Ray, S.P. Agarwal, New Delhi Concept Publishing Company.

Mukherjee, S.K. and Mukherjee, D.P., (1982). Contemporary Tribal and Political Movement among the Bodo-Kacharis of Assam, *Tribal Movement in India*, Vol. I ed., K.S. Singh, New Delhi, Manohar.

27

ETHNICITY WITH SPECIAL REFERENCE TO NORTH-EAST INDIA

GITA PYAL

Ethnicity defines individuals who consider themselves or are considered by others, to share common characteristics which differentiate them from the other collectivities in a society, within which they develop distinct cultural behaviour. The term ethnic is part of a family term of similar or related meaning such as minority group, nation and race and it is not often easy to make sharp distinction between them.

Ethnic group with a common cultural tradition and a sense of identity exists as a larger society. The members of an ethnic group differ with regard to certain cultural characteristics from the other members of their society. They may have their own language and religion as well as certain distinctive customs. Probably, the most important is their feeling of identification as a traditionally distinct group. The term is usually applied only to minority groups, but if there are number of cultural distinct groups in a society some writers also refer to the dominant cultural group as an ethnic group. It is possible for an ethnic group to be a racial group as well.

Members of an ethnic group may be identifiable in terms of racial attributes, they may also share other cultural characteristics such as religion, language, politics or occupation. Ethnic groups should also be distinguished from social classes, since membership generally cross-cuts the socio-economic satisfaction within society encompassing individuals who share common characteristics that supersede class. The Jews in the United States constitute a typical ethnic group, since they include individuals of different racial origins (from East Europe to North Africa), social classes, mother tongues, religious commitment and political beliefs.

The ethnic group refers basically to the vertical divisions of a society in contrast to the horizontal divisions. The horizontal divisions refer to class, the vertical divisions to ethnicity. Ethnicity broadly refers to any group of people within a cultural unit who identify themselves as a distinct entity. Ethnicity stands for ethnic quality or affiliation of a group bearing different meaning in varied situational contexts. Ethnicity was first used by David Reisman in 1953, but the concept itself is not new, it was merely labelled differently. The concept of ethnicity is particularly important when it forms the basis for social discrimination or for independence movements. Most sociologists and social scientists use ethnic group to mean a social group which shares some aspects of a common culture.

Referring to the phenomenon of ethnicity in the Indian context Punekar (1974) has identified caste, language, region and religion as the four major premises where ethnicity operates in a significant way in India. According to Fredrik Barth, problem of ethnic group is a theme of great, but neglected, importance to social anthropology. Ethnicity rests on the reasoning that cultural variation is discontinuous. There are groups of people who share a common culture and inter-connected differences that distinguish each such discrete culture from all others. Since culture is nothing but a way to describe human behaviour, it would follow that there are discrete groups of people, i.e. ethnic units, to correspond to each culture.

The cultural contents of ethnic group consists of two categories (i) Overt signal or size such as features of dress, language, house-form and general style of life; and (ii) Basic value orientation such as the standard of morality and excellence. Sometimes they also describe not only cultural features but also ascriptive characteristics such as race, colour and tribe. In some social system, minorities are considered to be ethnic groups.

Ethnic identity as a term is quite often used by writers. Identity reflects both likeness and uniqueness. It relates to the members of a group which share a certain culture in common, at the same time which differentiates it from others. Such attributes not only distinguish a group from other groups but also contribute to the sameness and oneness among its members for identification.

In North-East India, politics has generally followed the ethnic path.

Ethnic-cultural mobilization and ethnic movements launched by various ethnic groups in the region remain on-going processes. It is not difficult to determine that ethnic movement in the region started first with the identity around certain social problem followed by concretising the identity by forming an ethnic association claiming for a separate administrative unit. Differences among different ethnic groups arose where smaller communities tended to merge and form bigger identities making it convenient to raise political demands. The term ethnicity based on the concept of pure race is a myth in North-East India. It refers to any group of people within a cultural unit who identify themselves as a distinct group.

Based on ethnicity some demand for a separate administrative arrangement, so that the group concerned can preserve its cultural heritage, language and so on. As a next step it is demanded that separate political unit comprising the areas where the ethno-cultural group form a majority be formed. The population groups in some of the North-Eastern states formed after such ethnic movements have very little cultural affinity among themselves. After the formation of the state no common identity has really developed in any of these states with the result that various sub-groups again highlight their differences and demand separate political units. Otherwise conflict between these groups will emerge leading to violence.

Just after formation of Mizo District Council the Pawi-Lakhers demanded a separate District Council. So also the Jaintias achieved their separate District Council. In Nagaland though there has been a somewhat common Naga identity since the formation of the Naga Club, the tribal identities have remained strong. However, another phenomenon to be noted here is the merger of small identities to form bigger identities making it convenient to raise political demands.

The situation obtaining in the North-East is somewhat different from other parts of India. The reason for this difference can be traced to a number of factors. Some of these factors are the following :

(i) Location of the tribal groups in relatively isolated tracts, frequently in the hilly frontier regions;

(ii) The existence of tribes till recently as homogeneous groups within well defined tribal territories; and

(iii) The recent effective induction of the tribal population in the framework of the nation-state. These factors help us to understand, at least partly, why the region experienced ethnic movement. For instance, the Pan Kuki movement is trying to unite all the fragmented Kuki groups into a strong ethno-cultural identity, so that they can demand autonomy of their own.

There are evolving new identities attached to these administrative units these days. Ethnicity is determined by prevailing socio-cultural and political trends. The tribals of North-East India like any other ethnic groups are also affected by identity crises, in socio-cultural and political fields. Small tribal groups and larger non-tribal groups also face the spectre of identity crises which often lead to agitational programmes. The growing rise in secessionist movement in the North-East also added to the problem. The ethnic movement organised under the leadership of Phizo in Nagaland and under Laldenga in Mizoram gave rise to the call for secession from the Indian state. Of late, such type of movement has been organised by several groups in North-East notably by United Liberation Front of Assam to name among the few. There are genuine reasons for such movement. In terms of physical development the region comes at the lowest grade at the national scale.

The location of the region in close proximity of the international border makes it vulnerable to infiltration of foreign nationals from across the border which in its turn, creates not only socio-economic problems but law and order problem as well. Further there are also instances of the exploitation of the local people by the outsiders. The alienation of the local people is sometimes articulated by a demand for the extension of Inner Line Act for some areas like Meghalaya.

Migration to some North-Eastern state is subject to an inner line permit and it discourages non-tribal migrants. Urban centres in these states are markedly different from ordinary towns elsewhere in terms of their tribal and ethnic composition.

Geographical isolation, lack of cultural intercourse and above all the highlighting of distinctive features of various communities lead to gradual erosion of mutual trust and fellow feeling giving rise to frequent occurrences of communal tension in the region.

The ethnic intensity, awareness and behaviour of any people can be affected by impersonal social forces such as social and geographical mobility. There are also affected by human agencies as well, such as government and politicians.

Most of the regional political parties reflected their respective ethnic aspiration. In the hill areas of North-Eastern region, the important consideration for socio-economic modernization is not so much of class consciousness as ethnic consciousness. Regional imbalance thrives due to lack of common identity of culture, language, race or religion. Because of this, economic development through various Five Year Plans had failed to weaken ethnic formation as expected in the North-East India. The moment ethnic groups demand secession, the final stage of ethnic formation is supposed to have been reached and the formal process of nationality begins.

In North-East India, ethnic consciousness as a political force is gaining ground. Some ethnic groups are still dormant and others are either suppressed or calmed down by inducements. But group formation based on ethnicity is not weakened.

REFERENCES

Bhattacharjee, Chandana. (1996) *Ethnicity and Autonomy Movement : Case of Bodo Kacharis of Assam*, Vikas Publishing House Pvt. Ltd. Bangalore.

Das, N.K. (1989). *Ethnic Identity, Ethnicity and Social Stratification in North-East India.* Inter-India Publications, New Delhi.

Datta, P.S. (1995). *North-East and the Indian State : Paradoxes of a Periphery,* Vikas Publishing House Pvt Ltd., Bangalore.

Pakem, B. (1990). *Nationality, Ethnicity and Cultural Identity in North-East India,* Omsons Publications, Guwahati.

Subba, T.B. (1992). *Ethnicity, State and Development : A Case Study of Gorkhaland Movement in Darjeeling*, Vikas Publishing House Pvt. Ltd., Delhi.

28

IDENTITY CRISIS OF BOROS (BODOS) IN BRAHMAPUTRA VALLEY

PREMALATA DEVI

Introduction

North–Eastern region of India is a melting pot of multi-ethnic and multi-linguistic groups. Assam is one of the states of this region where many tribes and non-tribes too have settled together. The largest plain area of this region is Brahmaputra valley of Assam where the Boros are considered to be the largest tribe. There are as many as eighteen sub-groups of scheduled castes and scheduled tribes in Assam. Out of them Chutiya, Moran, Deori, Saraniya, Borahi, Koch/Rajbanshis and Sonowals claimed as Hindus and refused to identify as Kachari by themselves.

The Kacharis are represented by different terms in different places, like the Mech in western part, the Boro in central part and the Sonowal and Thengal in the eastern part of the Brahmaputra valley of Assam. They are oldest inhabitants within the geographical boundaries of Assam and despite having different tribe names with different group identity as Mech, Boro, Sonowal, etc. people used to call them as Assamese in broader sense.

Origin of the Boros

Anthropologists and social scientists, through their somatometric study clearly stated that Boros are the true representative of Tibeto-Burmese linguistic group of Indo-Mongoloid stock. They started to settle in the plain area of Assam since the second millennium B.C. The Boros migrated through two major flows from the north and north-east into the rich valley of river Brahmaputra. The first flow was into the western Assam via north-east Bengal through the valley of Tista, Dharla, Sankosh river and it founded the powerful kingdom of Kamrup. The second flow was through the Subansiri, Dibang and Dihang valley into the eastern Assam and it established a powerful Chutia kingdom. A part of western migrants settled in the Jalpaiguri district of West Bengal and Kokrajhar, Bongaigaon, Dhubri and Goalpara districts of Assam are known as 'Mech'. It is believed that the Boro-Kachari living on the bank of the river 'Michi' flowing through Nepal called themselves 'Mech' or 'Meche'. Another part of western migrants settled in the Barpeta, Nalbari and Kamrup districts is known as 'Kachari'. The eastern migrants, on the other hand, are known as Chutiya, Moran and Borahis. Outside the Brahmaputra valley, Boros are also found in the contiguous areas North-Cachar (as Dimasa Kachari), Tripura (as Tippera or Barman), Garo Hills (as Garo, Hajong) etc. They all belong to the Indo-Mongoloid group. The Boro-Kacharis are also mentioned as 'Kirata' in *Vedas*. The extensive work on racial elements in Assam by B.M. Das[1] and study on Boro language and literature by P.C. Bhattacharya[2] clarify the fact that the Boros are the descendants of Kiratas later known as Boro-Kachari. According to P.C. Bhattacharya, Boro is a large linguistic group of Kachari tribes, closely related to Tiwa (Lalung), Rava, Hajong and Koche languages. He along with Robin Burling found that "Boro and Garo separated from a common ancestral language about two thousand years ago. Their glotto-chronicle or laxico-statistic account shows that Boro and Dimasa separated from each other about one thousand years ago. Thus, Dimasa is nearer to Boro than Garo."

Ethnic Identity

During the colonial period when the tribals like Khasis, Nagas, Kukis, and Mizos of North-Eastern region professed Christianity, the Boro-Kacharis and the Mishing etc. adopted Hindu ritual and their ways of life have become partly Sanskritized. Most of them have concern over the social status in the society. In general no tribe wanted to emulate a higher caste to achieve an enhanced status[3]. Their main orientation is to emulate Hinduism to get a notion of 'pure ethnic group' and the notion of 'sanskritization' can be ascribed to the detribalization process in Assam.

According to some scholars, the Deoris are a branch of the Boros of Assam who once dominated the entire Upper Assam. The term 'Deori' means the priest. As per the popular belief the Deoris were the priest group in Chutiya kingdom in Sadiya of Upper Assam. The Chutiya kingdom was there in Sadiya till it fell to the Ahoms by 1535 A.D. The Ahoms were honoured and offered privileges to construct *thaan* (temples) for ritual practice and worship during the reign of king Dihingia.

During the Burmese invasion in 1822-25 A.D. the Chutiyas migrated to the south-western part of Assam. They stayed for few days there in south bank of river Brahmaputra and made a *thaan* (temple) as a mark of cordial relations between hills and plain tribes. The *thaan* is a common place of worship and sacrifice by all the three sub-groups which are known as Dibongia. Tengapania and Bargonia. Interestingly, these three sub-groups of Deori tribe believe in three different supernatural powers like Dibongias worship *Kundi Mama*, Tengapanias worship *Boliya-Baba* and Borgonias worship *Tamreswari*.

Besides the different traditional beliefs, the tribes of Assam have accepted the Vaishnava sect of Hindu religion. Among all the tribes, the Sonowal Kacharis of Upper Assam are the most highly detribalized group of Boro-Kacharis of the valley. The followers of Vaishnavism were initiated to spread neo-Vaishnavism among the tribals and low-caste people. They offered several incentives to attract the attention of the tribal people. They assured them higher social status and economic upliftment in social life. But they could not preach on the Sonowal-Kacharis, because they themselves became the disciple of the 'Aoniati Satra', that was in the mainstream of the original neo-Vaishnava religion. During the Burmese invasion the social mobility was accompanied with caste mobility and the high caste people were able to get higher status as policy-makers. In order to get social privilege and dignity, the tribal people had to change their social identity. The Sonowal-Kacharis changed their original surnames and adopted caste surnames like Das, Bora, Dekabarua, Hazarika, Saikia etc.

Like the Sonowal-Kacharis, some of the Boro-Kacharis of Lower Assam also became the disciples of Kalicharan Brahma, the founder of 'Brahma Religion'. They gave up their traditional practices and followed the Brahma religion where they performed *Jajna/Ahuti* followed by sprinkling of ghee, rice, frankincense etc. in the fire. The ritual begins with the *mantras*. Guru Kalicharan Brahma along with the propagation of Brahma religion launched campaigns for social reforms. He encouraged trade, business, weaving, carpentry etc., and changed the bride price at exorbitant rates. He urged the then British Government for schools in the Boro dominated areas in English language, where educated unemployed youths could get opportunities to teach.[4] Guru Kalicharan also pleaded before the Simon Commission for the reservation of seats in the Legislative Assembly and jobs in the government.[5] Despite these efforts in social reforms by Guru Kalicharan the Boro people could not bear with his ideals. This was so because he had made some restrictions in the society in rearing pigs and poultry, apart from prohibition of drinking beer etc. As Christianity is very simple and low cost religious faith there being no such type of restriction to perform religious practices in Christianity, a fraction of Boro people were influenced by Christianity. But most of the Christian Boros still practice their traditional religion and drink rice beer, ate meat, fish during the religious practices. They could not maintain the code of conduct of Guru Kalicharan's ethics. The conversion of tribal religion to other folds let the people to a modern socio-religious environment where they have not attained the equal status of life till today. This development seems to have created intra-tribal conflicts among them. The negligence of their own traditional religious practices is leading them to the loss of socio-cultural identity following which identity crisis cropped up among the Boros of Brahmaputra valley of Assam. The traditional religious beliefs of Boro are almost going to be extinct and there is a strong conflict between the neo-converts and the traditional ones. As a result there is a trend to revive their traditional identity through socio-religious practices.

The Bodoland Movement

Multiple factors sparked off the multifaceted problems of Boros, which led to a Bodoland Movement. These were (i) non-tribal including tea garden labourers poured into the tribal land from other parts of the states and from neighbouring Bangladesh, (ii) non-implementation of the Assam Land Regulation (Amendment) Act, 1947, (iii) non-implementation of the Constitutional provisions under Sixth Schedule of the constitution of India, and (iv) fractional division into different religious fragments among the Boros. Thus, the Boros had to struggle much and there was no alternative left but to take up agitational path and ultimately turned into the movement which continued under different banners of leaderships.

At the first instance, creation of separate state in Boro dominated areas of Assam came to their mind and Plains Tribals Council of Assam (PTCA) was formed in 1967. To achieve their rights, the PTCA were firm in their demand for an autonomous region for the plains tribals to be named as 'Udayachal'. This movement continued over two decades and underwent a radical change within it and gave rise to United Tribal Nationalist Liberation Front (UTNLF) in 1984. Their movement was also launched for creation of Union Territory in tribal dominated areas of Assam.[6] The Boros who had joined hands with the All Assam Students Union (AASU) during the six-year long movement (1979-85) have now deadly rivalry over the Bodoland issue.[7] The 'Assam Accord' of 1985 did not cover the interest of the Boros. Henceforth in 1988, the All Bodo Students Union (ABSU) began to support actively the UTNLF for a common issue, *i.e.* the Bodoland in Assam. To gain momentum of the movement and popularize the issue among the masses, another Bodo People's Action Committee (BPAC) was formed in the same year. When the movement turned violent, there was series of talks of bipartite and tripartite nature held with the State Government, the Central Government and ABSU-BPAC representatives to solve the demand of the Boros. Finally, the 'Boroland Accord' was signed creating 'Bodoland Autonomous Council' (BAC) on February 20, 1993. This accord was reached with the objective of providing maximum autonomy to the Boros for social, economic, educational, ethnic and cultural advancement within the framework of Indian Constitution.

Revivalism

The multitude of all the factors mentioned above describe the emerging event of the Boros in recent past. Though most of them have converted to different religions like Hinduism, Christianity, neo-Vaishnavism and Brahma *dharma*, the new generation of Boros are trying to revive their traditional religious norms. Even they are very much concerned with their own script and dialect. The Boros students' organization are trying to change their mode of script from Assamese to Devanagri. Boro language has already been accepted as the medium of instruction at certain level of education. They have formed the 'Boro Sahitya Sabha' and activated it in various places of the region every year. *Bathou*, the traditional religion of Boros is alternatively used as compulsive force to revive their ethnic identity. To expose their ethnic identity to the outer world the Boros are now-a-days observing *Bathou Puja, Kherai Puja* and *Garja Puja*, the rites and rituals of age old traditional processes for the welfare of the community.

Conclusion

Boros, being one of the eight largest tribes of India and earliest inhabitants of Brahmaputra Valley, are worried about the extinction of their traditional identity due to conversion into new faith. The movement of the Boros under different banners over a period of time resulted in Autonomous Council in Boro dominated areas of Assam. The series of movement of the Boros made the new generation very much conscious of the need for revivalism and retribalisation for their own identity.

NOTES

1. B.M. Das, (1987). *The People of Assam*, Gian Publishing House, Delhi.
2. Bhattacharya, P.C. "The Boro Language and Literature", *The Assam Tribune*. March 3, Guwahati 1992.
3. Sonowal, C.J., (1996). "Religious Trend and Identity Crisis : A Cross Cultural Study among Three Plains Tribes of Assam", in *Peoples of North-East India*, edt. Sarthak Sengupta, Gyan Publishing House, New Delhi.
4. Singh, K.S., (1982). *Tribal Movements in India*, edt. Vol. I. Manohar Publishers.
5. Basumatary, Jayanarayan, (1981). "Boroni Bathou Dhoromni Bijap", Self Published, Kokrajhar.
6. Swargiary, Noas, (1997). "The Bodo Mass Movements since Independence" in *The Bodos : Children of Bhulumbutter*, edt. Thomas Pulloppillil & Jacob Aluckal, Spectrum Publications, Guwahati.
7. Chattopadhyya, D.K., (1990). *History of the Assamese Movement since 1947*, Minerva Associates (Publications) Pvt. Ltd., Calcutta.

29

AN OVERVIEW OF THE DIMASA SOCIETY

MINAKSHI CHAKRABORTY

North Cachar Hills District is the homeland of heterogeneous tribes and races. The common feature of all these tribes and races is that they have a rich tradition of local initiatives and institutions. They maintain their distinct languages, cultures, manners and customs without slightest interference from one another. The Dimasas, popularly known as the Hill Kacharis, are the dominant tribe in N.C. Hills and as a distinct ethnic group in India is endowed with a rich store of legends, myths, traditions, dances, songs, art and architecture. They could really boast of a glorious political past with a superior culture of their own.

Dimasas are found in Karbi-Anglong, Cachar and Nowgong districts of Assam and the Dhansiri region of Nagaland but are highly concentrated in N.C. Hills District and claim that they have their own originality and tradition. It is simply obvious that society can never be a static one, rather it is a process of change with which every society adapts itself. In Dimasa society also cultural assimilation is on the process of setting the community on its threshold.

The Dimasas of N.C. Hills, slowly but steadily, observed the socio-politico-economic dimensions of independent India. After independence, the Constitution of India in the Sixth Schedule provides for district autonomy for the hill districts of erstwhile Assam. Thus, it was given a District Council as early as 1952 with Mikir Hills and only in February 1970, N.C. Hills was made a full-fledged district of Assam with an Autonomous District Council. Along with the establishment of District Council, the political consciousness started to develop rapidly among the tribal population of this part of our country. Political consciousness awakened them to think over their distinctive identity.

The North-Eastern states of India are facing the problem of preservation of their distinct identity. Thus, identity problems of various tribes are alike in this region. Firstly, long economic deprivation from Centre is the core of grievances of the tribal people. Secondly, isolation from the national mainstream compelled them to think that they have been turned into second-class citizens and, therefore, placed a demand for separate homeland. Thirdly, they are looking for more political liberty and extension of overall protection of culture and life so that they could retain their identity. Taking all these infrastructural elements they built their own nationalistic ideas. Dimasas, as a North-Eastern tribe, are facing all these problems and a new wave of thought developed.

The influx of immigrants from neighbouring regions has drawn a change in the demographic line of N.C. Hills. It has divided the local population along communal lines and has been the cause of increasing tension between the outsiders and the locals. Dimasas are aware of the extent to which they differ from others who live in the state. They are able to compare their characteristics with those of others. This ethnic self-awareness helped them to organize a move to drive out the outsiders from N.C. Hills district in 1975-76. In Maibang, Mahur and Harangajao area, wall writing and postering is seen with the slogan "*Bideshi phire jaao*", Foreigners go back. In fact, it has not been ascertained who the foreigners are permanent Residential Certificate (P.R.C.) is issued by the Autonomous District Council to all the tribal and non-tribal people subject to the fulfilment of certain specified conditions. Still a penumbra of tension always existed between the outsiders and the locals.

The Central Government acceded to the demands for statehood by several tribal communities, e.g., Naga tribes were given their own state Nagaland; the Mizos formed Mizoram; the various ethno-cultural hills tribes of the North-East Frontier formed Arunachal Pradesh. But the creation of these administrative units with groups of communities poorly solved the political problems of the North-Eastern tribal people; rather it developed an instinct of self-preservation.

A separate political identity has been claimed for the N.C. Hills and Karbi Anglong districts, which falls in the domain of territorial identity in India. The individuals, who assert territorial identification, believe that their identity can be legitimized only if they achieve statehood.

The Autonomous State Demand Committee emerged as political party of Karbi-Anglong and N.C. Hills districts enjoying massive popular support for ending the hegemony of Dispur and demanding separate autonomous state within India. Their struggle, like other tribes demanding autonomy is more directly against the chauvinism of the politico-economically advanced community.

It is to be clear here that the Autonomous State Demand Committee (A.S.D.C.) as a political party tried to obtain a full-fledged state within India and has not shown separatist or secessionist attitude. It is the deep-rooted anger of the people against the existing system of corruption and for uplifting the socio-politico-economic condition of the people to ensure equal development to all ethnic and minority nationalities. "*Desh Humara Hukum Tumhara Nehin Chalega*", (No State – No Rest), "We Demand Autonomous State" are the popular slogans of ASDC party and everywhere wall-writing is seen with these slogans.

The Dimasa Women Society (DWS), Dimasa Students Union (DSU) as the grassroots organizations are working under A.S.D.C. banner. They organized workshop and sent delegation to Dispur and Delhi to realize their cherished goals. Their commitment forced the Government to sign a Memorandum of Understanding (MoU) on 1st April, 1995 in New Delhi delegating unconditional powers of thirty (30) departments. Although the MoU has not achieved autonomous state as yet, the party is working hard to get it. The A.S.D.C. has promised to promote dying ethnic culture of the hills. The District Council has granted financial assistance to various ethnic groups and facilitated the observance of their colourful traditional and religious festivals with official local holidays. In North Cachar Hills the A.S.D.C. promised to the people of their community eradication of some evil norms through revival of old heritage.

The rising demand for statehood is a by-product of the language agitation. The decision of the Government to create linguistic states precipitated similar demands by smaller linguistic groups and by a variety of other social identities, for each ethnic group perceived that statehood was the most effective means of legitimizing its claim for a separate cultural identity.

The movement for a separate hill state was intensified in 1960 after the passing of the bill to make the Assamese language the official language of Assam. The imposition of the Assamese language became a most repugnant move to the Bodos, Karbis and Dimasa Kacharis. Language has all along remained a mobilizing symbol of nationality formation of the Dimasas.

Though historical evidences support the fact that Dimasa language has no script of its own, the Dimasa elites tried to introduce the language with Roman script at the school level. Since its formation in 1972 "Dimasa Jalairaoni Hoshom" (Dimasa Youth Organization) has been demanding the introduction of Dimasa in the primary schools of N.C. Hills. The Assam Text Book Production and Publication Board published Dimasa text books for primary classes in 1972 which ended up rotting in the godowns of the District Council. Again in 1986, with the aim to preserve the distinct linguistic identity in the multi-lingual setting of Assam, the Dimasa elite decided to introduce Bodo as the medium of instruction which met with little success.

It was found that there is a gap between the demand for equality and the level of capacity. Dimasa language is not yet capable of being used as medium of instruction even at the school level but the question of linguistic-cultural identity agitates the minds of the Dimasas.

At one time Dimasa elite agreed to assimilate with greater Bodo language and decided to participate in the deliberations of Bodo Sahitya Sabha to ameliorate the Dimasa literature. The founder president of Bodo Sahitya Sabha was Shri Sonaram Thaosen. But recently from 1999 onwards Dimasa intellectuals and elite started a move to establish their separate identity in the field of literature and organize a Dimasa Sahitya Sabha or "Dimasa Lairidim Mel" in Dimasa populated areas. The first Dimasa Sahitya Sabha was held at Hawraghat. In November 2000 the second Dimasa Sahitya Sabha was held at Maibang with seminar discussion on the issue of Dimasa Script and was participated by scholars, writers and others. There were some scholars who favoured English script while some organizations like Waimijing, Dimasa Students Union of Delhi and N.C. Hills advocated Roman script as the phonology of the Dimasa language would not be perfect in English. Thus, the issue is yet to be settled.

Introduction of Autonomous District Council in the district moulded the political aspiration of the people as each ethnic entity has its own aspiration. The Autonomous District Council is entrusted with the power to make laws for the areas covered in respect of occupation, transfer, management and use of land, forests and water resources, agriculture, police, public health, education, cattle, fisheries, roads, markets, inheritance of property, marriage, social customs, administration of justice etc. The people who believe in territorial identification assert that the indigenous population has a special claim to the region: a first claim on employment, schools, housing, positions in the administrative services and even control over the state political system.

On 24th May, 1980 'WAIMIJING' published the following news: "*NEEPCO hmalaini hatani subungse hmalailai lab suguba, erani subung muchibo rijaoya*" (People coming from outside have derived all benefits from NEEPCO and the people of this district got nothing). Dimasa elite favour industrialization of their district while dislike the idea of outsiders taking up jobs. That is why even today preferences are given to the indigenous people in jobs and other opportunities available within the district.

Another means of identity preservation is found in the celebration on the 'Bihu' or 'Bushu' festival. Bushu is commonly celebrated as a harvesting festival of the Dimasas. Recently 27th January is declared as a fixed date to celebrate "Bushu Dima". They have granted the "Bushu" as an occasion to cultivate their cultural traits and protect their distinctive tribal identity.

Insurgency, now-a-days is a regular phenomenon and North Cachar Hills is no exception. It is to be acknowledged that insurgency in this district is following the secessionist way. The extremist organization of the soil "Dima Halam Dauga" (DHD) is walking on the line of NSCN and ULFA with a dream to achieve a sovereign Dimasa homeland. Their aim is also to revive and popularize Dimasa culture and traditions. They appeal to the Dimasa women, girls and students to wear Dimasa traditional dress (Rigu) every Monday and Friday in office, schools and college. Girls wearing trendy dresses like jeans, salwar kurta are harassed and punished in open daylight by the cadres.

Dimaraji Revival Demand Committee (DRDC), a political organization, was established with the aim to create a greater Dimasa state comprising a portion of Nagaland, Nagaon, Cachar along with N.C. Hills districts. To create pressure on Government to realize

'Dimaraji' they call for 'Bandh' of forty-eight to seventy-two hours from time to time and paralyse the normal life.

The inter-tribal conflict though not manifested is rather latent here. The political aspirations of the people of various communities sometimes bring this issue to limelight. Thus, the college election in Haflong Government College has been suspended since 1992 on the question of Dimasa and Hmar students representation. During college social week the inter-tribal conflict raises its ugly head. Students of Dimasa, Hmar, Kuki, and Naga etc. communities come forward to perform their cultural items and try to show their distinct ethnic identities.

This overview of the Dimasa society gives certain clues to understand the identity aspiration move by the elites. Modern concept of global village through the 'Dot Com Revolution' assists cultural assimilation process, which puts the Dimasa culture on threshold. The process of modernization has exposed them to a more complicated and competitive world order. The norms of the traditional society are being shattered everyday by the onslaught of modernization.

Amidst all these antagonism the Dimasa drives on the problem of being a marginal group in the wider national context. In independent India no group should be deprived of its rightful place in economy and government. The complex ethnic plank has again and again brought into focus the indigenous and outsiders question in North-East India. The Dimasas of this district are fighting to establish their social norms and practices, cultural heritage and territorial identity through autonomy movement against the plain people's hegemony over language, education, culture etc. It is the responsibility of the Dimasa elite and educated youth to make the coming generation aware about their past heritage to preserve and instil their ethno-culture identity.

REFERENCES

1. Assam Sahitya Sabha. *Dimasa Bhasa Aru Sanskriti.*
2. Bhattacharjee, J.B., (ed.), *Sequences of Development in North-East India.*
3. Dipali G. Dande. *Among the Dimasa of Assam.*
4. Haflong *Nisarga's,* Bengali magazine published .
5. *Nisarga,* Bengali magazine published from Haflong.
6. Pankaj Thakur. (ed.). *India's North-East.*

30

SPATIAL DISTRIBUTION AND SOCIO-ECONOMIC WELL-BEING OF SCHEDULED TRIBE POPULATION IN ASSAM

MOMITA GOSWAMI AND LAKHAHIRA DATTA

Assam located in the heart of the north-east India has diverse population base with various ethnic, cultural and economic background. The "Scheduled Tribes" account for a sizable proportion of the population of Assam and constitute an important segment of the social fabric of the state. A perusal of the census data reveals that their spatial distribution is characterized by a striking tendency of clustering and concentration in pockets within an environmental setting which is, by and large, away from the crowded industrial/urban areas. This contributed significantly the concentration of single ethnic group in a specific area resulting lack of adequate interaction not only between the tribal and non-tribal communities but also various tribal groups within the population of the state.

Perhaps, constrained by harsh environmental condition, which has fostered physical social and cultural isolation for ages, the different tribal communities living in different areas have developed their own traditional mode of living. However, it may be noted here that the *genre de vie* of the tribal communities have been modified to some extent by the exogenous forces and have a symbiotic relationship with the ecological conditions and the resource base of the enclaves of their concentration. These weaker sections of the rural community generally belong to the lowest income group people living in abject poverty and are also surviving in severe under-nutritional condition.

According to 1991 census, out of the total population of Assam,

12.82 per cent is scheduled tribe population. As per the scheduled caste and scheduled tribe lists (modification under 1956), there are as many as 23 major tribal communities in Assam, of whom 9 are plain tribes and 14 are hill tribes. The Constitution of India identified them as socio-economically backward section of people in the society. After independence many plans and programmes have been formulated and implemented by the Central as well as the State governments, for their development, but except a fraction of their effort, all are in vein. Probably, low level of literacy among the tribals is the main cause for which they cannot perfectly perceive and utilise the facilities available for them in the demographic polity of India. Sometimes, even they are victimised by some political leaders which creates an imbalance situation and threatens the integrity of our country. The gap between the tribals and the non-tribals have been widening and the feeling of discontentment ultimately leads to the emergence of some specific demands like creation of separate state/autonomous district, preservation of their cultural identity etc. Thus ethnic clashes and problems have been gaining ground in Assam.

Assam is blended with hills and plains and it has different tribal groups belonging to both hill and the plain distributed in different districts. Among the plain tribes Boro-Kacharis are the most predominant group distributed mainly in Kokrajhar, Goalpara, Bongaigaon, Nalbari, Barpeta and Darrang districts.

The Miris also known as Mishings constitute the second highest group concentrated mainly in the flood prone areas of Dhemaji, Lakhimpur and Sonitpur districts. The Sonowal Kachari constitutes the third highest group distributed mainly in the Dibrugarh and Golaghat districts. On the other hand, overwhelming chunk of Rabha population whose position is fourth in size mainly is concentrated in the southern bank of the river Brahmaputra specially in the Goalpara and Kamrup districts.

The Tiwa community known as Lalung is the fifth largest group mainly found in the Morigaon and Nagaon districts. In addition to these, a few Lalung villages are also found in Dhemaji district.

Deori community, a riverine tribal is the sixth largest group in size found mainly in Lakhimpur, Dibrugarh, Jorhat and Sibsagar districts. The next group is the Barman of Cachar found exclusively in the

Cachar district. The Mech, a small group is found in the southern part of Dhubri and Kokrajhar district while another small group is found in the Hojai Lanka area, i.e. south-eastern part of Nagaon district.

Among the hill tribes the Karbis and the Dimasas are the most important groups. Karbis are concentrated in the Karbi Anglong district and in the foothill areas of Nagaon and Kamrup districts, while the Dimasa Kacharis are mainly found in the North Cachar hill district of Assam. Besides, Hajong, Hmar, Rengma, Naga, Kuki, Garo are also dominant groups inhabited in Assam hills.

Among the districts of Assam, N.C. Hills has recorded the highest percentage of scheduled tribe population (65.54% to total population) which is followed by Karbi Anglong (51.56%), Dhemaji (43.92%) and Kokrajhar (41.14%). The percentage of scheduled tribe population is recorded lowest in Hailakandi district (0.16%) followed by Karimganj (0.17%). Using Location Quotient method the core and peripheral distribution of S.T. population is calculated and presented in the Tables 30.1 and 30.2.

Table 30.1 clearly shows the spatial variation and concentration of Scheduled Tribe population in Assam.

It may be noted here that land alienation and indebtedness are the chronic problems of the tribal areas. Due to poverty most of the poor people used to sell their land to other non-tribal people at a very low price and they used to spend the money mainly for consumption of liquor. Thus gradually socio-economic conditions of the tribal people has been deteriorating.

In order to preserve the tribal culture on one hand and to give socio-economic security on the other, the exclusive pockets of the tribals in plains of Assam were identified by the government as tribal belts and blocks and in these pockets restrictions have been imposed on handing over of tribal lands to the non-tribals. Table 30.2 has also highlighted the spatial concentration of tribal population in tribal belts of blocks in the plain areas of Assam.

Table 30.2 clearly reveals that the Boro Kachari belts/blocks are concentrated in Kokrajhar, Kamrup, Nalbari and Barpeta districts whereas the Miri (Mishing) belts/Blocks are located in Sonitpur, North Lakhimpur and Dhemaji districts. On the other hand the Tiwas are spread in the tribal belts/blocks of Nagaon and Morigaon districts.

Table 30.1 : Spatial Distribution and Concentration of S.T. Population in Assam, 1991

Districts		Percentage of Scheduled Tribe population 1991	L.Q. Value
1.	Dhubri	2.42	0.18
2.	Kokrajhar	41.15	3.21
3.	Bongaigaon	17.53	1.37
4.	Goalpara	17.23	1.34
5.	Barpeta	7.97	0.62
6.	Nalbari	17.67	1.38
7.	Kamrup	10.72	0.84
8.	Darrang	17.32	1.35
9.	Sonitpur	10.71	0.83
10.	Lakhimpur	23.57	1.84
11.	Dhemaji	43.92	3.42
12.	Morigaon	15.40	1.20
13.	Nagaon	3.69	0.28
14.	Golaghat	10.25	0.80
15.	Jorhat	12.09	0.94
16.	Sivasagar	3.80	0.29
17.	Dibrugarh	7.95	0.62
18.	Tinsukia	5.35	0.41
19.	Karbianglong	51.56	4.02
20.	North Cachar Hills	65.54	5.11
21.	Karimganj	0.17	0.01
22.	Hailakandi	0.16	0.01
23.	Cachar	1.36	0.10
	Assam	12.82	

Source : Census of India, 1991, Series-A, Part II-B, Assam.

Table 30.2: Spatial Distribution of Tribal Belts and Blocks in the plain of Assam

	Name of the Belt/Block	Major Plain tribe within the Belt and Block
1.	Sidli Tribal Belt (Kokrajhar)	Boro-Kachari
2.	Bijni Tribal Block (Bongaigaon)	Boro-Kachari
3.	Rani Chaygaon Tribal Belt (Kamrup)	Rabha
4.	Khetri Sonapur Tribal Belt (Kamrup)	Rabha Lalung
5.	Tamulpur Tribal Belt (Nalbari)	Boro-Kachari
6.	Baska Tribal Belt (Nalbari)	Boro-Kachari
7.	Chapaguri Tribal Belt (Barpeta)	Boro-Kachari
8.	Kharija Bijni Tribal Block (Barpeta)	Boro-Kachari
9.	Bejegaon Tribal Block (Barpeta)	Boro-Kachari
10.	Gabardhana Tribal Block (Barpeta)	Boro-Kachari
11.	Gohpur Tribal Block (Sonitpur)	Miri
12.	Balipara Tribal Belt (Sonitpur)	Boro-Kachari
13.	Teteli Bhanguria Tribal Block (Darrang)	Boro-Kachari
14.	Kacharipara Tribal Block (Darrang)	Boro-Kachari
15.	Dalgaon Tribal Block (Darrang)	Boro-Kachari
16.	Lalai Tribal Belt (Darrang)	Boro-Kachari
17.	Tezial Tribal Block (Darrang)	Boro-Kachari
18.	Bhuiankhat Tribal Block (Darrang)	Boro-Kachari
19.	North Lakhimpur Tribal Belt (Lakhimpur)	Miri
20.	Murkong Selek Jonai Tribal Belt (Dhemaji)	Miri
21.	Bihpuria Subansiri Tribal Block (Lakhimpur)	Miri & Deori
22.	Abor-Misimi Tirap Tribal Belt (Tinsukia)	Miri & Deori Sonowal Kachari
23.	Boro-Kachari Tribal Belt (Nagaon)	Lalung
24.	Amgurichang Phulgurichang Tribal Block (Nagaon)	Lalung
25.	Bordalang, Lankabheta Tribal Block (Nagaon)	Lalung
26.	Baguriguri Tribal Block (Nagaon)	Lalung
27.	Barchoi Tribal Block (Nagaon)	Lalung
28.	Borchila Tribal Block (Nagaon)	Lalung
29.	Borpathar Tribal Block (Kamrup)	Lalung
30.	Jamadari Tribal Block (Morigaon)	Lalung
31.	Borogoni Pathar Tribal Block (Morigaon)	Lalung
32.	Changana Tribal Block (Morigaon)	Lalung
33.	Tetelia Tribal Block (Morigaon)	Lalung
34.	Gobha Tribal Block (Morigaon)	Lalung
35.	Rhulaguri Tribal Block (Morigaon)	Lalung
36.	Bagariguri Tribal Block (Morigaon)	Lalung
37.	Bhulukjari Tribal Block (Morigaon)	Lalung

The Sonowal Kachari are concentrated in the tribal belts/ blocks of Dibrugarh and Tinsukia districts. However, it may be noted here that all the plain tribal people of Assam are not distributed within the tribal belts/blocks. A sizeable number of them are either distributed in the peripheral location of these belts and blocks or are found in other areas interspersed with non-tribal habitations.

In order to understand the socio-economic welfare of the scheduled tribes in Assam, the analysis of the demographic and socio-cultural and economic characteristics is presented.

Demographic Profile

The sex ratio is by and large balanced in case of scheduled tribe population. The scheduled tribe population being the least mobile group with higher gender equality presents a high sex ratio (963.30/1000) than the other groups, viz. scheduled caste population (909.56/1000) and non-Scheduled population (908.56/1000). The sex ratio among the scheduled tribe population is highest in Barpeta (1002/1000) and lowest in Karimganj (904/1000).

The percentage of young population in the age group 0-6 among the tribals is however higher than the general population recording 20.09 per cent as against 19.51 per cent for the non-scheduled population which is due to the weak socio-economic conditions. It may be noted here that the average household size which is determined by natural increase of population coupled with socio-economic factor is found to be high (6.29%) in the case of tribals. The lowest household size (4.81%) is recorded by N.C. Hills and highest by Lakhimpur district (8.09%). For general non-scheduled population, the figures are 5.30 per cent in Jorhat (lowest) and 7.53 per cent) in Nalbari (highest).

Literacy Pattern

Literacy is the important determining factor of socio-economic development of any society. The literacy rate of the scheduled tribe population in Assam is only 49.16 against 52.89 general population in Assam. There is however gender disparity in respect of literacy. Male percentage of literacy for scheduled tribe population in Assam is 61.90 which is almost same with the general non-scheduled tribe population

(61.75%). Interestingly it is lower than the scheduled caste population of the state (64.10%). The highest male literacy is recorded by Dibrugarh (83.74%). While the lowest male literacy is recorded by Dhemaji (35.48%). On the other hand the average female literacy rate of the scheduled tribe population is 43.03 per cent which is almost same with the female literacy of the general population (43.24%).

Participation in Economic Activity

Sex-wise work participation rate clearly indicates that there is variation between male and female. Male work participation rate is 48.87 per cent in case of tribals as against 32.02 per cent for the female. As the economy is based primarily on agriculture there is insignificant spatial variation in respect of participation rate.

The dependency ratio (percentage of non-worker to total workers) is also relatively lower and in case of scheduled tribe population (48.09%) than the general non-scheduled population (82.31%). Among the tribals, out of the total workers (9,70,305), 89.39 per cent is engaged in primary sector, 1.67 per cent in secondary sector while 8.94 per cent is in tertiary sector of economy which clearly indicates that agriculture is the main stay of economy of the major section of the tribal people.

Size of Operational Holding

The field study in seven selected tribal villages reveals that the size of operational holding for 88 per cent of the households is below the size of 2 hectares. A major section of them live in a poor condition and the land is not sufficient to maintain their family.

Food and Nutrition

From the field survey it is observed that on an average per head per day calorie intake is 2215 (standard requirements 2400) of which 75 per cent is available from cereals mainly rice. Intake of milk and milk product is negligible, while flesh food is very common. They also eat pulses, sugar and molasses. Root and leafy vegetables are common foodstuff and intake of oil and fats from outside is very insufficient.

Summary of Selected Indicators of Socio-economic Well-being of Scheduled Tribe Population in Assam, 1991

Indicators	Average	Lowest	Highest
1. Sex ratio	963.30	904 Karimganj	1002 Barpeta
2. Population in Age Group 0-6 in p.c.	20.09	15.61 Dibrugarh	24.09 Dhemaji
3. Literacy in p.c.	49.16	22.38 Karimganj	73.07 Dibrugarh
4. Male literacy in p.c.	61.90	35.48 Karimganj	83.74 Dibrugarh
5. Female literacy in p.c.	43.03	20.33 Karimganj	89.50 Dibrugarh
6. Urban population in p.c.	3.51	0.11 Nalbari	11.82 Karimganj
7. Work Participation			
Primary	87.30	70.16 Hailakandi	93.76 Karbianglong
Secondary	1.99	0.71 Lakhimpur	6.85 Hailakandi
Tertiary	10.71	4.91 Karbianglong	22.99 Hailakandi
8. Dependency ratio in p.c.	148.09	122.70 Dhemaji	210.87 Karimganj
9. Male work participation	48.87	44.05 Lakhimpur	58.53 Hailakandi
10. Female work participation	32.02	12.96 Karimganj	43.84 Dhemaji

Almost 90 per cent of the population drink the country made liquor. As a result of low nutrition the health condition of the people of the sample villages is far from satisfactory.

Conclusion

The above analysis clearly indicates that the socio-economic well-being of scheduled tribe population in the state is not satisfactory. Therefore, intensive development programme should be launched for different tribal groups living in different ecological conditions considering their emotions and sentiments. Special attention should be given to enhance the educational standard for common people so that they can take part in different developmental programmes extended to them. The rural tribal people should be trained so that they can use new scientific methods in agriculture to derive maximum production from their small holdings.

As most of them are landless peasants, vocational training should be given to them to develop their cottage industries using the local resources available to them. Specially financial assistance and other facilities should be given to them to develop their traditional culture mainly handloom industry. This will help to minimise their socio-economic problems. It may be noted here that low economic level is the main cause of discontentment among the tribal resulting social tensions and other problems. Therefore, decentralisation of economy mainly through Panchayat is essential in these remote areas which will perhaps help to develop the socio-economic conditions of the tribal people.

REFERENCES

Bulletin of the Tribal Research Institute, Assam, Guwahati, Vol.1, No. 1, 1983, 1990-1999.

Census of India (1991). *Primary Census Abstract,* Assam.

—(1991) *Primary Census Abstract for Scheduled Castes and Scheduled Tribes,* Assam.

—(1991), *Union Primary Census Abstract for Scheduled Castes and Scheduled Tribes,* Assam, India.

Kar, B.K. (1996), Socio-economic well-being of different population groups in Assam, *North-Eastern Geographer,* Vol. 27, No. 1 & 2, pp. 26-36.

Pant, B.R. (1997). Social well-being of scheduled castes population in the Uttarakhand region, India, *National Geographer,* Vol. 32, No. 1.

Raja, Moonis. *Tribal Atlas of India.*

INDEX